WRITING
IN THE SOCIAL SCIENCES

JOYCE S. STEWARD
University of Wisconsin—Madison

MARJORIE SMELSTOR
University of Texas at San Antonio

Scott, Foresman and Company
Glenview, Illinois

Dallas, Tex.   Oakland, N.J.   Palo Alto, Calif.
Tucker, Ga.   London, England

An Instructor's Manual is available. It may be obtained through your local Scott, Foresman representative or by writing to English Editor, College Division, Scott, Foresman and Company, 1900 East Lake Avenue, Glenview, IL 60025.

Library of Congress Cataloging in Publication Data
Steward, Joyce S.
  Writing in the social sciences.

  Bibliography: p.
  Includes index.
  1. English language—Rhetoric.   2. Social sciences—
Authorship.   3. Readers—Social sciences.   4. College
readers.   5. Social sciences—Addresses, essays, lectures.
I. Smelstor, Marjorie.   II. Title.
PE1479.S62S73   1984   808'.0663   83–19573
ISBN 0–673–15460–2

Acknowledgments

Chapter 2
From "In Search of History," pages 16–21. Copyright © 1963 by Alma Tuchman, Lucy T. Eisenberg and Jessica Tuchman Matthews. Reprinted from *Practicing History* by Barbara W. Tuchman, by Alfred A. Knopf, Inc.
"Writing and Typing" from *Annals of an Abiding Liberal* by John Kenneth Galbraith. Copyright © 1979 by John Kenneth Galbraith. Reprinted by permission of Houghton Mifflin Company.
"Politics and the English Language" by George Orwell. Copyright 1946 by Sonia Brownell Orwell; renewed 1974 by Sonia Orwell. Reprinted from *Shooting an Elephant and Other Essays* by George Orwell by permission of Harcourt Brace Jovanovich, Inc., the estate of the late Sonia Brownell Orwell and Martin Secker & Warburg Ltd.
"Politics and the American Language" by Arthur Schlesinger, Jr., *American Scholar,* Autumn 1974. Revised and expanded from an article in *Today's Education,* September/October 1974. Reprinted by permission of the author.
Acknowledgements continue on page 337.

1 2 3 4 5 6 - RRC - 88 87 86 85 84 83

PREFACE

Writing in the Social Sciences grew out of our experiences with students writing in such fields as psychology, sociology, anthropology, history, and economics. Tutoring in cross-curriculum writing centers, teaching special short courses for students majoring in the social sciences, and working and talking with other teachers, we began to see the need for such a collection as we offer here. We discovered that our students both need and want to read articles and papers related to their particular studies. This collection, drawn from the work of both professionals and other students, can help your students discover ideas and patterns, content and techniques to apply in their own writing.

The Writing Process

The materials here fall into four parts. Part One centers on the writing process by asking students to think about how they compose and by offering descriptive and critical essays from professional writers. At the end of each selection in this part, we have summarized practical advice from such respected writers as Barbara W. Tuchman, John Kenneth Galbraith, Geroge Orwell, and Arthur Schlesinger, Jr. Although ways of going about writing are always personal and individual, both the advice and examples should guide students in related writing tasks and lead them to discover their own "best ways."

A Variety of Writing Purposes

Part Two, the largest portion of the book, presents papers written for a variety of purposes. The selections are, of course, not exact models for imitation. Rather, they are examples of good writing about the social sciences, often by eminent authors and scholars such as Hannah Arendt, Isaiah Berlin, and Henry Steele Commager, to name but a few. These selections reveal their purposes and audiences; they demonstrate the research writers do to fulfill those purposes and reach audiences; they illustrate various ways of organizing; and they exemplify a variety of styles. We believe, also, that they are worthwhile reading because they deal with subjects that are of current or continuing interest. While each chapter in Part Two focuses on a specific writing purpose, Chapter 7 is unique in addressing several forms of writing—the abstract, the book review, the annotated bibliography, and the literature review—that social scientists often use but that are usually not included in general collections of essays for student writers.

Part Two illustrates that, while a specific article may relate to only one of the many social science fields, the *way* a writer conveys a message transcends the single field and suggests ideas and methods common to all. Following Jacques Barzun's point about the similarities among the "sister disciplines," we have tried to emphasize this quality of kinship among the social sciences. After each selection, Questions for Discussion direct students to probe not just content but how the writing is made clear and effective, to discover methods that will in turn be useful as they choose among the subsequent Suggestions for Writing that challenge them to research, and to think and express themselves in their major fields.

Focus on Rhetorical Choices

Part Three includes two specially focused chapters. The first, by grouping papers that treat the same subject in different ways, illustrates how purpose influences rhetorical choices. Such comparative study should help students develop sensitivity to the ways a writer influences readers and should raise thoughtful questions: How much content is enough? When is less than all "untruth"? How does stance change effect? What dangers or advantages arise from using connotative language? The second chapter in Part Three consists of two student research papers. Since basic instruction in the process of research is found in college handbooks and rhetoric texts, we offer these papers as examples of the *products* of research in the social sciences. From them students can infer how the authors have found and selected materials, presented and documented evidence in effective organized form, and achieved (or failed to achieve) clear expression. The finished papers should help students set realistic goals for their own writing.

Guide to Research Tools

Part Four is a rich guide to resources for students and professional writers in the social sciences. Completed with the assistance of Ann Thompson, librarian at the University of Texas at San Antonio, to whom we owe great appreciation, this guide to reference materials, nonprint media, and writing resources in the social sciences represents what we have often wished our students had in hand. We believe that the bibliography included here will fulfill that need.

Finally, this book is intended not just for classrooms—for those classes labeled composition or those in social sciences where writing plays a major part—but for individuals, for those students and even those professionals who struggle to improve their writing on their own. The models throughout and the guides in Part Four will be of value to them.

No preface is complete without a note of thanks, and we owe many such notes: Judith Cohen of Harvard University, Constance Coiner of the University of California at Los Angeles, John Harper of the University of Iowa, Robert Keefe of the University of Massachusetts at Amherst, and Carolyn Mullins of Indiana University helped with critical reviews of selections. Anthropology professors Joel Gunn and Thomas Hester and psychology professor David Schneider of the University of Texas at San Antonio, sociology professor Daniel Rigney of St. Mary's University, anthropology professor Thomas Greaves of Trinity University, and economics professor W. Lee Hansen of the University of Wisconsin-Madison answered questions, lent us books, read parts of apparatus, and shared student papers and assignments from their courses. Mary Berthold and Joyce Sexton of the University of Wisconsin-Madison Writing Laboratory surveyed needs of incoming graduate students whom they tutor. Many people at Scott, Foresman helped all along the line: Harriett Prentiss and Amanda Clark provided the impetus and gave encouragement; Molly Gardiner and Linda Bieze saw us through the editorial process. To all these, and to the students who in the first place made their needs apparent, we give our thanks.

JS
MS

CONTENTS

Part One

ABOUT WRITING

1

YOU AS A WRITER

Writing in history and the social sciences is, of course, like writing in general: you must have something you want to say to someone and you must find the best way to say it. Because anyone studying the social sciences or entering the professions connected with them will inevitably do a lot of writing, it is particularly important that you discover your way of writing and master the necessary skills for communicating effectively.

Although you must find your personal way of going about the work of writing, some general suggestions may help you get started. These suggestions are offered here as a series of steps, although they do not always occur sequentially and may, in fact, overlap. For instance, you might in doing your writing find that you need to further narrow a topic or you might in doing research discover some material that leads you to change your original purpose or emphasis. But normally all these steps are parts of a writer's approach and must occur somewhere in the process of completing a paper.

Getting Started

1. Size up the task by analyzing the assignment (if one is given), its purpose and the special stipulations for handling it; or, define your own task if you are free to choose. Either way, be sure to settle on a topic or an angle that you really want to write about. Interest—whether you *care* or not—inevitably shows.

2. Ask yourself useful questions to discover what you already know (your background on the subject) and to determine the directions you might take.

Try various ways of brainstorming:

- think through the topic—talk to yourself
- talk the topic over with others
- make notes or lists
- jot down questions
- talk into a cassette recorder

Try the journalist's approach—5 Ws and H:

- Who
- What
- When
- Where
- Why
- How

Try devising a drama as Kenneth Burke does with what he calls a *pentad:*

- Action: What is happening?
- Agent: Who is doing it?
- Agency: How is it being done?
- Scene: Where and when?
- Purpose: Why?

(Such questions may lead you to the two kinds of research explained later.)

3. Write a purpose statement: "What I want to show is _____ and I shall do it by [this means]." If possible, turn that statement into a control sentence or *thesis,* a single

sentence summary of what you think your paper will say or prove. As you go about writing, you will test and probably modify this thesis somewhat, but at this point, such a sentence (or two) will give you something to aim at.

Choosing a Stance

1. Identify your attitude toward a topic—decide where you stand.
2. Decide how you want to sound on paper: knowledgeable, formal or informal, exploring, sharing, questioning, persuasive.
3. Use questions to define your position: Am I a teacher? Am I an advocate? Am I an impartial observer?

Analyzing the Audience

Determine the context in which you write and the group you are writing for:
1. Will your readers be specialists or generalists, people who know a lot or a little about the subject?
2. Will your audience require persuading? Must you offer convincing evidence or explanatory examples, what kinds and how much?
3. What sort of vocabulary will the audience understand? Is technical or specialized language appropriate or must such terms be explained?

Doing the Research

Original knowledge + research = necessary background for writing.
1. Distinguish between primary and secondary sources:

- **primary**—newspapers, speeches, films, novels, diaries, journals, firsthand information from interviews, and so on

- **secondary**—secondhand reports, reviews and criticism, commentary on the firsthand sources

2. Be thorough and fair: you cannot afford to trap yourself by overlooking or ignoring important information. If you cannot find everything you want, say so.

3. Keep careful records of your sources for citation and (when necessary) documentation.

Making a Preliminary Plan

Make a "blueprint" for yourself, knowing that you may revise it later. That blueprint can take various forms:

1. If you have not done so earlier, try now to frame a thesis or control sentence.

2. Make a tentative outline, including in it both major points and supportive facts or materials.

3. List in order the questions your paper may set up and answer.

4. Draw a diagram of what your paper may look like:

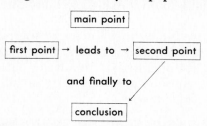

5. Or simply write a rough draft as a way to explore, to discover gaps, to find a pattern of organization.

Doing the Writing

As you write, keep your goal in mind:

1. Assess your material (knowledge, facts, research) and draw inferences carefully from the information.

2. Arrange the facts and interpretive comments or inferences to show their relationship.

3. When a section of a paper (or an entire short paper) falls into one of the common patterns of development, check to see that you follow the basic guidelines for that kind of development:

- Examples: choose sufficient examples that clearly relate to the central idea; control arrangement for effect or logic.
- Tracing: keep the time sequence of steps in the process clear. (Narration is a form of tracing.)
- Comparison/contrast: be certain that subjects have a common basis so that points of comparison or contrast are observable and valid; follow either unit-by-unit or point-by-point pattern (unit treats one object/idea first, then the other; point-by-point treats both objects/ideas together, covering points of comparison and contrast.)
- Causal analysis: include genuine causes, not superficial ones; show relationship between these essential causes and the result being discussed.
- Classification or division: choose a single method of dividing or classifying, and make sure that all items in the sample under consideration fall into one of these classes.
- Definition: follow the process of logical definition by placing the item in a class and then showing its distinguishing features; avoid "circularity" (defining the item in terms of itself) and expand by giving examples, describing, and so on.

These patterns of development may occur in single paragraphs or in larger units of a paper. Sometimes an entire paper follows one method. For instance, the paper may use a pattern of comparison/contrast, or set forth reasons for some event or decision. At other times, the patterns merge. A writer, especially in dealing with an essay test question that requires a specific task, may want in the first sentence or two to predict both content and pattern: "The old-fashioned school in a one-room log cabin had many of the freedoms that we have lost in a modern 'free' high school" as an opening sentence *predicts* or *obligates* a development by contrasts, either dealing with the old school and then the new, or structured according to points of difference between the two.

4. Plan subsections (sometimes with subheadings) as logical divisions within your paper by determining into what parts your material and thoughts about it fall. A short paper may be divided into only a few paragraphs; a longer paper may fall into sections of several paragraphs each.

5. Provide connections between sections (and between paragraphs and sentences) by using linking words and phrases, echoes and effective repetition.

6. Choose a beginning and ending that frame the paper, but avoid the formulaic "I intend to show" and "In conclusion, I have shown."

- Begin by catching interest, posing a problem, or making a prediction.
- End by drawing well-founded conclusions, pointing out implications, or suggesting further study.

Revising and Polishing the Whole

Revision falls into several steps and occurs at various times. Writing the paper (except for impromptu topics or essay-question answers, when your time is limited) always requires more than one draft. As you write, you may discover that you need more material, and you may revise by doing additional research and expanding your paper. You may also discover that you have been repetitive, and you may do some drastic cutting. But, primarily, revision requires that you check the organization of your paper and then move to polishing the presentation. These suggestions should help:

1. Reread the entire paper, perhaps by reading aloud:

- Does it fulfill your purpose? Does it meet the requirements of the assignment?
- Does it accurately reflect your knowledge and views?
- Will it reach the intended audience?
- Does it build to conclusions that are obviously well-founded in research or supporting data?

- Is the arrangement logical and easy to follow? Are connections clear?

A good test of the structure is to outline or make summary statements in the margins by noting what each section or paragraph contributes, a way of "balancing the checkbook."

2. Make necessary changes: add, delete, substitute or rearrange; clarify generalizations; insert links to give smoothness and show relationships.

3. Refine the style: consider word choice, special terms or jargon (distinguish jargon from necessary "shop talk"), length and variety of sentences, connecting words and phrases.

Although writers may compose in paragraphs (completing a thought or part of one), they revise finally at the sentence level. Check such items as the following:

- clarity, naturalness (ease of reading): most sentences will be in natural subject-verb order.
- emphasis: place subordinate and modifying elements to emphasize main ideas.
- economy: avoid using excess words and vague, meaningless, and insignificant ones.
- balance and unbalance (parallelism and subordination): avoid illogical unbalance, shifts in viewpoint or tenses, mixed constructions, shifts from active to passive, and so on.
- variety in pattern and length

4. Edit for items such as spelling, punctuation, usage. Check form of footnotes, cited materials, tables or graphs, format—the general presentation of your paper.

These steps are, of course, suggestions, but they are the suggestions that many writers, including those represented in this book, frequently follow. As you read the words of the professional writers who write about writing in the following pages, you will find other bits of advice that should help you write in the social sciences. You will also find, as you go on through the sample essays, both materials and models of various types of writing in your discipline.

As you write more, you may become like George Orwell, whose essay is in Chapter 2. He once wrote that although writing is a "horrible, exhausting struggle," a writer cannot resist that struggle. Even though writing is always work, gaining mastery over your material and method should bring you a feeling of achievement and power, of satisfaction in reaching your reader with something important.

2

PROFESSIONALS TALK ABOUT WRITING

One of the best ways to learn about an art or skill—and writing is both—is to consult professionals who can speak from and about their experience. They know what works for them and what does not, not because they have read about the task but because they practice it. Professional writers know about the challenges facing them each time they write: the struggle to get started, the demands of researching a topic, the excitement of finding the right words, the necessity to write and rewrite for specific audiences. And they can help apprentice writers learn about these challenges.

In this chapter some influential writers in the social sciences address three major concerns:

1. Getting started and doing research—Tuchman
2. Doing the actual writing—Galbraith
3. Choosing language, evolving a style—Orwell, Schlesinger

As you read the following articles, examine not only what the writers say about writing, but also how they themselves write. Since these writers practice what they preach, you can learn as much from their practice as from their preachment. After each essay, you will find a summary of useful suggestions and some writing tasks to give you practice in learning to write.

BARBARA W. TUCHMAN

In a collection of essays entitled *Practicing History,* Barbara W. Tuchman tells of the way she became interested in writing while she pursued information for her master's thesis. Now the author of such books as *The Guns of August, The Proud Tower,* and *A Distant Mirror,* and twice a winner of the Pulitzer Prize, Tuchman describes her writing process in a way that has practical application for students today.

From "In Search of History"

1 One learns to write, I have since discovered, in the practice thereof. After seven years' apprenticeship in journalism I discovered that an essential element for good writing is a good ear. One must *listen* to the sound of one's own prose. This, I think, is one of the failings of much American writing. Too many writers do not listen to the sound of their own words. For example, listen to this sentence from the organ of my own discipline, the *American Historical Review:* "His presentation is not vitiated historically by efforts at expository simplicity." In one short sentence five long Latin words of four or five syllables each. One has to read it three times over and take time out to think, before one can even make out what it means.

2 In my opinion, short words are always preferable to long ones; the fewer syllables the better, and monosyllables, beautiful and pure like "bread" and "sun" and "grass," are the best of all. Emerson, using almost entirely one-syllable words, wrote what I believe are among the finest lines in English:

> By the rude bridge that arched the flood,
> Their flag to April's breeze unfurled,
> Here once the embattled farmers stood,
> And fired the shot heard round the world.

Out of twenty-eight words, twenty-four are monosyllables. It is English at its purest, though hardly characteristic of its author.

3 Or take this:

On desperate seas long wont to roam,
  Thy hyacinth hair, thy classic face,
Thy Naiad airs have brought me home
  To the glory that was Greece,
  And the grandeur that was Rome.

Imagine how it must feel to have composed those lines! Though coming from a writer satisfied with the easy rhythms of "The Raven" and "Annabel Lee," they represent, I fear, a fluke. To quote poetry, you will say, is not a fair comparison. True, but what a lesson those stanzas are in the sound of words! What superb use of that magnificent instrument that lies at the command of all of us—the English language. Quite by chance both practitioners in these samples happen to be Americans, and both, curiously enough, writing about history.

To write history so as to enthrall the reader and make the subject as captivating and exciting to him as it is to me has been my goal since that initial failure with my thesis. A prerequisite, as I have said, is to be enthralled one's self and to feel a compulsion to communicate the magic. Communicate to whom? We arrive now at the reader, a person whom I keep constantly in mind. Catherine Drinker Bowen has said that she writes her books with a sign pinned up over her desk asking, "Will the reader turn the page?"   4

The writer of history, I believe, has a number of duties *vis-à-vis* the reader, if he wants to keep him reading. The first is to distill. He must do the preliminary work for the reader, assemble the information, make sense of it, select the essential, discard the irrelevant—above all, discard the irrelevant—and put the rest together so that it forms a developing dramatic narrative. Narrative, it has been said, is the lifeblood of history. To offer a mass of undigested facts, of names not identified and places not located, is of no use to the reader and is simple laziness on the part of the author, or pedantry to show how much he has read. To discard the unnecessary requires courage and also extra work, as exemplified by Pascal's effort to explain an idea to a friend in a letter which rambled on for pages and ended, "I am sorry to have wearied you with so long a letter but I did not have time to write you a short one."   5

The historian is continually being beguiled down fascinating byways and sidetracks. But the art of writing—the test of the artist—is to resist the beguilement and cleave to the subject.

6   Should the historian be an artist? Certainly a conscious art should be part of his equipment. Macaulay describes him as half poet, half philosopher. I do not aspire to either of these heights. I think of myself as a storyteller, a narrator, who deals in true stories, not fiction. The distinction is not one of relative values; it is simply that history interests me more than fiction. I agree with Leopold von Ranke, the great nineteenth-century German historian, who said that when he compared the portrait of Louis XI in Scott's *Quentin Durward* with the portrait of the same king in the memoirs of Philippe de Comines, Louis' minister, he found "the truth more interesting and beautiful than the romance."

7   It was Ranke, too, who set the historian's task: to find out *wie es eigentlich gewesen ist,* what really happened, or, literally, how it really was. His goal is one that will remain forever just beyond our grasp for reasons I explained in a "Note on Sources" in *The Guns of August* (a paragraph that no one ever reads but *I* think is the best thing in the book). Summarized, the reasons are that we who write about the past were not there. We can never be certain that we have recaptured it as it really was. But the least we can do is to stay within the evidence.

8   I do not invent anything, even the weather. One of my readers told me he particularly liked a passage in *The Guns* which tells how the British Army landed in France and how on that afternoon there was a sound of summer thunder in the air and the sun went down in a blood-red glow. He thought it an artistic touch of doom, but the fact is it was true. I found it in the memoirs of a British officer who landed on that day and heard the thunder and saw the blood-red sunset. The art, if any, consisted only in selecting it and ultimately using it in the right place.

9   Selection is what determines the ultimate product, and that is why I use material from primary sources only. My feeling about secondary sources is that they are helpful but pernicious. I use them as guides at the start of a project to find out the general scheme of what happened, but I do not take notes

from them because I do not want to end up simply rewriting someone else's book. Furthermore, the facts in a secondary source have already been pre-selected, so that in using them one misses the opportunity of selecting one's own.

I plunge as soon as I can into the primary sources: the 10 memoirs and the letters, the generals' own accounts of their campaigns, however tendentious, not to say mendacious, they may be. Even an untrustworthy source is valuable for what it reveals about the personality of the author, especially if he is an actor in the events, as in the case of Sir John French, for example. Bias in a primary source is to be expected. One allows for it and corrects it by reading another version. I try always to read two or more for every episode. Even if an event is not controversial, it will have been seen and remembered from different angles of view by different observers. If the event *is* in dispute, one has extra obligation to examine both sides. As the lion in Aesop said to the Man, "There are many statues of men slaying lions, but if only the lions were sculptors there might be quite a different set of statues."

The most primary source of all is unpublished material: 11 private letters and diaries or the reports, orders, and messages in government archives. There is an immediacy and intimacy about them that reveals character and makes circumstances come alive. I remember Secretary of State Robert Lansing's desk diary, which I used when I was working on *The Zimmermann Telegram.* The man himself seemed to step right out from his tiny neat handwriting and his precise notations of every visitor and each subject discussed. Each day's record opened and closed with the Secretary's time of arrival and departure from the office. He even entered the time of his lunch hour, which invariably lasted sixty minutes: "Left at 1:10; returned at 2:10." Once, when he was forced to record his morning arrival at 10:15, he added, with a worried eye on posterity, "Car broke down."

Inside the National Archives even the memory of Wid- 12 ener paled. Nothing can compare with the fascination of examining material in the very paper and ink of its original issue. A report from a field agent with marginal comments by the Secretary of War, his routing directions to State and Commerce, and the scribbled initials of subsequent readers can be a little history in itself. In the Archives I found the original decode of the Zimmermann Telegram, which I was able to have declassified and photostated for the cover of my book.

13   Even more immediate is research on the spot. Before writing *The Guns* I rented a little Renault and in another August drove over the battle areas of August 1914, following the track of the German invasion through Luxembourg, Belgium, and northern France. Besides obtaining a feeling of the geography, distances, and terrain involved in military movements, I saw the fields ripe with grain which the cavalry would have trampled, measured the great width of the Meuse at Liège, and saw how the lost territory of Alsace looked to the French soldiers who gazed down upon it from the heights of the Vosges. I learned the discomfort of the Belgian *pavé* and discovered, in the course of losing my way almost permanently in a tangle of country roads in a hunt for the house that had been British Headquarters, why a British motorcycle dispatch rider in 1914 had taken three hours to cover twenty-five miles. Clearly, owing to the British officers' preference for country houses, he had not been able to find Headquarters either. French army commanders, I noticed, located themselves in *towns,* with railroad stations and telegraph offices.

14   As to the mechanics of research, I take notes on four-by-six index cards, reminding myself about once an hour of a rule I read long ago in a research manual, "Never write on the back of anything." Since copying is a chore and a bore, use of the cards, the smaller the better, forces one to extract the strictly relevant, to distill from the very beginning, to pass the material through the grinder of one's own mind, so to speak. Eventually, as the cards fall into groups according to subject or person or chronological sequence, the pattern of my story will emerge. Besides, they are convenient, as they can be filed in a shoebox and carried around in a pocketbook. When ready to write I need only take along a packet of them, representing a chapter, and I am equipped to work anywhere; whereas if one writes surrounded by a pile of books, one is tied to a single place, and furthermore likely to be too much influenced by other authors.

15   The most important thing about research is to know when to stop. How does one recognize the moment? When I was

eighteen or thereabouts, my mother told me that when out with a young man I should always leave a half-hour before I wanted to. Although I was not sure how this might be accomplished, I recognized the advice as sound, and exactly the same rule applies to research. One must stop *before* one has finished; otherwise, one will never stop and never finish. I had an object lesson in this once in Washington at the Archives. I was looking for documents in the case of Perdicaris, an American—or supposed American—who was captured by Moroccan brigands in 1904. The Archives people introduced me to a lady professor who had been doing research in United States relations with Morocco all her life. She had written her Ph.D. thesis on the subject back in, I think, 1936, and was still coming for six months each year to work in the Archives. She was in her seventies and, they told me, had recently suffered a heart attack. When I asked her what year was her cut-off point, she looked at me in surprise and said she kept a file of newspaper clippings right up to the moment. I am sure she knew more about United States–Moroccan relations than anyone alive, but would she ever leave off her research in time to write that definitive history and tell the world what she knew? I feared the answer. Yet I know how she felt. I too feel compelled to follow every lead and learn everything about a subject, but fortunately I have an even more overwhelming compulsion to see my work in print. That is the only thing that saves me.

Research is endlessly seductive; writing is hard work. One has to sit down on that chair and think and transform thought into readable, conservative, interesting sentences that both make sense and make the reader turn the page. It is laborious, slow, often painful, sometimes agony. It means rearrangement, revision, adding, cutting, rewriting. But it brings a sense of excitement, almost of rapture; a moment on Olympus. In short, it is an act of creation.

ADVICE FROM BARBARA TUCHMAN

Practice—the only way to learn to write is to write.
Become enthralled with your subject—your enthusiasm can be transmitted to your reader.

Use primary sources for careful research.
Develop skill in the "mechanics" of research; through research you unearth those facts that are basic to writing.
Select among your facts and details—selection is the basis of "art." "To discard the unnecessary requires courage and . . . extra work."
Know when to stop the research and begin the work of writing.
Keep your prose economical, clear, direct; use your ear to test the sound of your sentences.

Activities and Writing Suggestions

1. With other members of your class, discuss the ways you go about writing:

- How do you find information?
- How much time do you spend planning, how much revising, and so on?
- How do you take notes? (cards, tablets?)
- How do you attempt to organize? by making an outline? in writing the rough draft?
- Do you test writing on your ear?

Consider how Tuchman's way differs from or is similar to your own or the ways of others in the group. Evaluate her suggestions.

2. Tuchman says, "One learns to write . . . in the practice thereof." Talk about your practice. How much time do you spend on a single composition? What proportion of time goes to finding content and what to changing the form? For the next two or three weeks, attempt to "practice" by keeping a journal or log, recording in it not just personal reactions but making notes on events of interest, conversations that are stimulating to thought, happenings of national or international interest. After keeping your record for a time, discuss the value of the journal as practice.

3. Tuchman is conscious of audience as she writes; she says that the historian has an obligation to "enthrall the reader." Choose a

non-fiction book or an article that you have found particularly interesting, and write a short paper telling *how* it "enthralls." For instance, does the writer use narrative incident, one of Tuchman's favorite methods? What does the writer's language contribute to interest?

JOHN KENNETH GALBRAITH

Economist John Kenneth Galbraith offers advice for beginning writers, suggesting various syndromes to avoid.

Writing, Typing and Economics

1   Six or seven years ago, when I was spending a couple of terms at Trinity College, Cambridge, I received a proposal of more than usual interest from the University of California. It was that I resign from Harvard and accept a chair there in English. More precisely, it was to be the chair in rhetoric; they assured me that rhetoric was a traditional and not, as one would naturally suppose, a pejorative title. My task would be to hold seminars with the young on what I had learned about writing in general and on technical matters in particular.

2   I was attracted by the idea. I had spent several decades attempting to teach the young about economics. And the practical consequences were not reassuring. When I entered the field in the early 1930s, it was generally known that the modern economy could suffer a serious depression, and that it could have a serious inflation. In the ensuing forty years my teaching had principally advanced to the point of telling that it was possible to have both at once. This was soon to be associated with the belief of William Simon and Alan Greenspan, the gifts of Richard Nixon and Gerald Ford to our science, that progress in this subject is measured by the speed of the return to the ideas of the eighteenth century. A subject where it can be believed that you go ahead by going back has many problems for a teacher. Things are better now. Mr. Carter's economists do not believe in going back. But they are caught in a delicate balance between their fear of inflation and unemployment and their fear of doing anything about them. It is hard to conclude that economics is a productive intellectual and pedagogical investment.

3   Then I began to consider what I could tell about writing.

My experience was certainly ample. I had been initiated by two inspired professors in Canada, O. J. Stevenson and E. C. McLean. They were men who deeply loved their craft and who were willing to spend endless hours with a student, however obscure his talent. I had been an editor of *Fortune,* which in my day meant mostly being a writer. Editor was thought a more distinguished title and justified more pay. Both as an editor proper and as a writer, I had had the close attention of Henry Robinson Luce. Harry Luce is in danger of being remembered for his political judgments, which left much to be desired; he found unblemished merit in John Foster Dulles, Robert A. Taft, and Chiang Kai-shek. But more important, he was an acute businessman and a truly brilliant editor. One proof is that while Time, Inc. publications have become politically more predictable since he departed, they have become infinitely less amusing.

Finally, as I reflected, among my qualifications was the amount of my life that I have spent at a typewriter. Nominally I have been a teacher. In practice I have been a writer—as generations of Harvard students have suspected. Faced with the choice of spending time on the unpublished scholarship of a graduate student or the unpublished work of Galbraith, I have rarely hesitated. Superficially, at least, I was well qualified for that California chair.

There was, however, a major difficulty. It was that I could tell everything I knew about writing in approximately half an hour. For the rest of the term I would have nothing to say except as I could invite discussion, this being the last resort of the empty academic mind. I could use up a few hours telling how a writer should deal with publishers. This is a field of study in which I especially rejoice. All authors should seek to establish a relationship of warmth, affection, and mutual mistrust with their publishers. This is in the hope that the uncertainty will add, however marginally, to compensation. But instruction on how to deal with publishers and how to bear up under the inevitable defeat would be for a very advanced course. It is not the sort of thing that the average beginning writer at Berkeley would find immediately practical.

So I returned to the few things that I could teach. The first lesson would have to do with the all-important issue of inspiration. All writers know that on some golden mornings they are touched by the wand—are on intimate terms with poetry and cosmic truth. I have experienced those moments myself. Their lesson is simple: It's a total illusion. And the danger in the illusion is that you will wait for those moments. Such is the horror of having to face the typewriter that you will spend all your time waiting. I am persuaded that most writers, like most shoemakers, are about as good one day as the next (a point which Trollope made), hangovers apart. The difference is the result of euphoria, alcohol, or imagination. The meaning is that one had better go to his or her typewriter every morning and stay there regardless of the seeming result. It will be much the same.

7   All professions have their own ways of justifying laziness. Harvard professors are deeply impressed by the jeweled fragility of their minds. More than the thinnest metal, these are subject terribly to fatigue. More than six hours teaching a week is fatal—and an impairment of academic freedom. So, at any given moment, they are resting their minds in preparation for the next orgiastic act of insight or revelation. Writers, in contrast, do nothing because they are waiting for inspiration.

8   In my own case there are days when the result is so bad that no fewer than five revisions are required. However, when I'm greatly inspired, only four revisions are needed before, as I've often said, I put in that note of spontaneity which even my meanest critics concede. My advice to those eager students in California would be, "Do not wait for the golden moment. It may well be worse." I would also warn against the flocking tendency of writers and its use as a cover for idleness. It helps greatly in the avoidance of work to be in the company of others who are also waiting for the golden moment. The best place to write is by yourself, because writing becomes an escape from the terrible boredom of your own personality. It's the reason that for years I've favored Switzerland, where I look at the telephone and yearn to hear it ring.

9   The question of revision is closely allied with that of inspiration. There may be inspired writers for whom the first draft is just right. But anyone who is not certifiably a Milton had better assume that the first draft is a very primitive thing. The

reason is simple: Writing is difficult work. Ralph Paine, who managed *Fortune* in my time, used to say that anyone who said writing was easy was either a bad writer or an unregenerate liar. Thinking, as Voltaire avowed, is also a very tedious thing which men—or women—will do anything to avoid. So all first drafts are deeply flawed by the need to combine composition with thought. Each later draft is less demanding in this regard. Hence the writing can be better. There does come a time when revision is for the sake of change—when one has become so bored with the words that anything that is different looks better. But even then it may be better.

For months in 1955–1956, when I was working on *The Affluent Society,* my title was "The Opulent Society." Eventually I could stand it no longer: the word opulent had a nasty, greasy sound. One day, before starting work, I looked up the synonyms in the dictionary. First to meet my eye was the word "affluent." I had only one worry; that was whether I could possibly sell it to the publisher. All publishers wish to have books called *The Crisis in American Democracy.* My title, to my surprise, was acceptable. Mark Twain once said that the difference between the right adjective and the next-best adjective is the difference between lightning and a lightning bug.

Next, I would stress a rather old-fashioned idea to those students. It was above all the lesson of Harry Luce. No one who worked for him ever again escaped the feeling that he was there looking over one's shoulder. In his hand was a pencil; down on each page one could expect, any moment, a long swishing wiggle accompanied by the comment: "This can go." Invariably it could. It was written to please the author and not the reader. Or to fill in the space. The gains from brevity are obvious; in most efforts to achieve brevity, it is the worst and dullest that goes. It is the worst and dullest that spoils the rest.

I know that brevity is now out of favor. The *New York Review of Books* prides itself on giving its authors as much space as they want and sometimes twice as much as they need. Even those who have read only Joyce must find their thoughts wandering before the end of the fortnightly article. Writing for television, I've learned in the last year or two, is an exercise in relentless condensation. It has left me with the feeling that even brevity can be carried to extremes. But the danger, as

I look at some of the newer fashions in writing, is not great.

13   The next of my injunctions, which I would impart with even less hope of success, would concern alcohol. Nothing is so pleasant. Nothing is so important for giving the writer a sense of confidence in himself. And nothing so impairs the product. Again there are exceptions: I remember a brilliant writer at *Fortune* for whom I was responsible, who could work only with his hat on and after consuming a bottle of Scotch. There were major crises in the years immediately after World War II, when Scotch was difficult to find. But it is, quite literally, very sobering to reflect upon how many good American writers have been destroyed by this solace—by the sauce. Scott Fitzgerald, Sinclair Lewis, Thomas Wolfe, Ernest Hemingway, William Faulkner—the list goes on and on. Hamish Hamilton, once my English publisher, put the question to James Thurber: "Jim, why is it so many of your great writers have ruined themselves with drink?" Thurber thought long and carefully and finally replied: "It's this way, Jamie. They wrote these novels, and they sold very well. They made a lot of money and so they could buy whiskey by the case."

14   Their reputation was universal. A few years before his death, John Steinbeck, an appreciative but not a compulsive drinker, went to Moscow. It was a triumphal tour; and in a letter that he sent me about his hosts, he said: "I found I enjoyed the Soviet hustlers pretty much. There was a kind of youthful honesty about their illicit intentions that was not without charm. And their lives are difficult under their four-party system [a reference that escapes me]. It takes a fairly deft or very lucky man to make his way upward in the worker's paradise." I later heard that one night, after a particularly effusive celebration, he decided to make his way back to the hotel on foot. On the way he was overcome by fatigue and the hospitality he had received and sat down on a bench in a small park to rest. A policeman, called a militiaman in Moscow, came along and informed John, who was now asleep, and his companion, who spoke Russian, that the benches could not be occupied at that hour. His companion explained, rightly, that John was a very great American writer and that an exception should be made. The militiaman insisted. The companion explained again, insisted more strongly. Presently a transcendental light came over the policeman's face. He looked at

Steinbeck asleep on the bench, inspected his condition more closely, recoiled slightly from the fumes, and said, "Oh, oh, Gemingway." Then he took off his cap and tiptoed carefully away.

We are all desperately afraid of sounding like Carry Nation. I must take the risk. Any writer who wants to do his best against a deadline should stick to Coca-Cola. If he doesn't have a deadline, he can risk Seven-Up.   15

Next, I would want to tell my students of a point strongly pressed, if my memory serves, by Shaw. He once said that as he grew older, he became less and less interested in theory, more and more interested in information. The temptation in writing is just the reverse. Nothing is so hard to come by as a new and interesting fact. Nothing is so easy on the feet as a generalization. I now pick up magazines and leaf through them looking for articles that are rich with facts; I do not care much what they are. Richly evocative and deeply percipient theory I avoid. It leaves me cold unless I am the author of it. My advice to all young writers is to stick to research and reporting with only a minimum of interpretation. And especially this is my advice to all older writers, particularly to columnists. As the feet give out, they seek to have the mind take their place.   16

Reluctantly, but from a long and terrible experience, I would urge my young writers to avoid all attempts at humor. It does greatly lighten one's task. I've often wondered who made it impolite to laugh at one's own jokes; it is one of the major enjoyments of life. And that is the point. Humor is an intensely personal, largely internal thing. What pleases some, including the source, does not please others. One laughs; another says, "Well, I certainly see nothing funny about that." And the second opinion has just as much standing as the first, maybe more. Where humor is concerned, there are no standards—no one can say what is good or bad, although you can be sure that everyone will. Only a very foolish man will use a form of language that is wholly uncertain in its effect. That is the nature of humor.   17

There are other reasons for avoiding humor. In our society the solemn person inspires far more trust than the one who laughs. The politician allows himself one joke at the beginning of his speech. A ritual. Then he changes his expression, affects   18 an aspect of morbid solemnity signaling that, after all, he is a totally serious man. Nothing so undermines a point as its association with a wisecrack—the very word is pejorative.

19   Also, as Art Buchwald has pointed out, we live in an age when it is hard to invent anything that is as funny as everyday life. How could one improve, for example, on the efforts of the great men of television to attribute cosmic significance to the offhand and hilarious way Bert Lance combined professed fiscal conservatism with an unparalleled personal commitment to the deficit financing of John Maynard Keynes? And because the real world is so funny, there is almost nothing you can do, short of labeling a joke a joke, to keep people from taking it seriously. A few years ago in *Harper's* I invented the theory that socialism in our time was the result of our dangerous addiction to team sports. The ethic of the team is all wrong for free enterprise. The code words are cooperation; team spirit; accept leadership; the coach is always right. Authoritarianism is sanctified; the individualist is a poor team player, a menace. All this our vulnerable adolescents learn. I announced the formation of an organization to combat this deadly trend and to promote boxing and track instead. I called it the C.I.A.—Congress for Individualist Athletics. Hundreds wrote in to *Harper's* asking to join. Or demanding that baseball be exempted. A batter is on his own. I presented the letters to the Kennedy Library.

20   Finally, I would come to a matter of much personal interest, intensely self-serving. It concerns the peculiar pitfalls of the writer who is dealing with presumptively difficult or technical matters. Economics is an example, and within the field of economics the subject of money, with the history of which I have been much concerned, is an especially good case. Any specialist who ventures to write on money with a view to making himself intelligible works under a grave moral hazard. He will be accused of oversimplification. The charge will be made by his fellow professionals, however obtuse or incompetent. They will have a sympathetic hearing from the layman. That is because no layman really expects to understand about money, inflation, or the International Monetary Fund. If he does, he suspects that he is being fooled. One can have respect only for someone who is decently confusing.

In the case of economics there are no important proposi- 21
tions that cannot be stated in plain language. Qualifications
and refinements are numerous and of great technical complexity. These are important for separating the good students from
the dolts. But in economics the refinements rarely, if ever,
modify the essential and practical point. The writer who seeks
to be intelligible needs to be right; he must be challenged if
his argument leads to an erroneous conclusion and especially
if it leads to the wrong action. But he can safely dismiss the
charge that he has made the subject too easy. The truth is not
difficult.

Complexity and obscurity have professional value—they 22
are the academic equivalents of apprenticeship rules in the
building trades. They exclude the outsiders, keep down the
competition, preserve the image of a privileged or priestly
class. The man who makes things clear is a scab. He is criticized less for his clarity than for his treachery.

Additionally, and especially in the social sciences, much 23
unclear writing is based on unclear or incomplete thought. It
is possible with safety to be technically obscure about something you haven't thought out. It is impossible to be wholly
clear on something you do not understand. Clarity thus ex-
poses flaws in the thought. The person who undertakes to
make difficult matters clear is infringing on the sovereign right
of numerous economists, sociologists, and political scientists
to make bad writing the disguise for sloppy, imprecise, or incomplete thought. One can understand the resulting anger.
Adam Smith, John Stuart Mill, John Maynard Keynes were
writers of crystalline clarity most of the time. Marx had great
moments, as in *The Communist Manifesto.* Economics owes very
little, if anything, to the practitioners of scholarly obscurity.
If any of my California students should come to me from the
learned professions, I would counsel them in all their writing
to keep the confidence of their colleagues. This they should
do by being always complex, always obscure, invariably a trifle
vague.

You might say that all this constitutes a meager yield for 24
a lifetime of writing. Or that writing on economics, as someone once said of Kerouac's prose, is not writing but typing.
True.

ADVICE FROM JOHN KENNETH GALBRAITH

Waiting for inspiration often leads to doing nothing.

A first draft is seldom effective; a writer must work at revision.

Experiment with words—study them, love them, find the "right" one.

Reject the false confidence of alcohol—a temptation for many writers.

Information is better than interpretation—facts more important than generalizing.

Beware of humor—it isn't funny to everyone.

Bad writing is often a disguise for sloppy thought— complexity and obscurity are indications of disregard for the reader.

Activities and Writing Suggestions

1. Write a short letter to Galbraith, telling him what in his essay you think will be helpful to you as a writer. Consider both ideas that may be new to you and those that are reinforced.

2. Because Galbraith is a popularizer of economics, he is sometimes looked down upon by academicians who scorn writing for a general audience. Would you like to see the qualities he advocates in writing and writers applied to scholarly books and textbooks? Why or why not? To what extent? Put your comments into a short letter to a publisher of scholarly materials.

3. From your reading in economics or another of the social sciences, choose some writing that you think meets Galbraith's standards for clarity. Then choose an example of writing that lacks such clarity. Write an analysis explaining why one is clear and the other is not. Share the examples in class as you discuss Galbraith's recommendations.

GEORGE ORWELL

Though he wrote this article nearly forty years ago, novelist George Orwell's observations and suggestions about the state of language are pertinent today.

Politics and the English Language

Most people who bother with the matter at all would admit that the English language is in a bad way, but it is generally assumed that we cannot by conscious action do anything about it. Our civilization is decadent and our language—so the argument runs—must inevitably share in the general collapse. It follows that any struggle against the abuse of language is a sentimental archaism, like preferring candles to electric light or hansom cabs to aeroplanes. Underneath this lies the half-conscious belief that language is a natural growth and not an instrument which we shape for our own purposes.

Now, it is clear that the decline of a language must ultimately have political and economic causes: it is not due simply to the bad influence of this or that individual writer. But an effect can become a cause, reinforcing the original cause and producing the same effect in an intensified form, and so on indefinitely. A man may take to drink because he feels himself to be a failure, and then fail all the more completely because he drinks. It is rather the same thing that is happening to the English language. It becomes ugly and inaccurate because our thoughts are foolish, but the slovenliness of our language makes it easier for us to have foolish thoughts. The point is that the process is reversible. Modern English, especially written English, is full of bad habits which spread by imitation and which can be avoided if one is willing to take the necessary trouble. If one gets rid of these habits one can think more clearly, and to think clearly is a necessary first step towards political regeneration: so that the fight against bad English is not frivolous and is not the exclusive concern of professional writers. I will come back to this presently, and I hope that by that time the meaning of what I have said here will have become clearer. Meanwhile, here are five specimens of the English language as it is now habitually written.

3   These five passages have not been picked out because they are especially bad—I could have quoted far worse if I had chosen—but because they illustrate various of the mental vices from which we now suffer. They are a little below the average, but are fairly representative samples. I number them so that I can refer back to them when necessary:

1. I am not, indeed, sure whether it is not true to say that the Milton who once seemed not unlike a seventeenth-century Shelley had not become, out of an experience ever more bitter in each year, more alien [*sic*] to the founder of that Jesuit sect which nothing could induce him to tolerate.

Professor Harold Laski (Essay in *Freedom of Expression*)

2. Above all, we cannot play ducks and drakes with a native battery of idioms which prescribes such egregious collocations of vocables as the Basic *put up with* for *tolerate* or *put at a loss* for *bewilder.*

Professor Lancelot Hogben *(Interglossa)*

3. On the one side we have the free personality: by definition it is not neurotic, for it has neither conflict nor dream. Its desires, such as they are, are transparent, for they are just what institutional approval keeps in the forefront of consciousness; another institutional pattern would alter their number and intensity; there is little in them that is natural, irreducible, or culturally dangerous. But *on the other side,* the social bond itself is nothing but the mutual reflection of these self-secure integrities. Recall the definition of love. Is not this the very picture of a small academic? Where is there a place in this hall of mirrors for either personality or fraternity?

Essay on Psychology in *Politics* (New York)

4. All the "best people" from the gentlemen's clubs, and all the frantic fascist captains, united in common hatred of Socialism and bestial horror of the rising tide of the mass revolutionary movement, have turned to acts of provocation, to foul incendiarism, to medieval legends of poisoned wells, to legalize their own destruction of proletarian organizations, and rouse the agitated petty-bourgeoisie to chauvinistic fervor on behalf of the fight against the revolutionary way out of the crisis.

Communist Pamphlet

5. If a new spirit *is* to be infused into this old country, there is one thorny and contentious reform which must be tackled, and that is the humanization and galvanization of the B.B.C. Timidity here will bespeak canker and atrophy of the soul. The heart of Britain may be sound and of strong beat, for instance, but the British lion's roar at present is like that of Bottom in Shakespeare's *Midsummer Night's Dream*—as gentle as any sucking dove. A virile new Britain cannot continue indefinitely to be traduced in the eyes or rather ears, of the world by the effete languors of Langham Place, brazenly masquerading as "standard English." When the voice of Britain is heard at nine o'clock, better far and infinitely less ludicrous to hear aitches honestly dropped than the present priggish, inflated, inhibited, school-ma'amish arch braying of blameless bashful mewing maidens!

Letter in *Tribune*

Each of these passages has faults of its own, but, quite apart from avoidable ugliness, two qualities are common to all of them. The first is staleness of imagery; the other is lack of precision. The writer either has a meaning and cannot express it, or he inadvertently says something else, or he is almost indifferent as to whether his words mean anything or not. This mixture of vagueness and sheer incompetence is the most marked characteristic of modern English prose, and especially of any kind of political writing. As soon as certain topics are raised, the concrete melts into the abstract and no one seems able to think of turns of speech that are not hackneyed: prose consists less and less of *words* chosen for the sake of their meaning, and more and more of *phrases* tacked together like the sections of a prefabricated hen-house. I list below, with notes and examples, various of the tricks by means of which the work of prose-construction is habitually dodged:

Dying Metaphors. A newly invented metaphor assists thought by evoking a visual image, while on the other hand a metaphor which is technically "dead" (e.g., *iron resolution*) has in effect reverted to being an ordinary word and can generally be used without loss of vividness. But in between these two classes there is a huge dump of worn-out metaphors which have lost all evocative power and are merely used because they save people the trouble of inventing phrases for themselves. Examples are: *Ring the changes on, take up the cudgels for, toe the line, ride roughshod over, stand shoulder to shoulder with, play into the hands of, no axe to grind, grist to the mill, fishing in troubled waters, on the order of the day, Achilles' heel, swan song, hotbed.* Many of these are used without knowledge of their meaning (what is a "rift," for instance?), and incompatible metaphors are frequently mixed, a sure sign that the writer is not interested in what he is saying. Some metaphors now current have been twisted out of their original meaning without those who use them even being aware of the fact. For example, *toe the line* is sometimes written *tow the line.* Another example is *the hammer and the anvil,* now always used with the implication that the anvil gets the worst of it. In real life it is always the anvil that breaks the hammer, never the other way about: a writer who stopped to think what he was saying would be aware of this, and would avoid perverting the original phrase.

6   *Operators or Verbal False Limbs.* These save the trouble of picking out appropriate verbs and nouns, and at the same time pad each sentence with extra syllables which give it an appearance of symmetry. Characteristic phrases are *render inoperative, militate against, make contact with, be subjected to, give rise to, give grounds for, have the effect of, play a leading part (role) in, make itself felt, take effect, exhibit a tendency to, serve the purpose of, etc., etc.* The keynote is the elimination of simple verbs. Instead of being a single word, such as *break, stop, spoil, mend, kill,* a verb becomes *a phrase,* made up of a noun or adjective tacked on to some general-purpose verb such as *prove, serve, form, play, render.* In addition, the passive voice is wherever possible used in preference to the active, and noun constructions are used instead of gerunds (*by examination of* instead of *by examining*). The range of verbs is further cut down by means of the *-ize* and *de-* formations, and the banal statements are given an appearance of profundity by means of the *not un-* formation. Simple conjunctions and prepositions are replaced by such phrases as *with respect to, having regard to, the fact that, by dint of, in view of, in the interests of, on the hypothesis that;* and the ends of sentences are saved from anticlimax by such resounding common-places as *greatly to be desired, cannot be left out of account, a development to be expected in the near future, deserving of serious*

consideration, brought to a satisfactory conclusion, and so on and so forth.

Pretentious Diction. Words like *phenomenon, element, individual* (as noun), *objective, categorical, effective, virtual, basic, primary, promote, constitute, exhibit, exploit, utilize, eliminate, liquidate,* are used to dress up simple statements and give an air of scientific impartiality to biased judgments. Adjectives like *epoch-making, epic, historic, unforgettable, triumphant, age-old, inevitable, inexorable, veritable,* are used to dignify the sordid processes of international politics, while writing that aims at glorifying war usually takes on an archaic color, its characteristic words being: *realm, throne, chariot, mailed fist, trident, sword, shield, buckler, banner, jackboot, clarion.* Foreign words and expressions such as *cul de sac, ancien régime, deus ex machina, mutatis mutandis, status quo, gleichschaltung, weltanschauung,* are used to give an air of culture and elegance. Except for the useful abbreviations *i.e., e.g.,* and *etc.,* there is no real need for any of the hundreds of foreign phrases now current in English. Bad writers, and especially scientific, political and sociological writers, are nearly always haunted by the notion that Latin or Greek words are grander than Saxon ones, and unnecessary words like *expedite, ameliorate, predict, extraneous, deracinated, clandestine, subaqueous* and hundreds of others constantly gain ground from their Anglo-Saxon opposite numbers.[1] The jargon peculiar to Marxist writing (*hyena, hangman, cannibal, petty bourgeois, these gentry, lacquey, flunkey, mad dog, White Guard,* etc.) consists largely of words and phrases translated from Russian, German or French; but the normal way of coining a new word is to use a Latin or Greek root with the appropriate affix and, where necessary, the *-ize* formation. It is often easier to make up words of this kind (*deregionalize, impermissible, extramarital, nonfragmentary* and so forth) than to think up the English words that will cover one's meaning. The result, in general, is an increase in slovenliness and vagueness.

Meaningless Words. In certain kinds of writing, particularly in art criticism and literary criticism, it is normal to come across long passages which are almost completely lacking in meaning.[2] Words like *romantic, plastic, values, human, dead, sentimental, natural, vitality,* as used in art criticism, are strictly meaningless, in the sense that they not only do not point to

7

8

any discoverable object, but are hardly ever expected to do so by the reader. When one critic writes, "The outstanding feature of Mr. X's work is its living quality," while another writes, "The immediately striking thing about Mr. X's work is its peculiar deadness," the reader accepts this as a simple difference of opinion. If words like *black* and *white* were involved, instead of the jargon words *dead* and *living,* he would see at once that language was being used in an improper way. Many political words are similarly abused. The word *Fascism* has now no meaning except in so far as it signifies "something not desirable." The words *democracy, socialism, freedom, patriotic, realistic, justice,* have each of them several different meanings which cannot be reconciled with one another. In the case of a word like *democracy,* not only is there no agreed definition, but the attempt to make one is resisted from all sides. It is almost universally felt that when we call a country democratic we are praising it: consequently the defenders of every kind of régime claim that it is a democracy, and fear that they might have to stop using the word if it were tied down to any one meaning. Words of this kind are often used in a consciously dishonest way. That is, the person who uses them has his own private definition, but allows his hearer to think he means something quite different. Statements like *Marshal Pétain was a true patriot, The Soviet Press is the freest in the world, The Catholic Church is opposed to persecution,* are almost always made with intent to deceive. Other words used in variable meanings, in most cases more or less dishonestly, are: *class, totalitarian, science, progressive, reactionary, bourgeois, equality.*

9   Now that I have made this catalogue of swindles and perversions, let me give another example of the kind of writing that they lead to. This time it must of its nature be an imaginary one. I am going to translate a passage of good English into modern English of the worst sort. Here is a well-known verse from *Ecclesiastes:*

> I returned and saw under the sun, that the race is not to the swift, nor the battle to the strong, neither yet bread to the wise, nor yet riches to men of understanding, nor yet favour to men of skill; but time and chance happeneth to them all.

Here it is in modern English:

Objective consideration of contemporary phenomena compels
the conclusion that success or failure in competitive activities exhibits no tendency to be commensurate with innate capacity, but
that a considerable element of the unpredictable must invariably
be taken into account.

This is a parody, but not a very gross one. Exhibit (3),
above, for instance, contains several patches of the same kind
of English. It will be seen that I have not made a full translation. The beginning and ending of the sentence follow the
original meaning fairly closely, but in the middle the concrete
illustrations—race, battle, bread—dissolve into the vague
phrase "success or failure in competitive activities." This had
to be so, because no modern writer of the kind I am discussing—no one capable of using phrases like "objective consideration of contemporary phenomena"—would ever tabulate his
thoughts in that precise and detailed way. The whole tendency
of modern prose is away from concreteness. Now analyze
these two sentences a little more closely. The first contains
forty-nine words but only sixty syllables, and all its words are
those of everyday life. The second contains thirty-eight words
of ninety syllables: eighteen of its words are from Latin roots,
and one from Greek. The first sentence contains six vivid images, and only one phrase ("time and chance") that could be
called vague. The second contains not a single fresh, arresting
phrase, and in spite of its ninety syllables it gives only a short-
ened version of the meaning contained in the first. Yet without a doubt it is the second kind of sentence that is gaining
ground in modern English. I do not want to exaggerate. This
kind of writing is not yet universal, and outcrops of simplicity
will occur here and there in the worst-written page. Still, if
you or I were told to write a few lines on the uncertainty of
human fortunes, we should probably come much nearer to my
imaginary sentence than to the one from *Ecclesiastes.*

As I have tried to show, modern writing at its worst does
not consist in picking out words for the sake of their meaning
and inventing images in order to make the meaning clearer.
It consists in gumming together long strips of words which
have already been set in order by someone else, and making
the results presentable by sheer humbug. The attraction of this
way of writing is that it is easy. It is easier—even quicker, once

10

11

you have the habit—to say *In my opinion it is not an unjustifiable assumption that* than to say *I think.* If you use ready-made phrases, you not only don't have to hunt about for words; you also don't have to bother with the rhythms of your sentences, since these phrases are generally so arranged as to be more or less euphonious. When you are composing in a hurry—when you are dictating to a stenographer, for instance, or making a public speech—it is natural to fall into a pretentious, Latinized style. Tags like *a consideration which we should do well to bear in mind* or a *conclusion to which all of us would readily assent* will save many a sentence from coming down with a bump. By using stale metaphors, similes and idioms, you save much mental effort, at the cost of leaving your meaning vague, not only for your reader but for yourself. This is the significance of mixed metaphors. The sole aim of a metaphor is to call up a visual image. When these images clash—as in *The Fascist octopus has sung its swan song, the jackboot is thrown into the melting pot*—it can be taken as certain that the writer is not seeing a mental image of the objects he is naming; in other words he is not really thinking. Look again at the examples I gave at the beginning of this essay. Professor Laski (1) uses five negatives in fifty-three words. One of these is superfluous, making nonsense of the whole passage, and in addition there is the slip *alien* for *akin,* making further nonsense, and several avoidable pieces of clumsiness which increase the general vagueness. Professor Hogben (2) plays ducks and drakes with a battery which is able to write prescriptions, and while, disapproving of the everyday phrase *put up with,* is unwilling to look *egregious* up in the dictionary and see what it means; (3), if one takes an uncharitable attitude towards it, is simply meaningless: probably one could work out its intended meaning by reading the whole of the article in which it occurs. In (4), the writer knows more or less what he wants to say, but an accumulation of stale phrases chokes him like tea leaves blocking a sink. In (5), words and meaning have almost parted company. People who write in this manner usually have a general emotional meaning—they dislike one thing and want to express solidarity with another—but they are not interested in the detail of what they are saying. A scrupulous writer, in every sentence that he writes, will ask himself at least four questions, thus: What am I trying to say? What words will express it? What image or idiom will make it clearer? Is this image fresh enough to have an effect? And he will probably ask himself two more: Could I put it more shortly? Have I said anything that is avoidably ugly? But you are not obliged to go to all this trouble. You can shirk it by simply throwing your mind open and letting the ready-made phrases come crowding in. They will construct your sentences for you—even think your thoughts for you, to a certain extent—and at need they will perform the important service of partially concealing your meaning even from yourself. It is at this point that the special connection between politics and the debasement of language becomes clear.

In our time it is broadly true that political writing is bad writing. Where it is not true, it will generally be found that the writer is some kind of rebel, expressing his private opinions and not a "party line." Orthodoxy, of whatever color, seems to demand a lifeless, imitative style. The political dialects to be found in pamphlets, leading articles, manifestos, White Papers and the speeches of undersecretaries do, of course, vary from party to party, but they are all alike in that one almost never finds in them a fresh, vivid, home-made turn of speech. When one watches some tired hack on the platform mechanically repeating the familiar phrases—*bestial atrocities, iron heel, bloodstained tyranny, free peoples of the world, stand shoulder to shoulder*—one often has a curious feeling that one is not watching a live human being but some kind of dummy: a feeling which suddenly becomes stronger at moments when the light catches the speaker's spectacles and turns them into blank discs which seem to have no eyes behind them. And this is not altogether fanciful. A speaker who uses that kind of phraseology has gone some distance towards turning himself into a machine. The appropriate noises are coming out of his larynx, but his brain is not involved as it would be if he were choosing his words for himself. If the speech he is making is one that he is accustomed to make over and over again, he may be almost unconscious of what he is saying, as one is when one utters the responses in church. And this reduced state of consciousness, if not indispensable, is at any rate favorable to political conformity.

12

13   In our time, political speech and writing are largely the defense of the indefensible. Things like the continuance of British rule in India, the Russian purges and deportations, the dropping of the atom bombs on Japan, can indeed be defended, but only by arguments which are too brutal for most people to face, and which do not square with the professed aims of political parties. Thus political language has to consist largely of euphemism, question-begging, and sheer cloudy vagueness. Defenseless villages are bombarded from the air, the inhabitants driven out into the countryside, the cattle machine-gunned, the huts set on fire with incendiary bullets: this is called *pacification.* Millions of peasants are robbed of their farms and sent trudging along the roads with no more than they can carry: this is called *transfer of population* or *rectification of frontiers.* People are imprisoned for years without trial, or shot in the back of the neck or sent to die of scurvy in Arctic lumber camps: this is called *elimination of unreliable elements.* Such phraseology is needed if one wants to name things without calling up mental pictures of them. Consider for instance some comfortable English professor defending Russian totalitarianism. He cannot say outright, "I believe in killing off your opponents when you can get good results by doing so." Probably, therefore, he will say something like this:

> While freely conceding that the Soviet regime exhibits certain features which the humanitarian may be inclined to deplore, we must, I think, agree that a certain curtailment of the right to political opposition is an unavoidable concomitant of transitional periods, and that the rigors which the Russian people have been called upon to undergo have been amply justified in the sphere of concrete achievement.

14   The inflated style is itself a kind of euphemism. A mass of Latin words falls upon the facts like soft snow, blurring the outlines and covering up all the details. The great enemy of clear language is insincerity. When there is a gap between one's real and one's declared aims, one turns as it were instinctively to long words and exhausted idioms, like a cuttlefish squirting out ink. In our age there is no such thing as "keeping out of politics." All issues are political issues, and politics itself is a mass of lies, evasions, folly, hatred and schizophrenia.

When the general atmosphere is bad, language must suffer. I should expect to find—this is a guess which I have not sufficient knowledge to verify—that the German, Russian, and Italian languages have all deteriorated in the last ten to fifteen years, as a result of dictatorship.

But if thought corrupts language, language can also corrupt thought. A bad usage can spread by tradition and imitation, even among people who should and do know better. The debased language that I have been discussing is in some ways very convenient. Phrases like *a not unjustifiable assumption, leaves much to be desired, would serve no good purpose, a consideration which we should do well to bear in mind,* are a continuous temptation, a packet of aspirins always at one's elbow. Look back through this essay, and for certain you will find that I have again and again committed the very faults I am protesting against. By this morning's post I have received a pamphlet dealing with conditions in Germany. The author tells me that he "felt impelled" to write it. I open it at random, and here is almost the first sentence that I see: "[The Allies] have an opportunity not only of achieving a radical transformation of Germany's social and political structure in such a way as to avoid a nationalistic reaction in Germany itself, but at the same time of laying the foundations of a cooperative and unified Europe." You see, he "feels impelled" to write—feels, presumably, that he has something new to say—and yet his words, like cavalry horses answering the bugle, group themselves automatically into the familiar dreary pattern. This invasion of one's mind by ready-made phrases *(lay the foundations, achieve a radical transformation)* can only be prevented if one is constantly on guard against them, and every such phrase anaesthetizes a portion of one's brain.

I said earlier that the decadence of our language is probably curable. Those who deny this would argue, if they produced an argument at all, that language merely reflects existing social conditions, and that we cannot influence its development by any direct tinkering with words and constructions. So far as the general tone or spirit of a language goes, this may be true, but it is not true in detail. Silly words and expressions have often disappeared, not through any evolutionary process but owing to the conscious action of a minority. Two recent examples were *explore every avenue* and *leave no stone unturned,* which were killed by the jeers of a few journalists. There is a long list of flyblown metaphors which could similarly be got rid of if enough people would interest themselves in the job; and it should also be possible to laugh the *not un-* formation out of existence,[3] to reduce the amount of Latin and Greek in the average sentence, to drive out foreign phrases and strayed scientific words, and, in general, to make pretentiousness unfashionable. But all these are minor points. The defense of the English language implies more than this, and perhaps it is best to start by saying what it does *not* imply.

17   To begin with it has nothing to do with archaism, with the salvaging of obsolete words and turns of speech, or with the setting up of a "standard English" which must never be departed from. On the contrary, it is especially concerned with the scrapping of every word or idiom which has outworn its usefulness. It has nothing to do with correct grammar and syntax, which are of no importance so long as one makes one's meaning clear, or with the avoidance of Americanisms, or with having what is called a "good prose style." On the other hand it is not concerned with fake simplicity and the attempt to make written English colloquial. Nor does it even imply in every case preferring the Saxon word to the Latin one, though it does imply using the fewest and shortest words that will cover one's meaning. What is above all needed is to let the meaning choose the word, and not the other way about. In prose, the worst thing one can do with words is to surrender to them. When you think of a concrete object, you think wordlessly, and then, if you want to describe the thing you have been visualizing you probably hunt about till you find the exact words that seem to fit it. When you think of something abstract you are more inclined to use words from the start, and unless you make a conscious effort to prevent it, the existing dialect will come rushing in and do the job for you, at the expense of blurring or even changing your meaning. Probably it is better to put off using words as long as possible and get one's meaning as clear as one can through pictures or sensations. Afterwards one can choose—not simply *accept*—the phrases that will best cover the meaning, and then switch round and decide what impression one's words are likely to

make on another person. This last effort of the mind cuts out all stale or mixed images, all prefabricated phrases, needless repetitions, and humbug and vagueness generally. But one can often be in doubt about the effect of a word or a phrase, and one needs rules that one can rely on when instinct fails. I think the following rules will cover most cases:

1. Never use a metaphor, simile, or other figure of speech which you are used to seeing in print.
2. Never use a long word where a short one will do.
3. If it is possible to cut a word out, always cut it out.
4. Never use the passive where you can use the active.
5. Never use a foreign phrase, a scientific word, or a jargon word if you can think of an everyday English equivalent.
6. Break any of these rules sooner than say anything outright barbarous.

These rules sound elementary, and so they are, but they demand a deep change of attitude in anyone who has grown used to writing in the style now fashionable. One could keep all of them and still write bad English, but one could not write the kind of stuff that I quoted in those five specimens at the beginning of this article.

I have not here been considering the literary use of language, but merely language as an instrument for expressing and not for concealing or preventing thought. Stuart Chase and others have come near to claiming that all abstract words are meaningless, and have used this as a pretext for advocating a kind of political quietism. Since you don't know what Fascism is, how can you struggle against Fascism? One need not swallow such absurdities as this, but one ought to recognize that the present political chaos is connected with the decay of language, and that one can probably bring about some improvement by starting at the verbal end. If you simplify your English, you are freed from the worst follies of orthodoxy. You cannot speak any of the necessary dialects, and when you make a stupid remark its stupidity will be obvious, even to yourself. Political language—and with variations this is true of all political parties, from Conservatives to Anarchists—is designed to make lies sound truthful and murder respectable, and to give an appearance of solidity to pure wind. One cannot change this all in a moment, but one can at least change one's own habits, and from time to time one can even, if one jeers loudly enough, send some worn-out and useless phrase—some *jackboot, Achilles' heel, hotbed, melting pot, acid test, veritable inferno* or other lump of verbal refuse—into the dustbin where it belongs.

Notes

1. An interesting illustration of this is the way in which the English flower names which were in use till very recently are being ousted by Greek ones, *snapdragon* becoming *antirrhinum, forget-me-not* becoming *myosotis,* etc. It is hard to see any practical reason for this change of fashion: it is probably due to an instinctive turning-away from the more homely word and a vague feeling that the Greek word is scientific.

2. Example: "Comfort's catholicity of perception and image, strangely Whitmanesque in range, almost the exact opposite in aesthetic compulsion, continues to evoke that trembling atmospheric accumulative hinting at a cruel, an inexorably serene timelessness. . . . Wrey Gardiner scores by aiming at simple bull's-eyes with precision. Only they are not so simple, and through this contented sadness runs more than the surface bitter-sweet of resignation." *(Poetry Quarterly)*

3. One can cure oneself of the *not un-* formation by memorizing this sentence: *A not unblack dog was chasing a not unsmall rabbit across a not ungreen field.*

SIX TIMELESS RULES FROM GEORGE ORWELL

Never use a metaphor, simile or other figure of speech which you are used to seeing in print.
Never use a long word where a short one will do.
If it is possible to cut a word out, always cut it out.
Never use the passive where you can use the active.
Never use a foreign phrase, a scientific word or a jargon word if you can think of an everyday English equivalent.
Break any of these rules sooner than say anything outright barbarous.

Activities and Writing Suggestions

1. The year 1984 will bring many reviews, articles, and conferences devoted to the contributions of George Orwell, whose novel *1984* predicted the changes that might occur by that time. Using

the research methods suggested by Barbara Tuchman, write a paper about Orwell's life and literary works, both his fiction and non-fiction. Concentrate, if you wish, on his thought about society and politics, about the human condition and what needs to be done to make it better.

2. Like Orwell, critics today sometimes label political language "doublespeak." Select a bill or a speech from current political publications and apply Orwell's six rules as a test of clarity. Or select examples from well-known persons in public life and write a set of rules that you think should be respected. Your rules may or may not be similar to Orwell's.

3. Sociologists are sometimes accused of employing a jargon labeled *sociologese;* educators, of using *educationese.* Make a list of words used in a special way in some course you are taking—sociology, psychology, education, literature. Report on that special vocabulary; consider the difference between jargon that obscures and useful shop talk.

4. Write a paper about computer language, a new vocabulary that many students now must master. Use your dictionary to discover which words are still unlisted there. Write seriously or satirically, as you wish.

ARTHUR SCHLESINGER, JR.

Applying Orwell's ideas to the American language, historian
Arthur Schlesinger, Jr., shows how and why our language has
collapsed and calls for a restoration of clear, precise prose.

Politics and the American Language

In our time, political speech and writing
are largely the defence of the indefensible.
—George Orwell

1   It takes a certain fortitude to pretend to amend Orwell on this
subject. But "Politics and the English Language"—which I
herewith incorporate by reference—was written more than a
generation ago. In the years since, the process of semantic collapse has gathered speed, verified all of Orwell's expectations
and added new apprehensions for a new age. Americans in
particular have found this a painful period of self-recognition.
In 1946 we comfortably supposed that Orwell was talking
about other people—Nazis and Stalinists, bureaucrats and sociologists, Professor Lancelot Hogben and Professor Harold
Laski. Now recent history has obliged us to extend his dispirit-
ing analysis to ourselves.

2   Vietnam and Watergate: these horrors will trouble the rest
of our lives. But they are not, I suppose, unmitigated horrors.
"Every act rewards itself," said Emerson. As Vietnam instructed us, at terrible cost, in the limit of our wisdom and
power in foreign affairs, so Watergate instructed us, at considerably less cost, in the limits of wisdom and power in the presidency. It reminded us of the urgent need to restore the original balance of the Constitution—the balance between
presidential power and presidential accountability. In doing
this, it has, among other things, brought back into public consciousness the great documents under which the American
government was organized.

3   The Constitution, the debates of the Constitutional Con-

vention, *The Federalist Papers*—how many of us read them with sustained attention in earlier years? A few eccentrics like Justice Black and Senator Ervin pored over them with devotion. The rest of us regarded them, beyond an occasional invocation of the Bill of Rights or the Fourteenth Amendment, as documents of essentially historical interest and left them undisturbed on the shelf. Then, under the goad first of Vietnam and then of Watergate, legislators, editors, columnists, even political scientists and historians—everyone, it would seem, except for presidential lawyers—began turning the dusty pages in order to find out what Madison said in the convention about the war-making power or how Hamilton defined the grounds for impeachment in the sixty-fifth Federalist. Vietnam and Watergate are hardly to be compared. One is high tragedy, the other low, if black, comedy. But between them they have given the American people a spectacular reeducation in the fundamentals of our constitutional order.

One cannot doubt that this experience will have abiding   4
political significance. The effect of Vietnam in exorcising our illusions and chastening our ambitions in foreign affairs has long been manifest. Now we begin to see the effect of Watergate in raising the standards of our politics. But I am less concerned initially with the political than with the literary consequences of this return to our constitutional womb. For, in addition to their exceptional qualities of insight and judgment, the historic documents must impress us by the extraordinary distinction of their language.

This was the age of the Enlightenment in America. The   5
cooling breeze of reason tempered the hot work of composition and argument. The result was the language of the Founding Fathers—lucid, measured and felicitous prose, marked by Augustan virtues of harmony, balance and elegance. People not only wrote this noble language. They also read it. The essays in defense of the Constitution signed Publius appeared week after week in the New York press during the winter of 1787–88; and the demand was so great that the first thirty-six Federalist papers were published in book form while the rest were still coming out in the papers. One can only marvel at the sophistication of an audience that consumed and relished pieces so closely reasoned, so thoughtful and analytical. To

compare *The Federalist Papers* with their equivalents in the press of our own day—say, with the contributions to the Op Ed page of the *New York Times*—is to annotate the decay of political discourse in America.

6   No doubt the birth of a nation is a stimulus to lofty utterance. The Founding Fathers had a profound conviction of historical responsibility. "The people of this country, by their conduct and example," Madison wrote in *The Federalist*, "will decide the important question, whether societies of men are really capable or not of establishing good government from reflection and choice, or whether they are forever destined to depend for their political constitutions on accident and force." The substitution of reflection and choice for accident and force proposed a revolution in the history of government; and the authors of *The Federalist* were passionate exemplars of the politics of reason.

7   The Founding Fathers lived, moreover, in an age when politicians could say in public more or less what they believed in private. If their view of human nature was realistic rather than sentimental, they were not obliged to pretend otherwise. *The Federalist,* for example, is a work notably free of false notes. It must not be supposed, however, that even this great generation was immune to temptation. When the Founding Fathers turned to speak of and to the largest interest in a primarily agricultural nation, they changed their tone and relaxed their standards. Those who lived on the soil, Jefferson could inanely write, were "the chosen people of God . . . whose breasts He has made His peculiar deposit for substantial and genuine virtue." Such lapses from realism defined one of the problems of American political discourse. For, as society grew more diversified, new interests claimed their place in the sun; and each in time had to be courted and flattered as the Jeffersonians had courted and flattered the agriculturists. The desire for success at the polls thus sentimentalized and cheapened the language of politics.

8   And politics was only an aspect of a deeper problem. Society as a whole was taking forms that warred against clarity of thought and integrity of language. "A man's power to connect his thought with its proper symbol, and so to utter it," said Emerson, "depends on the simplicity of his character, that is,

upon his love of truth, and his desire to communicate it without loss. The corruption of man is followed by the corruption of language. When simplicity of character and the sovereignty of ideas is broken up by the prevalence of secondary desires, the desire of riches, of pleasure, of power, and of praise . . . words are perverted to stand for things which are not."

"The prevalence of secondary desires," the desire of riches, pleasure, power and praise—this growing social complexity began to divert the function of words from expression to gratification. No one observed the impact of a mobile and egalitarian society on language more acutely than Tocqueville. Democracy, he argued, inculcated a positive preference for ambiguity and a dangerous addiction to the inflated style. "An abstract term," Tocqueville wrote, "is like a box with a false bottom; you may put in what you please, and take them out again without being observed." So words, divorced from objects, became instruments less of communication than of deception. Unscrupulous orators stood abstractions on their head and transmuted them into their opposites, aiming to please one faction by the sound and the contending faction by the meaning. They did not always succeed. "The word *liberty* in the mouth of Webster," Emerson wrote with contempt after the Compromise of 1850, "sounds like the word *love* in the mouth of a courtezan." Watching Henry Kissinger babbling about his honor at his famous Salzburg press conference, one was irresistibly reminded of another of Emerson's nonchalant observations: "The louder he talked of his honor, the faster we counted our spoons."

Other developments hastened the spreading dissociation of words from meaning, of language from reality. The rise of mass communications, the growth of large organizations and novel technologies, the invention of advertising and public relations, the professionalization of education—all contributed to linguistic pollution, upsetting the ecological balance between words and their environment. In our own time the purity of language is under unrelenting attack from every side—from professors as well as from politicians, from newspapermen as well as from advertising men, from men of the cloth as well as from men of the sword, and not least from those indulgent compilers of modern dictionaries who propound the suicidal thesis that all usages are equal and all correct.

11   A living language can never be stabilized, but a serious language can never cut words altogether adrift from meanings. The alchemy that changes words into their opposites has never had more adept practitioners than it has today. We used to object when the Communists described dictatorships as "people's democracies" or North Korean aggression as the act of a "peace-loving" nation. But we are no slouches ourselves in the art of verbal metamorphosis. There was often not much that was "free" about many of the states that made up what we used to call, sometimes with capital letters, the Free World; as there is, alas, very often little that is gay about many of those who seek these days to kidnap that sparkling word for specialized use. Social fluidity, moral pretension, political and literary demagoguery, corporate and academic bureaucratization and a false conception of democracy are leading us into semantic chaos. We owe to Vietnam and Watergate a belated recognition of the fact that we are in linguistic as well as political crisis and that the two may be organically connected. As Emerson said, "We infer the spirit of the nation in great measure from the language."

12   For words are not neutral instruments, pulled indifferently out of a jumbled tool kit. "Language," wrote Coleridge, "is the armoury of the human mind; and at once contains the trophies of its past, and the weapons of its future conquests." Language colors and penetrates the depths of our consciousness. It is the medium that dominates perceptions, organizes categories of thought, shapes the development of ideas and incorporates a philosophy of existence. Every political movement generates its own language-field; every language-field legitimizes one set of motives, values and ideals and banishes the rest. The language-field of the Founding Fathers directed the American consciousness toward one constellation of standards and purposes. The language-field of Vietnam and Watergate has tried to direct the national consciousness toward very different goals. Politics in basic aspects is a symbolic and therefore a linguistic phenomenon.

13   We began to realize this in the days of the Indochina War. In the middle 1960s Americans found themselves systemati-

cally staving off reality by allowing a horrid military-bureaucratic patois to protect our sensibilities from the ghastly things we were doing in Indochina. The official patter about "attrition," "pacification," "defoliation," "body counts," "progressive squeeze-and-talk," sterilized the frightful reality of napalm and My Lai. This was the period when television began to provide a sharper access to reality, and Marshall McLuhan had his day in court.

But the military-bureaucratic jargon could be blamed on generals, who, as General Eisenhower reminded us at every press conference, habitually speak in a dialect of their own. What we had not perhaps fully realized before Watergate was the utter debasement of language in the mouths of our recent civilian leaders. How our leaders really talk is not, of course, easy to discover, since their public appearances are often veiled behind speeches written by others. I know that President Kennedy spoke lucidly, wittily and economically in private. President Johnson spoke with force and often in pungent and inventive frontier idiom. President Nixon's fascinating contribution to oral history suggests, however, a recent and marked decline in the quality of presidential table talk. "A man cannot speak," said Emerson, "but he judges himself."

Groping to describe that degenerate mélange of military, public relations and locker-room jargon spoken in the Nixon White House, Richard N. Goodwin aptly wrote of "the bureaucratization of the criminal class." It was as if the Godfather spoke in the phrases of the secretary of health, education and welfare. When one read of "stroking sessions," of "running out of the bottom line," of "toughing it out," of going down "the hang-out road," or "how do you handle that PR-wise," one felt that there should be one more impeachable offense; and that is verbicide. But what was worse than the massacre of language, which after all displayed a certain low ingenuity, was the manipulation of meaning. The presidential speech preceding the release of the expurgated transcripts was syntactically correct enough. But it proclaimed in tones of ringing sincerity that the transcripts showed exactly the opposite of what in fact the transcripts did show. "He unveils a swamp," as the *New Yorker* well put it, "and instructs us to see a garden of flowers." In the Nixon White House, language not only fled the reality principle but became the servant of nightmare.

16   "The use of words," wrote Madison in the thirty-seventh *Federalist,* "is to express ideas. Perspicuity, therefore, requires not only that the ideas should be distinctly formed, but that they should be expressed by words distinctly and exclusively appropriate to them." Madison was under no illusion that this condition of semantic beatitude was easy to attain. "No language is so copious," he continued, "as to supply words and phrases for every complex idea, or so correct as not to include many equivocally denoting different ideas. . . . When the Almighty himself condescends to address mankind in their own language, his meaning, luminous as it must be, is rendered dim and doubtful by the cloudy medium through which it is communicated." Nevertheless, Madison and his generation thought the quest for precision worth the effort. It is an entertaining but morbid speculation to wonder what the Founding Fathers, returning to inspect the Republic on the eve of the two-hundredth anniversary of the independence they fought so hard to achieve, would make of the White House tapes.

17   The degradation of political discourse in America is bound to raise a disturbing question. May it be, as Tocqueville seemed to think, that such deterioration is inherent in democracy? Does the compulsion to win riches, pleasure, power and praise in a fluid and competitive society make the perversion of meaning and the debasement of language inevitable? One can certainly see specific American and democratic traits that have promoted linguistic decay. But a moment's reflection suggests that the process is by no means confined to the United States nor to democracies. Language degenerates a good deal more rapidly and thoroughly in communist and fascist states. For the control of language is a necessary step toward the control of minds, as Orwell made so brilliantly clear in *1984.* Nowhere is meaning more ruthlessly manipulated, nowhere is language more stereotyped, mechanical, implacably banal and systematically false, nowhere is it more purged of personal nuance and human inflection, than in Russia and China. In democracies the assault on language is piecemeal, sporadic and unorganized. And democracy has above all the decisive advantage that the preservation of intellectual freedom creates the

opportunity for counterattack. Democracy always has the chance to redeem its language. This may be an essential step toward the redemption of its politics.

One must add that it is idle to expect perfection in political   18 discourse. The problem of politics in a democracy is to win broad consent for measures of national policy. The winning of consent often requires the bringing together of disparate groups with diverging interests. This inescapably involves a certain oracularity of expression. One remembers de Gaulle before the crowd in Algeria, when the *pieds-noirs* chanted that Algeria belonged to France, replying solemnly, "Je vous comprends, mes camarades"—hardly a forthright expression of his determination to set Algeria free. Besides, oracularity may often be justified since no one can be all that sure about the future. The Founding Fathers understood this, which is why the Constitution is in many respects a document of calculated omission and masterful ambiguity whose "real" meaning—that is, what it would mean in practice—only practice could disclose. Moreover, as Lord Keynes, who wrote even economics in English, once put it, "Words ought to be a little wild, for they are an assault of thought upon the unthinking."

Keynes immediately added, however: "But when the seats   19 of power and authority have been attained, there should be no more poetic license." Madison described the American experiment as the replacement of accident and force by reflection and choice in the processes of government. The responsibility of presidents is to define real choices and explain soberly why one course is to be preferred to another—and, in doing so, to make language a means not of deception but of communication, not an enemy but a friend of the reality principle.

Yet presidents cannot easily rise above the society they   20 serve and lead. If we are to restore the relationship between words and meaning, we must begin to clean up the whole linguistic environment. This does not mean a crusade for standard English or a campaign to resurrect the stately rhythms of *The Federalist Papers.* Little could be more quixotic than an attempt to hold a rich and flexible language like American English to the forms and definitions of a specific time, class, or race. But some neologisms are better than others, and here one can demand, particularly in influential places, a modicum of discrimination. More important is that words, whether new or old, regain a relationship to reality. Vietnam and Watergate have given a good many Americans, I believe, a real hatred of double-talk and a hunger for bluntness and candor. Why else the success of the posthumous publication of President Truman's gaudy exercise in plain speaking?

21   The time is ripe to sweep the language-field of American politics. In this season of semantic malnutrition, who is not grateful for a public voice that appears to blurt out what the speaker honestly believes? A George Wallace begins to win support even among blacks (though ambition is already making Wallace bland, and blandness will do him in too). Here those who live by the word—I mean by the true word, like writers and teachers; not by the phony word, like public relations men, writers and teachers—have their peculiar obligation. Every citizen is free under the First Amendment to use and abuse the words that bob around in the swamp of his mind. But writers and teachers have, if anyone has, the custodianship of the language. Their charge is to protect the words by which they live. Their duty is to expel the cant of the age.

22   At the same time, they must not forget that in the recent past they have been among the worst offenders. They must take scrupulous care that indignation does not lead them to the same falsity and hyperbole they righteously condemn in others. A compilation of political pronouncements by eminent writers and learned savants over the last generation would make a dismal volume. One has only to recall the renowned, if addled, scholars who signed the full page advertisement in the *New York Times* of October 15, 1972, which read, as the *New Yorker* would say, in its entirety: "Of the two major candidates for the Presidency of the United States, we believe that Richard Nixon has demonstrated the superior capacity for prudent and responsible leadership. Consequently, we intend to vote for President Nixon on November 7th and we urge our fellow citizens to do the same."

23   The time has come for writers and teachers to meet the standards they would enforce on others and rally to the defense of the word. They must expose the attack on meaning and discrimination in language as an attack on reason in dis-

course. It is this rejection of reason itself that underlies the indulgence of imprecision, the apotheosis of usage and the infatuation with rhetoric. For once words lose a stable connection with things, we can no longer know what we think or communicate what we believe.

One does not suggest that the restoration of language is   24
all that easy in an age when new issues, complexities and ambiguities stretch old forms to the breaking point.

> . . . Words strain
> Crack and sometimes break, under the burden,
> Under the tension, slip, slide, perish,
> Decay with imprecision, will not stay in place,
> Will not stay still.

Each venture is therefore the new beginning, the raid on the inarticulate with shabby equipment always deteriorating in the general mess of imprecision of feeling. Yet, as Eliot went on to say, "For us, there is only the trying. The rest is not our business." As we struggle to recover what has been lost ("and found and lost again and again"), as we try our own sense of words against the decay of language, writers and teachers make the best contribution they can to the redemption of politics. Let intellectuals never forget that all they that take the word shall perish with the word. "Wise men pierce this rotten diction," said Emerson, "and fasten words again to visible things; so that picturesque language is at once a commanding certificate that he who employs it, is a man in alliance with truth and God."

SCHLESINGER'S WARNINGS AND ADVICE

Avoid the linguistic dangers of
—separating words from their meanings by hiding behind abstractions and euphemisms;
—manipulating meaning, saying one thing but meaning another, as Orwell warns with the concept of Doublespeak.

Improve your awareness of style by reading *The Federalist Papers* and other timeless documents.
Realize that character shows in writing; the writer reveals the inner self.

Activities and Writing Suggestions

1. Read (or reread) some of *The Federalist Papers* and the United States Constitution; hold a class discussion about the style of these early documents. Consider, for instance, the fact that political tracts two centuries ago were not subject to immediate dissemination by television and radio.

2. Choose a particularly memorable sentence from Schlesinger's essay and use it as a topic or thesis for a paper developed with examples from your experience or reading. For instance, illustrate, with examples of your own, the sentence "For words are not neutral instruments, pulled indifferently out of a jumbled tool kit" (par. 12).

3. Write a paper about "military dialect," the jargon of the military bureaucracy mentioned in paragraphs 13–14 and others in this essay. You might find supporting illustrations both in reading and by listening to radio and television reports.

4. Are words in political speeches always used (or even chiefly used) for duplicity rather than perspicuity, as Schlesinger charges? Answer this question by collecting examples you hear in the talk of politicians and government officials during the next several weeks.

Part Two

WRITING FOR MANY PURPOSES

3

PAPERS THAT INVESTIGATE AND REPORT

Many papers you write for classes in the social sciences require that you make a report based on an investigation of a particular topic. That investigation may involve what we call primary research; that is, you may actually look into a situation for yourself by studying your surroundings or people you know, or by collecting information through interviews or some other form of inquiry such as case studies or questionnaires. At other times you may supplement or even replace direct research by collecting information from reading about a problem that you are investigating. Whatever your sources and methods, you will probably start with a preliminary question or questions, something that you want to know and about which you have some guesses as to answers. That speculation leads you to formulate a hypothesis that you can then test, thus proving or disproving your initial idea by the facts you actually discover.

In writing your report you will sometimes explain not only the results but how you conducted the investigation. At other times you will merely identify the area of concern and report the facts that lead to your conclusions. Some of those facts, of course, may be in the form of statistics that you have gathered and that you perhaps present in the form of tables, charts, or graphs. Whatever is involved in your reporting, you must be thorough and honest. Even though you may not be able to convey to your reader every bit of information you collect, you should avoid any tendency to select only material that proves something you want to prove. Your paper must present sufficient evidence to show how you arrive at your answers, and it must be clear and orderly.

The five selections that follow exemplify various ways of conducting and reporting an investigation.

LAURA BOHANNAN

Laura Bohannan, an anthropologist, set out to test a hypothesis by direct investigation. She found some things that surprised her, as you will learn from her report of living among a group of West Africans whose culture she studied.

Shakespeare in the Bush

1 Just before I left Oxford for the Tiv in West Africa, conversation turned to the season at Stratford. "You Americans," said a friend, "often have difficulty with Shakespeare. He was, after all, a very English poet, and one can easily misinterpret the universal by misunderstanding the particular."

2 I protested that human nature is pretty much the same the whole world over; at least the general plot and motivation of the greater tragedies would always be clear—everywhere —although some details of custom might have to be explained and difficulties of translation might produce other slight changes. To end an argument we could not conclude, my friend gave me a copy of *Hamlet* to study in the African bush: it would, he hoped, lift my mind above its primitive surroundings, and possibly I might, by prolonged meditation, achieve the grace of correct interpretation.

3 It was my second field trip to that African tribe, and I thought myself ready to live in one of its remote sections—an area difficult to cross even on foot. I eventually settled on the hillock of a very knowledgeable old man, the head of a homestead of some hundred and forty people, all of whom were either his close relatives or their wives and children. Like the other elders of the vicinity, the old man spent most of his time performing ceremonies seldom seen these days in the more accessible parts of the tribe. I was delighted. Soon there would be three months of enforced isolation and leisure, between the harvest that takes place just before the rising of the swamps and the clearing of new farms when the water goes down. Then, I thought, they would have even more time to perform ceremonies and explain them to me.

4 I was quite mistaken. Most of the ceremonies demanded

the presence of elders from several homesteads. As the swamps rose, the old men found it too difficult to walk from one homestead to the next, and the ceremonies gradually ceased. As the swamps rose even higher, all activities but one came to an end. The women brewed beer from maize and millet. Men, women, and children sat on their hillocks and drank it.

People began to drink at dawn. By midmorning the whole   5 homestead was singing, dancing, and drumming. When it rained, people had to sit inside their huts: there they drank and sang or they drank and told stories. In any case, by noon or before, I either had to join the party or retire to my own hut and my books. "One does not discuss serious matters when there is beer. Come, drink with us." Since I lacked their capacity for the thick native beer, I spent more and more time with *Hamlet.* Before the end of the second month, grace descended on me. I was quite sure that *Hamlet* had only one possible interpretation, and that one universally obvious.

Early every morning, in the hope of having some serious   6 talk before the beer party, I used to call on the old man at his reception hut—a circle of posts supporting a thatched roof above a low mud wall to keep out wind and rain. One day I crawled through the low doorway and found most of the men of the homestead sitting huddled in their ragged cloths on stools, low plank beds, and reclining chairs, warming themselves against the chill of the rain around a smoky fire. In the center were three pots of beer. The party had started.

The old man greeted me cordially. "Sit down and drink."   7 I accepted a large calabash full of beer, poured some into a small drinking gourd, and tossed it down. Then I poured some more into the same gourd for the man second in seniority to my host before I handed my calabash over to a young man for further distribution. Important people shouldn't ladle beer themselves.

"It is better like this," the old man said, looking at me approvingly and plucking at the thatch that had caught in my   8 hair. "You should sit and drink with us more often. Your servants tell me that when you are not with us, you sit inside your hut looking at a paper."

The old man was acquainted with four kinds of "papers":   9 tax receipts, bride price receipts, court fee receipts, and letters. The messenger who brought him letters from the chief used them mainly as a badge of office, for he always knew what was in them and told the old man. Personal letters for the few who had relatives in the government or mission stations were kept until someone went to a large market where there was a letter writer and reader. Since my arrival, letters were brought to me to be read. A few men also brought me bride price receipts, privately, with requests to change the figures to a higher sum. I found moral arguments were of no avail, since in-laws are fair game, and the technical hazards of forgery difficult to explain to an illiterate people. I did not wish them to think me silly enough to look at any such papers for days on end, and I hastily explained that my "paper" was one of the "things of long ago" of my country.

10   "Ah," said the old man. "Tell us."

11   I protested that I was not a storyteller. Story-telling is a skilled art among them; their standards are high, and the audiences critical—and vocal in their criticism. I protested in vain. This morning they wanted to hear a story while they drank. They threatened to tell me no more stories until I told them one of mine. Finally, the old man promised that no one would criticize my style "for we know you are struggling with our language." "But," put in one of the elders, "you must explain what we do not understand, as we do when we tell you our stories." Realizing that here was my chance to prove *Hamlet* universally intelligible, I agreed.

12   The old man handed me some more beer to help me on with my storytelling. Men filled their long wooden pipes and knocked coals from the fire to place in the pipe bowls; then, puffing contentedly, they sat back to listen. I began in the proper style, "Not yesterday, not yesterday, but long ago, a thing occurred. One night three men were keeping watch outside the homestead of the great chief, when suddenly they saw the former chief approach them."

13   "Why was he no longer their chief?"

14   "He was dead," I explained. "That is why they were troubled and afraid when they saw him."

15   "Impossible," began one of the elders, handing his pipe

on to his neighbor, who interrupted, "Of course it wasn't the dead chief. It was an omen sent by a witch. Go on."

Slightly shaken, I continued. "One of these three was a man who knew things"—the closest translation for scholar, but unfortunately it also meant witch. The second elder looked triumphantly at the first. "So he spoke to the dead chief saying, 'Tell us what we must do so you may rest in your grave,' but the dead chief did not answer. He vanished, and they could see him no more. Then the man who knew things—his name was Horatio—said this event was the affair of the dead chief's son, Hamlet."   16

There was a general shaking of heads round the circle. "Had the dead chief no living brothers? Or was this son the chief?"   17

"No," I replied. "That is, he had one living brother who became the chief when the elder brother died."   18

The old men muttered: such omens were matters for chiefs and elders, not for youngsters; no good could come of going behind a chief's back; clearly Horatio was not a man who knew things.   19

"Yes, he was," I insisted, shooing a chicken away from my beer. "In our country the son is next to the father. The dead chief's younger brother had become the great chief. He had also married his elder brother's widow only about a month after the funeral."   20

"He did well," the old man beamed and announced to the others, "I told you that if we knew more about Europeans, we would find they really were very like us. In our country also," he added to me, "the younger brother marries the elder brother's widow and becomes the father of his children. Now, if your uncle, who married your widowed mother, is your father's full brother, then he will be a real father to you. Did Hamlet's father and uncle have one mother?"   21

His question barely penetrated my mind; I was too upset and thrown too far off balance by having one of the most important elements of *Hamlet* knocked straight out of the picture. Rather uncertainly I said that I thought they had the same mother, but I wasn't sure—the story didn't say. The old man told me severely that these genealogical details made all the   22 difference and that when I got home I must ask the elders about it. He shouted out the door to one of his younger wives to bring his goatskin bag.

23   Determined to save what I could of the mother motif, I took a deep breath and began again. "The son Hamlet was very sad because his mother had married again so quickly. There was no need for her to do so, and it is our custom for a widow not to go to her next husband until she has mourned for two years."

24   "Two years is too long," objected the wife, who had appeared with the old man's battered goatskin bag. "Who will hoe your farms for you while you have no husband?"

25   "Hamlet," I retorted without thinking, "was old enough to hoe his mother's farms himself. There was no need for her to remarry." No one looked convinced. I gave up. "His mother and the great chief told Hamlet not to be sad, for the great chief himself would be a father to Hamlet. Furthermore, Hamlet would be the next chief: therefore he must stay to learn the things of a chief. Hamlet agreed to remain, and all the rest went off to drink beer."

26   While I paused, perplexed at how to render Hamlet's disgusted soliloquy to an audience convinced that Claudius and Gertrude had behaved in the best possible manner, one of the younger men asked me who had married the other wives of the dead chief.

27   "He had no other wives," I told him.

28   "But a chief must have many wives! How else can he brew beer and prepare food for all his guests?"

29   I said firmly that in our country even chiefs had only one wife, that they had servants to do their work, and that they paid them from tax money.

30   It was better, they returned, for a chief to have many wives and sons who would help him hoe his farms and feed his people; then everyone loved the chief who gave much and took nothing—taxes were a bad thing.

31   I agreed with the last comment, but for the rest fell back on their favorite way of fobbing off my questions: "That is the way it is done, so that is how we do it."

32   I decided to skip the soliloquy. Even if Claudius was here thought quite right to marry his brother's widow, there re-

mained the poison motif, and I knew they would disapprove
of fratricide. More hopefully I resumed, "That night Hamlet
kept watch with the three who had seen his dead father. The
dead chief again appeared, and although the others were
afraid, Hamlet followed his dead father off to one side. When
they were alone, Hamlet's dead father spoke."

"Omens can't talk!" The old man was emphatic. 33

"Hamlet's dead father wasn't an omen. Seeing him might 34
have been an omen, but he was not." My audience looked as
confused as I sounded. "It *was* Hamlet's dead father. It was
a thing we call a 'ghost.' " I had to use the English word, for
unlike many of the neighboring tribes, these people didn't believe in the survival after death of any individuating part of
the personality.

"What is a 'ghost?' An omen?" 35

"No, a 'ghost' is someone who is dead but who walks 36
around and can talk, and people can hear him and see him but
not touch him."

They objected. "One can touch zombis." 37

"No, no! It was not a dead body the witches had animated 38
to sacrifice and eat. No one else made Hamlet's dead father
walk. He did it himself."

"Dead men can't walk," protested my audience as one 39
man.

I was quite willing to compromise. "A 'ghost' is the dead 40
man's shadow."

But again they objected. "Dead men cast no shadows." 41

"They do in my country," I snapped. 42

The old man quelled the babble of disbelief that arose im- 43
mediately and told me with that insincere, but courteous,
agreement one extends to the fancies of the young, ignorant,
and superstitious, "No doubt in your country the dead can
also walk without being zombis." From the depths of his bag
he produced a withered fragment of kola nut, bit off one end
to show it wasn't poisoned, and handed me the rest as a peace
offering.

"Anyhow," I resumed, "Hamlet's dead father said that his 44
own brother, the one who became chief, had poisoned him.
He wanted Hamlet to avenge him. Hamlet believed this in
his heart, for he did not like his father's brother." I took an-

other swallow of beer. "In the country of the great chief, living in the same homestead, for it was a very large one, was an important elder who was often with the chief to advise and help him. His name was Polonius. Hamlet was courting his daughter, but her father and her brother . . . [I cast hastily about for some tribal analogy] warned her not to let Hamlet visit her when she was alone on her farm, for he would be a great chief and so could not marry her."

45   "Why not?" asked the wife, who had settled down on the edge of the old man's chair. He frowned at her for asking stupid questions and growled, "They lived in the same homestead."

46   "That was not the reason," I informed them. "Polonius was a stranger who lived in the homestead because he helped the chief, not because he was a relative."

47   "Then why couldn't Hamlet marry her?"

48   "He could have," I explained, "but Polonius didn't think he would. After all, Hamlet was a man of great importance who ought to marry a chief's daughter, for in his country a man could have only one wife. Polonius was afraid that if Hamlet made love to his daughter, then no one else would give a high price for her."

49   "That might be true," remarked one of the shrewder elders, "but a chief's son would give his mistress's father enough presents and patronage to more than make up the difference. Polonius sounds like a fool to me."

50   "Many people think he was," I agreed. "Meanwhile Polonius sent his son Laertes off to Paris to learn the things of that country, for it was the homestead of a very great chief indeed. Because he was afraid that Laertes might waste a lot of money on beer and women and gambling, or get into trouble by fighting, he sent one of his servants to Paris secretly, to spy out what Laertes was doing. One day Hamlet came upon Polonius's daughter Ophelia. He behaved so oddly he frightened her. Indeed"—I was fumbling for words to express the dubious quality of Hamlet's madness—"the chief and many others had also noticed that when Hamlet talked one could understand the words but not what they meant. Many people thought that he had become mad." My audience suddenly became much more attentive. "The great chief wanted to know

what was wrong with Hamlet, so he sent for two of Hamlet's age mates [school friends would have taken long explanation] to talk to Hamlet and find out what troubled his heart. Hamlet, seeing that they had been bribed by the chief to betray him, told them nothing. Polonius, however, insisted that Hamlet was mad because he had been forbidden to see Ophelia, whom he loved."

"Why," inquired a bewildered voice, "should anyone bewitch Hamlet on that account?"   51

"Bewitch him?"   52

"Yes, only witchcraft can make anyone mad, unless, of course, one sees the beings that lurk in the forest."   53

I stopped being a storyteller, took out my notebook and demanded to be told more about these two causes of madness. Even while they spoke and I jotted notes, I tried to calculate the effect of this new factor on the plot. Hamlet had not been exposed to the beings that lurk in the forests. Only his relatives in the male line could bewitch him. Barring relatives not mentioned by Shakespeare, it had to be Claudius who was attempting to harm him. And, of course, it was.   54

For the moment I staved off questions by saying that the great chief also refused to believe that Hamlet was mad for the love of Ophelia and nothing else. "He was sure that something much more important was troubling Hamlet's heart."   55

"Now Hamlet's age mates," I continued, "had brought with them a famous storyteller. Hamlet decided to have this man tell the chief and all his homestead a story about a man who had poisoned his brother because he desired his brother's wife and wished to be chief himself. Hamlet was sure the great chief could not hear the story without making a sign if he was indeed guilty, and then he would discover whether his dead father had told him the truth."   56

The old man interrupted, with deep cunning, "Why should a father lie to his son?" he asked.   57

I hedged: "Hamlet wasn't sure that it really was his dead father." It was impossible to say anything, in that language, about devil-inspired visions.   58

"You mean," he said, "it actually was an omen, and he knew witches sometimes send false ones. Hamlet was a fool not to go to one skilled in reading omens and divining the   59 truth in the first place. A man-who-sees-the-truth could have told him how his father died, if he really had been poisoned, and if there was witchcraft in it; then Hamlet could have called the elders to settle the matter."

60   The shrewd elder ventured to disagree. "Because his father's brother was a great chief, one-who-sees-the-truth might therefore have been afraid to tell it. I think it was for that reason that a friend of Hamlet's father—a witch and an elder—sent an omen so his friend's son would know. Was the omen true?"

61   "Yes," I said, abandoning ghosts and the devil; a witch-sent omen it would have to be. "It was true, for when the storyteller was telling his tale before all the homestead, the great chief rose in fear. Afraid that Hamlet knew his secret he planned to have him killed."

62   The stage set of the next bit presented some difficulties of translation. I began cautiously. "The great chief told Hamlet's mother to find out from her son what he knew. But because a woman's children are always first in her heart, he had the important elder Polonius hide behind a cloth that hung against the wall of Hamlet's mother's sleeping hut. Hamlet started to scold his mother for what she had done."

63   There was a shocked murmur from everyone. A man should never scold his mother.

64   "She called out in fear, and Polonius moved behind the cloth. Shouting, 'A rat!' Hamlet took his machete and slashed through the cloth." I paused for dramatic effect. "He had killed Polonius!"

65   The old men looked at each other in supreme disgust. "That Polonius truly was a fool and a man who knew nothing! What child would not know enough to shout, 'It's me!' " With a pang, I remembered that these people are ardent hunters, always armed with bow, arrow, and machete; at the first rustle in the grass an arrow is aimed and ready, and the hunter shouts "Game!" If no human voice answers immediately, the arrow speeds on its way. Like a good hunter Hamlet had shouted, "A rat!"

66   I rushed in to save Polonius's reputation. "Polonius did speak. Hamlet heard him. But he thought it was the chief and wished to kill him to avenge his father. He had meant to kill

him earlier that evening. . . ." I broke down, unable to describe to these pagans, who had no belief in individual afterlife, the difference between dying at one's prayers and dying "unhousell'd, disappointed, unaneled."

This time I had shocked my audience seriously. "For a   67
man to raise his hand against his father's brother and the one who has become his father—that is a terrible thing. The elders ought to let such a man be bewitched."

I nibbled at my kola nut in some perplexity, then pointed   68
out that after all the man had killed Hamlet's father.

"No," pronounced the old man, speaking less to me than   69
to the young men sitting behind the elders. "If your father's brother has killed your father, you must appeal to your father's age mates; *they* may avenge him. No man may use violence against his senior relatives." Another thought struck him. "But if his father's brother had indeed been wicked enough to bewitch Hamlet and make him mad that would be a good story indeed, for it would be his fault that Hamlet, being mad, no longer had any sense and thus was ready to kill his father's brother."

There was a murmur of applause. *Hamlet* was again a good   70
story to them, but it no longer seemed quite the same story to me. As I thought over the coming complications of plot and motive, I lost courage and decided to skim over dangerous ground quickly.

"The great chief," I went on, "was not sorry that Hamlet   71
had killed Polonius. It gave him a reason to send Hamlet away, with his two treacherous age mates, with letters to a chief of a far country, saying that Hamlet should be killed. But Hamlet changed the writing on their papers, so that the chief killed his age mates instead." I encountered a reproachful glare from one of the men whom I had told undetectable forgery was not merely immoral but beyond human skill. I looked the other way.

"Before Hamlet could return, Laertes came back for his   72
father's funeral. The great chief told him Hamlet had killed Polonius. Laertes swore to kill Hamlet because of this, and because his sister Ophelia, hearing her father had been killed by the man she loved, went mad and drowned in the river."

73   "Have you already forgotten what we told you?" The old man was reproachful. "One cannot take vengeance on a madman; Hamlet killed Polonius in his madness. As for the girl, she not only went mad, she was drowned. Only witches can make people drown. Water itself can't hurt anything. It is merely something one drinks and bathes in."

74   I began to get cross. "If you don't like the story, I'll stop."

75   The old man made soothing noises and himself poured me some more beer. "You tell the story well, and we are listening. But it is clear that the elders of your country have never told you what the story really means. No, don't interrupt! We believe you when you say your marriage customs are different, or your clothes and weapons. But people are the same everywhere; therefore, there are always witches and it is we, the elders, who know how witches work. We told you it was the great chief who wished to kill Hamlet, and now your own words have proved us right. Who were Ophelia's male relatives?"

76   "There were only her father and her brother." Hamlet was clearly out of my hands.

77   "There must have been many more; this also you must ask of your elders when you get back to your country. From what you tell us, since Polonius was dead, it must have been Laertes who killed Ophelia, although I do not see the reason for it."

78   We had emptied one pot of beer, and the old men argued the point with slightly tipsy interest. Finally one of them demanded of me, "What did the servant of Polonius say on his return?"

79   With difficulty I recollected Reynaldo and his mission. "I don't think he did return before Polonius was killed."

80   "Listen," said the elder, "and I will tell you how it was and how your story will go, then you may tell me if I am right. Polonius knew his son would get into trouble, and so he did. He had many fines to pay for fighting, and debts from gambling. But he had only two ways of getting money quickly. One was to marry off his sister at once, but it is difficult to find a man who will marry a woman desired by the son of a chief. For if the chief's heir commits adultery with your wife, what

can you do? Only a fool calls a case against a man who will someday be his judge. Therefore Laertes had to take the second way: he killed his sister by witchcraft, drowning her so he could secretly sell her body to the witches."

I raised an objection. "They found her body and buried it. Indeed Laertes jumped into the grave to see his sister once more—so, you see, the body was truly there. Hamlet, who had just come back, jumped in after him."

"What did I tell you?" The elder appealed to the others. "Laertes was up to no good with his sister's body. Hamlet prevented him, because the chief's heir, like a chief, does not wish any other man to grow rich and powerful. Laertes would be angry, because he would have killed his sister without benefit to himself. In our country he would try to kill Hamlet for that reason. Is this not what happened?"

"More or less," I admitted. "When the great chief found Hamlet was still alive, he encouraged Laertes to try to kill Hamlet and arranged a fight with machetes between them. In the fight both the young men were wounded to death. Hamlet's mother drank the poisoned beer that the chief meant for Hamlet in case he won the fight. When he saw his mother die of poison, Hamlet, dying, managed to kill his father's brother with his machete."

"You see, I was right!" exclaimed the elder.

"That was a very good story," added the old man, "and you told it with very few mistakes. There was just one more error, at the very end. The poison Hamlet's mother drank was obviously meant for the survivor of the fight, whichever it was. If Laertes had won, the great chief would have poisoned him, for no one would know that he arranged Hamlet's death. Then, too, he need not fear Laertes' witchcraft: it takes a strong heart to kill one's only sister by witchcraft.

"Sometime," concluded the old man, gathering his ragged toga about him, "you must tell us some more stories of your country. We, who are elders, will instruct you in their true meaning, so that when you return to your own land your elders will see that you have not been sitting in the bush, but among those who know things and who have taught you wisdom."

81

82

83

84

85

86

Points for Discussion

1. What hypothesis does Bohannan set out to test? Where does she state the hypothesis directly?

2. In paragraph 4 Bohannan points out that she was "quite mistaken" about the amount of time she thought the elders would give to performing ceremonies and explaining them to her. Why does she state this explicitly so early in the article? What does the statement foreshadow?

3. In observing the customs of the West Africans, Bohannan includes many details from her observation. For instance, she says "important people shouldn't ladle beer themselves" (par. 7). Point out other details that indicate her care in observation. Why is noting such small details important in research and reports such as this?

4. Besides observing closely, the anthropologist needs to ask questions. How do Bohannan's question about the "two causes of madness" (par. 54) and the answer she finds assist in testing her hypothesis?

5. In recording someone's written or spoken words, all writers are faced with the challenge not only of reporting accurately but also of using the quotations in an interesting way. Variety of presentation helps make writing interesting. Find examples of Bohannan's use of direct and indirect quotations, paraphrases, and summaries of speakers' words. For instance, paragraph 26 has a paraphrase of the man's question about marrying the wives of the dead chief, and paragraphs 27–28 contain two direct quotations. Find still other ways in which Bohannan reports what she hears.

6. What does her experience with the West Africans teach Laura Bohannan? How do you know what she learned from the experience? What then is the effect of concluding the article with the old man's words rather than Bohannan's own words?

Suggestions for Writing

1. Observe the customs and beliefs of some group of persons around you, studying them as Laura Bohannan did the West African tribe by noting their reactions to a particular form of art or entertainment. For instance, you might make some notes on your classmates' tastes and responses to a type of music, to a popular motion picture, or to a television serial. Make notes on your observations, jotting down actual comments that you hear. Decide after your study what the reactions and comments show about the group under study and report your findings in a paper. An example: on some college campuses there is considerable interest in soap opera, at times even a particular soap opera. Analyze the group's various comments and responses to this form of entertainment and determine what is revealed about the background, beliefs, and actions of the interested group.

2. Using quotations skillfully is essential for reporting the results of interviews or other investigations. Interview someone on one of these questions and report your findings in a paper:

- Is storytelling a lost art?
- Why is Shakespeare still popular although his plays were written for English audiences nearly four hundred years ago?
- What causes people to believe in witches, ghosts, or some form of the occult?

When you write your paper, use direct and indirect quotations, summaries, and paraphrases as Bohannan did.

If you have never done any interviewing, prepare yourself by reading about interview techniques. Here are a few tips:

- Plan your questions ahead of time; make them specific and clear.
- Select the interviewee or interviewees carefully, but do not "stack the deck." Your purpose may define the group—teachers on education, students with regard to a school curriculum, and so on.
- Carry a notebook and take careful notes; some of these will be direct quotations; others you can summarize and paraphrase later.

- Introduce yourself and make your purpose clear; give the interviewee every chance to respond; and respect answers or shyness. Keep to the subject; avoid rambling but be tactful.

When you are ready to write, you will select and arrange material to show your conclusions or make your point, using the evidence from the interview.

JUDITH S. WALLERSTEIN AND JOAN B. KELLY

This selection from *Psychology Today* is adapted from the
authors' 1980 book, *Surviving the Break-up: How Children
Actually Cope with Divorce.* Notice that Wallerstein and Kelly
clearly set forth both their goals and their conclusions in the
first few paragraphs of their article. They then go on to prove
and illustrate the soundness of their methods by citing both
individual case studies and statistics for the sample group.

California's Children of Divorce

The conventional wisdom used to be that unhappily married 1
people should remain married "for the good of the children."
Today's conventional wisdom holds, with equal vigor, that an
unhappy couple might well *divorce* for the good of the children; that an unhappy marriage for the adults is unhappy also
for the children; and that divorce that promotes the happiness
of the adults will benefit the children as well.

Testing that new dogma was among our goals in 1971 2
when we started what became known as the Children of Divorce Project. We interviewed all the members of 60 families
with children that had recently gone through divorce, and re-
interviewed them 18 months later. Recently, we saw them
again, after a lapse of five years. Our study has no counterpart
in the United States or in Europe in the span of years it covers,
in the participation of so many children of different ages, and
in the kinds of questions that were posed.

Our results called into sharp question much more than the 3
idea that what is good for the parents is always good for the
kids. For example, we thought that by five years after the initial separation, new family structures would be an accepted
part of life, and our observations would be made within a social and psychological landscape that had come to rest. Yet we
found more people than we expected to find still in various
degrees of turmoil.

Our overall conclusion is that divorce produces not a sin- 4 gle pattern in people's lives, as the conventional wisdom of any era tends to claim, but at least three patterns, with many variations. Among both adults and children five years afterward, we found about a quarter to be resilient (those for whom the divorce was successful), half to be muddling through, coping when and as they could, and a final quarter to be bruised: failing to recover from the divorce or looking back to the predivorce family with intense longing. Some in each group had been that way before and continued unchanged; for the rest, we found roughly equal numbers for whom the divorce seemed connected to improvement and decline.

5   What made the biggest difference for the children was not the divorce itself, but the factors that make for good adjustment and satisfaction in intact families: psychologically healthy parents and children who are involved with one another in appropriate ways. Yet providing these optimal conditions is difficult in the postdivorce family, with its characteristic climate of anger, rejection, and attempts to exclude the absent parent.

6   *Changing Family Circumstances*   News of their parents' divorce clearly had been an unhappy shock to most of the children. We found that although many of them had lived for years in an unhappy home, they did not experience the divorce as a solution to their unhappiness, nor did they greet it with relief at the time, or for several years thereafter.

7   To be sure, as many of the children matured, they often acquired a different perspective. But at the time of the family disruption, many of the children considered their situation neither better nor worse than that of other families around them. They would, in fact, have been content to hobble along. The divorce was a bolt of lightning that struck them when they had not even been aware of a need to come in from the storm.

8   Five years later, there had been little shifting of the children from the custody of one parent to the other. Seventy-seven percent of the youngsters continued to live in the custody of their mothers. Eight percent now lived with the

fathers, a slight increase; another 3 percent shuttled back and forth from one home to the other, usually not in a planned joint-custody arrangement, but under duress when their relationship with one or the other parent became overwhelmed with ill will. An additional 11 percent of the children—adolescents—were now living on their own.

Almost two-thirds of the youngsters had changed their place of residence, and a substantial number of these had moved three or more times. The moves were generally within a radius of 30 miles, however; very few families left the region. The fathers tended to stay close by as well. One-half continued to live within the same county as their children, some still within biking distance. An additional 30 percent of the fathers were within a one-hour drive.   9

Twenty-four (43 percent) of the fathers had remarried in the intervening four years, of whom five were then redivorced and two subsequently remarried. Thus, 44 percent of the youngsters had a new stepmother. Nineteen of the mothers—one-third—had remarried; two of these women were then redivorced, and two widowed. Hence, nearly a quarter of the children lived with a stepparent.   10

The majority of the fathers (68 percent) had made their child-support payments with considerable regularity, and an additional 19 percent paid some support, but irregularly and in varying amounts. (Nationally, the estimated figures are considerably lower.) Only 13 percent were completely delinquent. Still, far more of the mothers than the fathers had traveled downward from their former economic status.   11

At the time of divorce, two-fifths of the families had been solidly upper class or upper middle class, whereas two-thirds of the women and their children were now either solidly middle class or lower middle class.   12

The Children's Differing Reactions   Hardly a child of divorce we came to know did not cling to the fantasy of a magical reconciliation between his parents. Danny, age seven, whose parents had been divorced for several years when we first saw him, softly confided his "best" fantasy. He had, he said, always wanted to fix up Hazel Street and Pine Street.   13

"They're all filled with mud and they don't join, but a long time ago, they did, and I'd like to cut the two streets so they join. But this," he sighed, "will be a long time off."

14   When we saw Danny again, he was 11. "Divorce is not as bad as you think . . . not near as bad as it looks in movies or on television," he said. He had thought a lot about divorce, he told us; and had just recently figured it all out. "It's something like if you break a glass and pick the pieces up right away, they will fit back together perfectly, but if you take one piece and sand the edge, it will never fit again."

15   Five years after the separation, 28 percent of the children strongly approved of their parent's divorce, 42 percent were somewhere in the middle, accepting the changed family but not taking a strong position for or against the divorce, and 30 percent strongly disapproved—a major shift from the initial count. Then, three-quarters of the children strongly disapproved. Still, the faithfulness of so many youngsters to their predivorce families was unsettling, and more loyal than many parents welcomed.

16   Nancy, now in the second grade, said, "when they first divorced, I was kind of sad." Then, she said, she found out life was still fun because "we got to see Daddy in his house. . . . There are lots of good things to do. . . . Things are not so different. . . . You can meet a lot of new dogs and new people."

17   Thirty-four percent of the children and adolescents appeared to be doing especially well psychologically at the five-year mark. Their self-esteem was high and they were coping competently with the tasks of school, playground, and home. There were no significant age or sex differences among these resilient youngsters. The boys appeared to have caught up with their sisters in the years since the first follow-up, which had found the boys lagging behind. Characteristic of these children was their sense of sufficiency: the divorce had not depleted their lives by removing a loving parent, or by pairing them with an angry, disturbed one. At times, they still felt lonely, unhappy, or sorrowful about the divorce, but these misgivings did not make them aggrieved or angry at either parent.

18   Roughly 29 percent of the children were in the middle

range of psychological health. They were learning at grade level at school and showing reasonably appropriate social behavior and judgment in their relationships with adults and children. They were considered average by their teachers. Nevertheless, islands of unhappiness and diminished self-esteem or anger continued to demand significant portions of their attention and energy, and sometimes hampered the full potential of their development.

Sonja, age 11, was typical of the middle group. "I don't   19 think about the divorce as much as I used to," she said. "Before, I wasn't right. I was all mad and yelling at Mom. . . . Usually, I still yell at her. I tell her I don't mean it, but I can't control myself." Disquietingly, Sonja talked with considerable pleasure about hurting and slapping people. She laughed excitedly as she recounted several stories of people, adults and children, getting into difficulties. Recently, Sonja was caught stealing some things from a shopping center and also from the school. Yet Sonja's mother indicated that the child is not as demanding as she used to be, and that, overall, her behavior is improving.

We found a final third of the children and adolescents to   20 be consciously and intensely unhappy and dissatisfied with their life in the postdivorce family. Among this group were those with moderate to severe depression, although at least half of the depressed children had islands of relatively unburdened development within them and were able to move ahead in ways appropriate for their age in several important parts of their lives, such as school.

We were struck as well by the high incidence of intense   21 loneliness that we observed in 27 percent of the children, a little higher than at the 18 month mark. These children complained of coming home to empty houses after school to await the return of the working parent. On weekends, these youngsters often felt left out of the social life of both divorced parents. Several also complained of loneliness within a remarriage, while recognizing ruefully that the newly married adults wanted privacy and time away from curious children.

Anger played a significant role in the psychological life of   22 23 percent of the children and adolescents, who were not coping well. Most of the anger was defensive and reflected the underlying fear, sorrow, and sense of powerlessness of these youngsters. Anger at the father was especially likely to be sustained, especially in older boys and adolescents. Three children had rejected their fathers' overtures, including Paul, who returned unopened his father's birthday present to him on his 14th birthday. Other children's anger took other forms, including explosive outbursts of temper and delinquent behavior, such as drug involvement and stealing.

23   *The Importance of Involved Fathers*   What accounted for the successful outcomes? Some children improved simply by escaping a disturbed and cruel parent to be left in the custody of a concerned and loving one. Some of these youngsters developed good relationships with a stepparent. Little boys, especially, appeared to spurt ahead with excitement and new growth with a stepfather whom they grew quickly to love.

24   A number of other factors seemed common to the children who dealt most resiliently with divorce. One factor, not surprisingly, was having a strong personality to start with. As we followed the course of the children whom we had placed initially within the ranks of the very well adjusted, it appeared that two-thirds of these resilient, successful copers were still functioning very well five years later. Sad to say, some boys and girls in all age groups who had been able to cope during a conflict-ridden marriage deteriorated notably in the post-separation period.

25   The most unpredictable change occurred among those children whose adjustment initially was a mixed bag of successes and failures. Very few of the boys and girls who were originally at the midpoint of the scale were still there after five years. Those youngsters were the most vulnerable to change, and stood in equal measure to either deteriorate or improve.

26   Perhaps the most crucial factor influencing a good readjustment was a stable, loving relationship with both parents, between whom friction had largely dissipated, leaving regular, dependable visiting patterns that the parent with custody encouraged. . . . Forty percent of the mother-child relationships were adequate to very good, with an additional 20 percent at the adequate mark. Occasionally, when the father had been abusive or was psychologically disturbed, a strong mother bore the emotional load by herself and seemed able

to give the children all the emotional support they needed. Usually, however, it took two, and a custodial parent's efforts to improve the child's life were burdened by the seeming disinterest of the other parent.

The contribution that the out-of-home parent could make emerged with clarity at five years. Frequent, flexible visiting patterns remained important to the majority of the children. Nearly one-quarter of the youngsters continued to see their fathers weekly, if not several times weekly. An additional 20 percent visited two to three times a month. Thus, 45 percent of the children and adolescents continued to enjoy what society deems "reasonable visitation," although many of the children continued to complain of not enough contact.   27

The 17 percent of youngsters with erratic visits (less than once a month) continued to be anguished by the father's inconstancy; the passage of five years had not lessened their wish to be loved by both parents. The same percentage as before (9 percent) had no contact.   28

Overall, we found that 30 percent of the children had an emotionally nurturant relationship with their father five years after the marital separation, and that this sense of a continuing, close relationship was critical to the good adjustment of both boys and girls.   29

These men had worked hard to earn the parenthood that fathers in intact families customarily take for granted. Some had persevered despite such irritations as one former wife who, four years after the separation, was still regularly calling her former husband during their son's visits with him to order the boy to shower. One man described the special personalities of his three children so vividly that hearing him talk, one would have been hard put to know that there had been a divorce in the family five years earlier. The children of these men, in turn, were spared the sense of loss and rejection that many less fortunate children experienced.   30

In contrast to the youngsters who yearned for more visits, almost one-fifth of the youngsters did not find the visits pleasurable or gratifying. A number of them resented being used to carry hostile messages between parents. Noted Larry, a 13-year-old, "My father has to understand that when he shoots arrows at my mother, they first have to go through our bodies before they reach her."   31

32   In the most unsatisfactory visiting arrangements, a range of parental behavior, from outright abandonment to general unreliability, often disappointed a child repeatedly, usually leading the child to feel rejected, rebuffed, and unloved and unlovable. Anger at the rejecting father usually did not undo the child's unhappy conclusion about his or her essential unlovability to the father. Lea, for example, was an abnormally quiet girl whose teacher said she did not believe she could succeed at anything. We interviewed her at home. When asked about her father, she brought out a box containing all of the letters her father had written to her during the past three years. These letters, possibly 15 in number, were dog-eared, folded and refolded, and the interviewer couldn't help but be reminded of a precious collection of love letters that had been read and reread with tears. The father had actually visited only once in the past two years.

33   Peter, age nine, had not seen his father, who lives nearby, more than once every two to three months. We expected that he would be troubled, but we were entirely unprepared for the extent of this child's misery. The interviewer observed: "I asked Peter when he had last seen his dad. The child looked at me blankly and his thinking became confused, his speech halting. Just then, a police car went by with its siren screaming. The child stared into space and seemed lost in reverie. As this continued for a few minutes, I gently suggested that the police car had reminded him of his father, a police officer. Peter began to cry and sobbed without stopping for 35 minutes."

34   Even though the majority of fathers and children continued to see each other fairly often, by the five-year mark three-quarters of these relationships offered the children little in fully addressing the complex tasks of growing up. Yet, paradoxically, by his absence a father continued to influence the thoughts and feelings of his children; most particularly, the disinterested father left behind a legacy of depression and damaged self-esteem.

35   Except in extreme cases in which a father was clearly abusing children or seriously disturbed, some contact seemed better than none at all. The father's presence kept the child from a worrisome concern with abandonment and total rejection and from the nagging self-doubts that follow such worry. The

father's presence, however limited, also diminished the child's vulnerability and aloneness and total dependency on the one parent.

A few other factors that we had expected to be significant   36
in helping children adjust turned out not to be. Children were incapable of using friends to make up for troubled conditions at home; rather, those with comparatively stable homes were the ones most likely to have friends outside. Grandparents provided some solid supports for both divorced mothers and their children—when they supported the idea of the divorce—but were not a strong enough influence to make up for problems elsewhere. Most children did not seem to be influenced either for good or ill if their mother worked, although some of the youngest boys appeared to do significantly better in school and in their overall adjustment when the mother did not work full time.

One-third of the children once again confronted   37
far-reaching change in their daily lives when one or both of their divorced parents remarried. (Only two of the fathers with custody remarried.) The arrival of a stepfather seemed to create particular friction for a short while. Most of the stepfathers had been married before, expected to assume the role of parent to their wives' children, and, encouraged by the women, moved quickly into the prerequisites, prerogatives, and authority that this position traditionally conveyed. Only a few men appeared sensitive to the need to cultivate a relationship with stepchildren gradually and to make due allowance for suspiciousness and resistance in the initial stages.

Still, after some early tensions, the relationships with the   38
children from two to eight years old took root fairly quickly and were happy and gratifying to both child and adult. Yet children with a stepfather seemed particularly sensitive to friction between parents.

Many people expect children to experience conflict as they   39
turn from father to stepfather during their growing-up years. This was not borne out by our observations. Nor was the expectation that in the happily remarried family the biological father was likely to fade out of the children's lives. The great majority of fathers in the remarried families continued to visit, much as they had earlier. Mostly, children enlarged their view

of the family and made room for three major figures. Jerry, age 10, when asked how often he saw his father, responded, "Which dad do you mean?" When a child did experience painful psychological conflict between the father and the stepfather, the adults were likely to be jealous or competitive, pulling hard in opposite directions.

40   The most tragic situations for the child were those in which mother and stepfather demanded that the child renounce his or her love for the father as the price for acceptance and affection within the remarried family. Such children were severely troubled and depressed, too preoccupied with the chronic unresolvable conflict to learn or to develop at a normal pace.

41   *Eventual Softening of the Strains*   Most of the adults in our study, especially the women, were feeling better five years after divorce than they had when we first saw them, despite the greater economic pressure and the many stresses of the postdivorce family. But among the children, although individuals had improved or worsened, the percentages within broad categories of good and poor adjustment had remained relatively stable. Hence, it seems that a divorced family per se is neither more nor less beneficial for children than an unhappy marriage. Unfortunately, neither unhappy marriage nor divorce is especially congenial for children. Each imposes its own set of differing stresses.

42   Our other major finding about how important it is for a child to keep a relationship with both original parents points to the need for a concept of greater shared parental responsibility after divorce. In this condition, each parent continues to be responsible for, and genuinely concerned about, the well-being of his or her children, and allows the other parent this option as well.

43   The concept of joint legal custody, in which each parent has the right to make important decisions about the life of the child, is a step in the right direction. The newer idea of shared *physical* custody, whether parents share the children 50-50, 80-20, or in other proportions, may also be a positive step, but it needs to be studied to determine its advantages and disadvantages for children at different developmental stages.

Many people object that parents who cannot agree during marriage certainly cannot be expected to reach agreement on child-related matters after divorce. Indeed, some infuriated or disturbed parents will never chart a rational course with regard to their children. Yet it seems clear that our society must encourage fathers and mothers to accept the importance of continuity in parent-child relationships after divorce. Perhaps in changing legal expectations, we can take the first steps in a necessary re-education about meeting the needs of children in the postdivorce family.

Unfortunately, it seems clear that the divorced family is,   44
in many ways, less adaptive economically, socially, and psychologically to the raising of children than the two-parent family, or at least the two-adult family. This does not mean that it cannot be done. But the fact remains that the divorced family in which the burden falls entirely or mostly on one parent is more vulnerable to stress, has more limited economic and psychological reserves, and lacks the supporting or buffering presence of another adult for the expected and unexpected crises of life.

In order to fulfill the responsibility of child-rearing and   45
provide even minimally for the needs of the adult, many divorced families are in urgent need of a network of services that are not now available in most communities, ranging from educational, vocational, and financial counseling to enriched child care and after-school programs. At the five-year point in our own study, two-fifths of the men and a somewhat greater number of the women characterized the brief counseling we offered as useful and supportive and were still following suggestions that we had made at the first meetings five years earlier.

Divorcing with children requires in adults the capacity to   46
maintain entirely separate social and sexual roles while they continue to cooperate as parents. This is very difficult. We began our work with the conviction that divorce should remain a readily available option to adults who are locked into an unhappy marriage. Our findings, although somewhat graver than expected, have not changed our conviction. They have given greater impetus to our interest in easing the family rupture for children and adults alike.

Notes
"The Children of Divorce as Adults" by Carin Rubenstein, *Psychology Today*, January 1980. Reprinted by permission from *Psychology Today Magazine.* Copyright © 1980 Ziff-Davis Publishing Company.

Points for Discussion

1. What are the major findings of Wallerstein and Kelly's study? Why—and how—do their conclusions disprove what they call the "new dogma" that "what is good for the parents is always good for the kids"? What factor do they conclude "made the biggest difference for the children" of divorced parents? Which, if any, of their findings surprise you? Explain your reactions.

2. We speak of research as primary or secondary, and we may use one or the other or both in order to find material (evidence) for providing information or for leading to conclusions. What is the method of the research reported here? Why is it natural, perhaps inevitable, that reporters of this type of research devote considerable space to explaining the methods of their investigation?

3. In paragraph 2 Wallerstein and Kelly explain clearly the size of their sample and its relationship to other studies. Why is it important to give this information at the outset of their report?

4. What is the importance of the statistical evidence—especially the percentages cited in such topics as remarriage (par. 10), regularity of support (par. 11), and measurement of attitudes toward a divorce (pars. 17–18)—in a report of this type? What is the purpose of the case studies—the short narrative accounts and quotations from specific children (Danny, Nancy, and Sonja)? Draw some conclusions about the relative space given to reporting of facts (concreteness) and the generalizations that the writers draw from these facts.

5. Investigators embark on their research with previously held notions or hypotheses, and their findings may prove or disprove these ideas. What is the significance of Wallerstein and Kelly's direct statement that some findings were not what they expected?

6. Choose two or three paragraphs from this essay and examine the ways that the writers link their ideas and sentences. Function

words and phrases, repetition, echoes of an idea in different words, and repeated patterns in phrases or sentences all give coherence.

You might construct a diagram showing the linking devices like this diagram for paragraph 7:

> To be sure, as many of the children matured, they often acquired a different perspective. But at the time of the family disruption many of the children considered their situation neither better nor worse than that of other families around them. They would, in fact, have been content to hobble along. The divorce was a bolt of lightning that struck them when they had not even been aware of a need to come in from the storm.

- *To be sure*—phrasal link to paragraph preceding
- *But*—connects by contrast the ideas from sentence 1 to sentence 2
- *children*, (s. 1) to *children* (s. 2) to pronouns *they* (throughout paragraph), repetition and reference
- *family disruption* echoed in *divorce*
- *bolt of lightning* idea echoed in *storm*

Suggestions for Writing

1. Conduct a before-and-after investigational study by interviewing a group of people involved in some situation that you know well. Here are a few suggestions:

- Interview a group of classmates before test week (midterms perhaps) or before an extensive paper is due to determine such items as attitudes, habits or plans for study, estimates of grades. Interview the group again after the test period or due date to determine changes in feelings, actual practice followed, grades attained. Draw some conclusions about the relationship between study habits and apprehension and the eventual achievement.
- To determine how "fixed" study habits are by the time students come to college, interview a group of new freshmen

about their practices—time of study, length of period spent,
location, and so on. Later in the semester talk to the same students again to determine what changes, if any, they have
made, and why.

- Survey a group of persons, probably fellow students, who are
about to have a vacation. Determine expectations, good or
bad, the various members have about the holiday. Recheck
after the period to determine the degree to which expectations influenced outcomes.

- Early in a semester, sample a group of faculty members by
asking them to explain expectations or beliefs about student
writing abilities. Later that same semester, interview again to
correlate their suppositions with findings they make about a
particular group of students or an entire class.

- Use a before-and-after survey to determine opinions and reactions regarding a film or reading selection. For instance, you
might design an interview about a book around such questions as these:
—Will you read this book gladly or only because it is assigned?
—What reviews have you read and what opinions about it
have the reviewers offered?
—How has the book been introduced in your class?
—Have you talked with others about it?
Again, use the second interview to determine how various beforehand factors influence the experience of reading the book
or viewing the film.

2. Make a study of the politics of some group of persons you
know by conducting interviews before an election and again after
it is over. Determine any change in attitudes—disappointment, ela-
tion over unexpected success, change of mind after seeing popular
expression. If possible, conduct a third interview as a follow-up after
the newly elected officials have taken office. (You, of course, need
not use a national election as the occasion.) Write a paper reporting
your findings. Titles such as these may suggest possibilities: "Survey
Shows People Get Behind the Men Elected," "I Wasted My
Vote—the New Lament."

ALBERT ROTHENBERG

Finding the facts—gathering them by interview, reading, questionnaires and surveys, any type of "observations"—is the business of the researcher in social sciences, just as experiment and observation in the laboratory or field furnish information for the scientist. When the writer comes to present what he or she has found, those collected bits of information provide examples to support whatever conclusion is possible—the facts are the clue to a message, the force behind an argument, the substance that the generalization rests upon. Rothenberg's explanation of creative achievement rests upon many examples—they reveal how fully he has thought about his subject and delved into it to gather the evidence he needs to conclude that creativity is marked by a certain type of thinking.

Creative Contradictions

While working on an essay for the *Yearbook of Radioactivity and Electronics* in 1907, Albert Einstein had what he called "the happiest thought of my life." Einstein's happy thought was the key to the most far-reaching scientific breakthrough of the 20th century: the general theory of relativity. The unusual circumstances surrounding it were revealed for the first time in another essay, unpublished and discovered only recently, entitled, "Fundamental Ideas and Methods of Relativity Theory, Presented in Their Development."

Einstein had already developed the special theory of relativity, which holds that since the speed of light is constant for all frames of reference, perceptions of time and motion depend upon the relative position of the observer. He had been forced to postulate the theory, he said, to explain the seeming contradictions in electromagnetic phenomena; that "one is dealing here with two fundamentally different cases was, for me, unbearable." Einstein was trying to modify Newton's classical theory of gravitation so that it could be encompassed within a broad relativity principle. And here, again, it seemed that what was lacking was a physical basis for bringing together Newton's theory and his own special theory.

3   Pondering those seemingly irreconcilable constructs, Einstein reached a startling conception: "For an observer in free fall from the roof of a house," he realized, "there exists, during his fall, no gravitational field . . . in his immediate vicinity. If the observer releases any objects, they will remain, relative to him, in a state of rest. The [falling] observer is therefore justified in considering his state as one of 'rest.' "

4   The general theory itself is highly complex, and the points of connection to Einstein's "happiest thought" are not simple to explicate or trace. But the specific structure of the key step is clear: Einstein had concluded that a person falling from the roof of a house was both in motion and at rest *at the same time.* The hypothesis was illogical and contradictory in structure, but it possessed a superior logic and salience that brought Newtonian physics and his own into the same overall conceptual scheme.

5   I describe this cognitive process as "janusian thinking," after Janus, the Roman god of doorways and beginnings, whose faces (he is variously portrayed as having two, four, and even six of them) look in different directions at the same time. Janusian thinking lies at the heart of the most striking creative breakthroughs. Contrary to the romantic notion that creativity grows largely out of inspiration, the "primary process" thinking of dreams, or some unconscious source, I have found janusian thinking—a major element of the creative process—to be a fully conscious, intentional, rational process.

6   In janusian thinking, two or more opposites or antitheses are conceived *simultaneously,* either as existing side by side, or as equally operative, valid, or true. In an apparent defiance of logic or of physical possibility, the creative person consciously formulates the simultaneous operation of antithetical elements and develops those into integrated entities and creations. It is a leap that transcends ordinary logic. What emerges is no mere combination or blending of elements: the conception does not only contain different entities, it contains opposing and antagonistic elements, which are understood as coexistent. As a self-contradictory structure, the janusian formulation is surprising when seriously posited in naked form. Though it usually appears modified and transformed in the

final product, it leaves the mark of implicit unexpectedness and paradox on the work.

Janusian thinking operates in diverse types of creativity—in the visual arts, literature, and music, as well as in science and philosophy. I discovered the mode after a number of different studies of the creative process, over the past 15 years, which included efforts to collect data on creative thinking in the work and testimony of people like Einstein, O'Neill, Conrad, Mozart, and Picasso, and through intensive interviews with 54 highly creative artists and scientists living in the United States and England. 7

Most of the living subjects were chosen because they were nominated to me by their peers and had won major recognition: a Nobel Prize, a National Book Award, a Pulitzer Prize, or membership in societies like the National Academy of Science, the American Academy of Arts and Letters, or the Royal Society of London. Moreover, I selected a number of highly rated but less-known subjects who were also recommended by peers and colleagues in their fields. I similarly interviewed an unusual group of controls who were matched in age, sex, and social status to the writers—successful but not creative persons, as assessed by their employers, counselors, and peers. To study their approach to a creative task, I asked each of the controls to embark on writing a piece of imaginative literature. Some wrote a poem; others, a short story. 8

In all, I have carried out 1,690 hours of interviewing to date. The sessions are weekly or biweekly, and the subjects have been assured of confidentiality. Rather than reporting on their personal history, they talk about their current work and the thoughts, dreams, and emotions connected with it. Before the sessions start, they give me material from their current projects, which forms the focus of our discussions. We talk extensively about general themes as well as specific details, such as what revisions take place as the work unfolds, and we attempt to trace the generating psychological factors throughout the entire period of creation—in most cases, over months and even years. 9

Janusian thinking seldom appears in the final artistic product, but it occurs at crucial points in the generation and devel- 10 opment of the work. In the initial phases of interviews with some of the writers, they reported using numerous opposite ideas, images, and concepts, but there were usually no clues at that point to the importance of those ideas. Their plays, novels, and poems showed elements of conflict, irony, tragic tension, and ambiguity as major elements, but there was no reason to believe that those elements derived from a factor like janusian thinking, or that such thinking played any major role in key creative conceptions. It was generally only after weeks or months of interviewing, and the development of some confidence and rapport, that the research subjects revealed the precise—and self-contradictory—nature of the critical ideas in their creations.

11   For instance, a Pulitzer Prize-winning novelist told me, after we had discussed for some months the novel he was working on, that he had developed the key idea as he sat in a lawn chair reading Erik Erikson's book on Martin Luther's rebellion. He thought of constructing a novel about another rebel, a revolutionary hero who, he said, "was responsible for the deaths of hundreds of people, but he himself would kill only one person with his own hand—and this was the one person who had been very kind to him and the one person he loved." In another case, a major American playwright told me he had come up with the specific idea for a play while traveling through Germany: "Driving on the autobahn, I suddenly felt amazed and overwhelmed at how beautiful Germany had become." He then thought of writing a play that would simultaneously express both the beauty of modern Germany and Hitler's destructiveness. "And then, I remembered a story I'd been told about a sacrifice made by an Austrian nobleman for a Jew in a Nazi official's waiting room." Later, the playwright incorporated the sacrifice into his play.

12   Two poets described initial conceptions that were only implicitly present in their finished poems. Because I had been conducting regular interviews with them during the writing of the poems, I knew that their recall of circumstances and thoughts was quite exact. One said that he had been walking on a beach and became interested in the quality of some rocks along the sand. As he touched the surface of the rocks, he noted that they seemed to feel like human skin. But they were also hard, heavy objects—violent weapons. The idea that the

rocks were at once sensual objects and weapons led to a conception of the simultaneous operation of sex and violence in the world, and the writer elaborated those aspects separately in the final version of the poem.

On another occasion, this poet was sitting at his desk and   13
he thought of a poetic line connoting rest and motion as operating simultaneously in the action of long-distance running. The thought led him to write a poignant poem about marathon racing, and the ravages of time and age, which elaborated on, and modified, the initial line.

The other poet, also sitting at his desk, had been thinking   14
about an incident in which a horse had appeared at a lonely desert site, when it occurred to him that horses are animals who "renounce their own kind in order to live our lives." The idea that horses live human lives, that they are both beast and not-beast simultaneously, generated a vibrant poem with a central image and theme of a happy and intense relationship between a young person and a horse, followed by a sad, resigned separation.

When, after a year's interviewing, I directed one novelist   15
to the earliest idea for his book, he referred to a line in it indicating that love and hate were the same. The phrase had also guided the novel's whole construction. Similarly, a poet said her first idea for a certain poem was the line, "Cream of celery soup has a soul of its own." She had been thinking, she recalled, about the simultaneously formed and unformed qualities of both soul and soup. And a playwright said that the earliest formulations in one of his works grew out of ideas and phrases that came to him while imagining that the white knight in a TV commercial was a black man.

A novelist-poet told me that he was doing his morning ex-   16
ercises when he thought of a series of lines that, as he described them, would use the last word of each line as the first word of the next—a juxtaposition that sets one word to opposite functions, both ending and beginning a poetic thought. In the end, his poem implicitly retained that structure.

Janusian thinking appeared and reappeared throughout   17
the interviews and studies of creative people. But the controls never displayed it in their thoughts or in any aspect of the writing assignment they were asked to do.

Those subjects approached the writing in various ways: 18 constructing a story outline, trying to think of a good ending, or merely trying to write out every thought that came to them. As with the creative group, I discussed with them the general themes and detailed revisions they made during the course of writing from week to week. Some persevered to complete an imaginative work, but many gave up. Though some occasionally wrote interesting lines and found fairly interesting themes, their earliest conceptions, and those along the way, were devoid of simultaneous antithesis. And no new or fresh creation appeared from their labors.

19   Because creativity is defined as something that "stands the test of time," I used another empirical method to study it in great works of the past. This involved doing statistical assessments of patterns of revisions in manuscripts by Eugene O'Neill, Maxwell Anderson, and Stephen Vincent Benét, developing specific hypotheses and predictions about their behavior in the course of writing the works, and then interviewing surviving family members to assess the predictions.

20   I first identified janusian thinking through reconstructing O'Neill's work on *The Iceman Cometh.* After examining all manuscript versions of the play, as well as the final work, and performing a special statistical type of content analysis, I discovered evidence for the author's persistent preoccupation with a simultaneous antithesis in an event whose meaning he had come to understand only years after it happened: a friend and roommate of his youth committed suicide because he was distressed over his wife's infidelity—but also because he had wanted her to be unfaithful to him. The idea produced the focus on infidelity, both religious and sexual, in the substance and title of the play.

21   Similarly, Maxwell Anderson created the prizewinning play *High Tor* with the idea of presenting characters who were both alive and dead at the same time. The characters were not merely ghosts but lost persons struggling to survive, to understand what had happened to them. Much of the action in the play turns on the dual nature of their existence as survivors of a Dutch explorer's ship who interact with modern inhabitants of the Hudson River Palisades.

22   Conceiving the important novel *Nostromo,* Joseph Conrad followed a janusian sequence, which he described in the pref-

ace. Conrad was struck by a story he had heard about an "unmitigated rascal" who had stolen a large quantity of silver somewhere on the seaboard of South America during a revolution. "I did not see anything at first in the mere story," he recalled. Then: "It dawned upon me that the purloiner of the treasure need not necessarily be a confirmed rogue, that he could even be a man of character." This key idea of the criminal as both rogue and man of character was elaborated in the story of a land that was both good and evil simultaneously. As Conrad reported, "It was only then that I had the first vision of a twilight country . . . with . . . its high, shadowy sierra and its misty campo for mute witnesses of events flowing from the passions of men short-sighted in good and evil. Such are in very truth the obscure origins of *Nostromo*—the book. From that moment, I suppose, it had to be."

We can trace janusian thinking in some of the most profound creations in music and the visual arts, as well. Successive sketches for Picasso's mural *Guernica,* for instance, reveal that the painter initially conceived of a female figure oriented spatially in opposite directions. In the first sketch, Picasso represented the figure (who is holding a torch in the completed mural) as both looking into a room and looking out to a courtyard at the same time. In successive sketches, he made this feature of the figure less obvious. However, the entire mural portrays human carnage both inside a room and without at the same time. 23

Other artists, among them Leonardo da Vinci, Vincent van Gogh, and John Constable, as well as members of the modern schools, have provided descriptions of similar formulations. The celebrated British sculptor Henry Moore said: "To know one thing, you must know the opposite . . . just as much, else you don't know that one thing. So that, quite often, one does the opposite as an expression of the positive." And the late Josef Albers, the influential painter of the "hard edge" school, described his own approach: "I start from experiences and read . . . always between polarities . . . loud and not-loud . . . young and old . . . spring and winter. . . . If I can make black and white behave together instead of shooting at each other only, I feel proud. . . ." 24

Recently, in a brilliant series of Harvard lectures on music, 25

Leonard Bernstein described the simultaneous operation of the antithetical factors of diatonicism (the tone relationships among the notes within the traditional scales) and chromaticism (relationship among the various keys) in the construction of virtually all types of music. Using a Mozart piece to make his point, Bernstein demonstrated such conceptualization in Mozart's creative process and left little doubt that it is an important aspect of his own work.

26   Finally, another outstanding scientific achievement of the 20th century reveals, on close inspection, the clear imprint of janusian thinking. In discovering the double-helical structure of DNA and the key to genetic replication, James Watson and Francis Crick made possible an enormous acceleration of knowledge of natural processes in the field of microbiology. Describing the events leading up to the discovery in *The Double Helix,* Watson recounted a long and arduous series of trials and errors, and collation of the work of others. One day, he was trying to construct a large-scale model of a DNA molecule, as he and others had been doing for some time. He was briefly interrupted by a colleague who entered the lab, but he went back to thinking about the problem, shifting segments of the molecule with his hands, and considering various ways in which they might fit together. He realized that, instead of a structure based on the pairing of like-with-like segments, the molecule could consist of *identical but spatially opposed chains.*

27   "Suddenly," Watson said, "I became aware . . . that both pairs could be flip-flopped over and still have their . . . bonds facing in the same direction." Unhesitatingly, he concluded: "It strongly suggested that the backbones of the two chains run in opposite directions."

28   To make that discovery, Watson had to conceive of opposites operating simultaneously, a conception none of the many colleagues searching for the same answer were able to do at the time. Like Einstein, he was fully conscious, aware, and logical at that moment—but in that creative leap, he was able to transcend the bounds of ordinary logic and cognition.

29   Characteristically, as in the Einstein and Conrad examples, janusian concepts occur early in the creative process. They do not, of course, account for the entire creation: they are key steps, often initial formulations, that are later elaborated and

transformed. Einstein's enormous intellect and capacity for both inductive and deductive logic certainly played a major role in the development of his theory. So did his ability to combine separate symbols, his intense concentration, his profound understanding of the categories of science and mathematics, and, in a special way, his use of mental imagery. Conrad's facility with language, his personal experience with sailing and exotic lands, his dual identity as an Englishman and the son of Polish intellectual gentry, all entered into the arduous creation of *Nostromo.*

Commonly, in the final product or creation—the scientific theory or crucial experiment, the poem, play, musical composition, or work of architecture—there is little overt sign of the janusian constructs that have occurred along the way. Several of the world's religions, however, have achieved integrations that retain a clear simultaneity, and tension, between opposite or antithetical factors.   30

In Taoism, the yin and the yang are two opposite and universal moral principles operating together as a single force. In Buddhism, nirvana, the end of the cycle of rebirth, is opposed to and unified with samsara, the endless series of incarnations and reincarnations of living things. And nirvana itself is both nonlife and nondeath. Some Western theology postulates a similar tension in the opposing powers of God and the devil.   31

In philosophy, simultaneous opposition and antithesis are manifest in the pre-Socratic conceptions of being and becoming, in Nietzsche's Dionysian and Apollonian principles, in Kierkegaard's belief by virtue of the absurd, and in Sartre's representation of being and nothingness. In psychology, there are Freud's formulation of the conscious operating together with the unconscious, the theory of the dually functioning but opposed instincts of sex and aggression, and Jung's animus and anima.   32

Janusian thinking differs from the types of creative cognition that other writers have hypothesized. In the Einstein example, the scientist could not have come to his theory merely by associating two incompatible elements, as Arthur Koestler proposes. It was by consciously formulating the givens in a different way, by conceiving the inconceivable—attributing the   33 possibility of rest to the state of falling—that Einstein was able to see the larger context of relativity. That is not merely association, in which any number of alternatives could fit the definition. In janusian thinking, the creative person is fully rational and intentional at the time he selects particular opposites and juxtaposes them.

34   Clearly, bringing together any opposites at all won't do. It matters very much which opposites are selected, and how the janusian formulation is elaborated in a particular work. In artistic fields, the creator chooses and develops those opposites and antitheses that most meaningfully crystallize and express personal as well as universal values, experiences, and feelings. The scientist also selects and elaborates the context to some extent, but he has the specific task of determining which opposites derived from the world of natural events are significant at a particular point in the evolution and growth of theory and knowledge.

35   The action of janusian thinking in creative processes helps to explain, among other things, some of the sense of newness and surprise when creations first appear. Always surprising is the discovery that the opposite of a previously held idea, concept, or belief is operative or true. Even more surprising is this: not only is the opposite true but *both* the opposite and the previously held idea are operative or true. Nothing could jar our expectations more.

Points for Discussion

1. What is the effect of opening with an example as Rothenberg does? In what way could that example be said to lead to others throughout the essay?

2. Rothenberg (unlike Laura Bohannan, p. 58) states his thesis directly. Where is it stated, and why is it placed at that point?

3. Reread the essay and observe how it is organized. What, basically, is Rothenberg's outline?

4. About how many examples does the author use to prove his thesis about creativity? What use does he make of direct quotation?

Point out the element most of the quotations have in common. (See especially pars. 11, 14, 15, 22, others.)

5. Transition words connecting paragraphs and sentences within paragraphs contribute unity to writing. Note how Rothenberg uses such words. In paragraph 11 he opens with the phrase "for instance," showing the connection between that paragraph and the preceding one; the same phrase connects the first and second sentences of paragraph 23. Find several other such words or phrases and explain their function.

6. Rothenberg opens several paragraphs with introductory adverbs: *recently* (par. 25), *finally* (par. 26), *characteristically* (par. 29), *commonly* (par. 30) are such words. Comment on the repetition of this type of connective. If you find it monotonous, how would you revise the sentences without losing the coherence?

7. Paragraph 32 contains an allusion to Arthur Koestler. What does the use of this allusion suggest about the audience for whom "Creative Contradictions" is intended? If you don't know the source of the allusion, how can you check its meaning?

8. What is the function of the colons in paragraphs 1, 4, 6, and 34?

Suggestions for Writing

1. The task of finding just the right example to introduce a paper, and then selecting and arranging additional examples to develop the thesis, is a challenge. Like a good story, examples *show* the readers what they need to know instead of merely telling them. For instance, when Rothenberg uses examples of the two poets who were inspired (pars. 12–14), he is showing us janusian thinking and not merely telling us about it.

Practice the art of using examples by writing an article for a general but educated audience (like that of *Psychology Today,* the magazine in which Rothenberg's article appeared) on a topic dealing with creativity. These possibilities relate to different disciplines:

- creative children
- the creative process of the scientist
- right and left sides of the brain as these influence the creative
- relationship between war and creative outpourings
- the influence of television on creativity

2. Set up a hypothesis or a question to investigate, something you have only a notion about now but want to know more about. From your observation and reading collect a number of examples to test that hypothesis or answer the question. Note each example on a card. After a period of collecting—say two weeks—formulate a thesis from the examples you have found. It may be different (slightly or wholly) from the hypothesis, or it may be a restatement of it. Then select and arrange several of the examples in a short paper proving the thesis you have formulated. The subject for investigation may come from any course you are now taking. For instance, if you are taking an economics course, you might set out to investigate the commonly held notion that stores advertising as "outlets" sell at lower prices than other stores. Or, if you are studying political science, you might test a hypothesis such as this: "Students on this campus would vote [Democratic, Republican] in [a certain] election." Another commonly held notion is that students now are indifferent to politics; you might test any generalization such as that.

WILLIAM GRAYBEAL

Many reports and papers in the social sciences require that you handle statistics as well as cite examples from observation and quote printed material or persons interviewed. In this article from *Today's Education,* William Graybeal, a research specialist with the National Education Association, analyzes demographic changes and makes predictions about their effects upon colleges and universities. His presentation of various types of statistics in tables, charts, and graphs illustrates expert handling of quantifiable information.

How Changes in Enrollment Will Affect Higher Education

The next 15 years will be an era of significant changes in higher education that will accompany changes in many aspects of American life and work. The primary causes of these developments are demographic and economic. Because colleges and universities across the nation are not feeling the impact of these factors equally and because many places have already introduced responses to them, many faculties have concluded—mistakenly—that changes will not affect them. While it is true that the effects will be less severe for some faculties, the majority of those employed in higher education will have to deal with pressures resulting from these changes.

What follows is a brief review of some facts about current and future developments in higher education, some responses being made to them, likely effects of these conditions upon faculties, and responses faculties may need to consider.

Higher education in the 1980's and early 1990's will change primarily as a result of reductions in the number of Americans reaching the "traditional" age of college enrollment. The sharp reduction in the rate of growth of this age group during the 1970's, accompanied by a surplus labor market, particularly for jobs traditionally filled by college graduates, has contributed to several changes already under way. These are likely to continue or grow during the next 15 years.

Reduction in the rate of economic growth, accompanied

1

2

3

4

by severe inflation, has contributed to financial constraints upon students, parents, alumni, and government agencies that provide vital support for higher education. The outlook of continued high inflation, low to moderate economic growth, relatively high unemployment, increases in government spending for older persons and national defense, and high energy costs precludes a serious expectation of improved levels of financial support for higher education—at least during the first half of the 15-year era.

5   *Population Decreases.*   A decrease in the number of Americans reaching the age of traditional college enrollment is the basic factor that will influence student enrollment levels during the 1980's and 1990's. Figure 1 shows the decrease in two ways: the number of Americans reaching the age of 18 and the number between the ages of 18 and 24 in designated years between 1960 and 2000. Because the potential college freshmen of the 1980's and most of the 1990's have already been born, the size of the traditional college-age population for these two decades can be estimated fairly accurately.

6   The decline in their numbers, of course, reflects declines in the number of annual births that began in 1963 and continued through 1973 (with the exception of small increases in the period 1969–71). After remaining near the 1973 level for the next three years, the number of annual births increased by 150,000 in 1977, by 30,000 in 1978, and by almost 100,000 in 1979. Thus, the number of persons reaching 18 will decline each year until 1992, with the exception of the period 1987–89, when the number will rise slightly each year.

7   The changes in birth rates did not occur equally among the states, and population migration also has contributed to differences among the states in the timing and severity of the estimated declines in the population aged 18–24. Figure 2 shows for each state the timing and severity of changes expected in the number of public high school graduates over the 15-year period from 1979 to 1994.

8   At five-year intervals, the size of each state's graduating class is expressed as a percentage of its class of 1979. The type

style of the state abbreviation indicates the extent of decline predicted by 1984—italic, for a severe drop; regular, for a moderate one; bold, for a small decline.

Location on the grid signals the change anticipated be-   9
tween 1979 and 1989 in the vertical columns and between 1979 and 1994 in the horizontal ones. States located in the lower left-hand corner will have the most severe declines in both periods. The projections used in the Figure result from applying recent trends in migration and school holding power to current enrollments in grades 1–12.

Some states (Arizona, Idaho, Nevada, Texas, Utah, and   10
Wyoming) are facing rather small decreases that will disappear after five or six years. Other places face severe declines throughout the next 15 years (Connecticut, Delaware, District of Columbia, Illinois, Maryland, Massachusetts, Michigan. Minnesota, New Jersey, New York, Ohio, Rhode Island, Wisconsin). A third grouping—Iowa, North Dakota, and South Dakota—will have severe decreases during the next five years, but no further significant decreases over the following 10 years.

Students aged 18–24 who have graduated from high   11
school still constitute the majority of higher education enrollments, and provision for their education involves a significant proportion of higher education faculty members. The growing proportion of students in higher education who are above age 24 offers one of the most promising approaches to alleviating the severity of enrollment declines. The facts in Figure I emphasize the importance of identifying strategies for increasing the proportion of enrollees whose ages are above the traditional 18–24-year-old range.

Changes Under Way. It is difficult to assess the impact of   12
conditions that may have contributed to higher than "normal" enrollments in higher education by members of some subgroups in the 1970's. It is also difficult to assess their impact on enrollments in the next 15 years. Some of these conditions are the following:

• The surplus labor market
• Increasing numbers of higher level job opportunities for women and ethnic minorities

Figure 1. Number of 18-Year-Olds and 18–24-Year-Olds 1960–2000

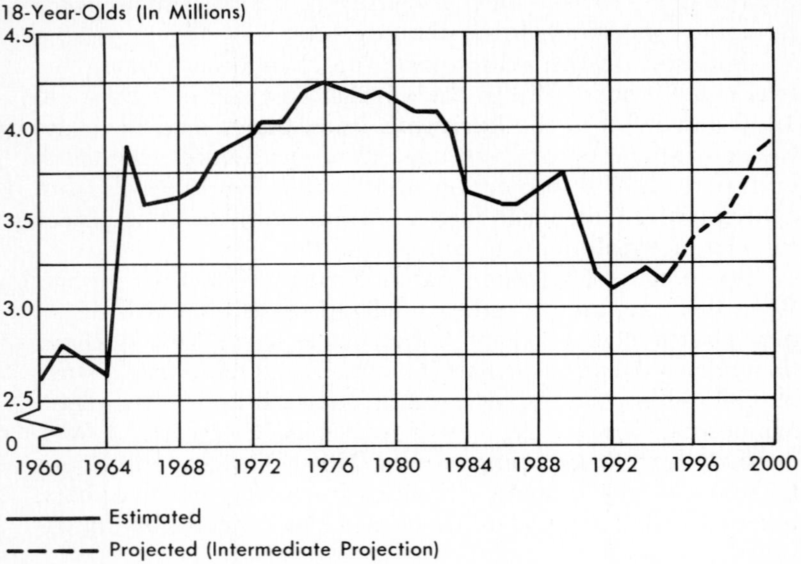

18-Year-Olds (In Millions)

———— Estimated

— — — Projected (Intermediate Projection)

18–24-Year-Olds
(In Millions)

1960 = 16.1	1970 = 24.7	1980 = 29.5	1990 = 25.1

2000 = 24.7

Sources: 1, 2, 3, 4

- Low birth rates that may have enlarged the labor force participation rate of women
- The contribution of high inflation to decisions of many women to enter the labor force.

13   Conditions affecting higher education enrollment changed in the 1970's and will likely continue to change in the same direction or remain near their present status for several more years. Table 1, "Selected Information About Higher Education in the 1970's," summarizes some indicators

Figure 2. Projected Change in Numbers of Public High School Graduates: How the States Will Differ

The classes of 1984, 1989, 1994 as percentages of the class of 1979

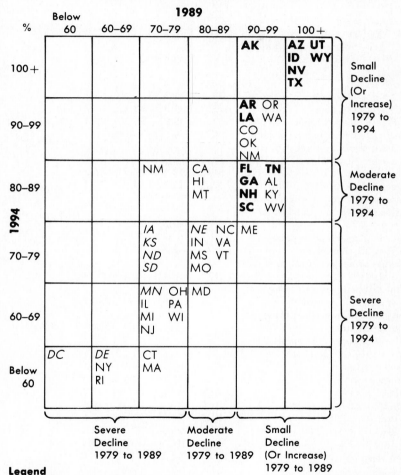

1994 \ 1989 %	Below 60	60–69	70–79	80–89	90–99	100+	
100+					AK	AZ UT ID WY NV TX	Small Decline (Or Increase) 1979 to 1994
90–99					AR OR LA WA CO OK NM		
80–89			NM	CA HI MT	FL TN GA AL NH KY SC WV		Moderate Decline 1979 to 1994
70–79			IA KS ND SD	NE NC IN VA MS VT MO	ME		
60–69			MN OH IL PA MI WI NJ	MD			Severe Decline 1979 to 1994
Below 60	DC	DE NY RI	CT MA				
		Severe Decline 1979 to 1989		Moderate Decline 1979 to 1989	Small Decline (Or Increase) 1979 to 1989		

Legend

States with severe early decline: Class of 1984 = 70–79% of Class of 1979

States with moderate early decline: Class of 1984 = 80–89% of Class of 1979

States with small early decline: Class of 1984 = 90–99% of Class of 1979

Table 1: Selected Information About Higher Education in the 1970s

Item		1968	1973	1976	1978	Projected 1988
	SOURCE					
Total fall enrollment, 50 states and DC (000's)	(9)	7,513	9,602	11,185	11,259	11,048
Total fall enrollment, aggregated United States (000's)	(6)	7,572	9,964	11,291	11,392	
Percent in						
Universities	(6)	36.8	27.4	25.4	24.6	
Other 4-year colleges		39.5	41.3	39.2	39.7	
2-year institutions		23.7	31.3	35.4	35.7	
Percent in private institutions	(6,7,8)	27.6	22.9	21.2	22.4	
Number receiving federal student financial aid as percent of enrollment (some duplication of students)	(10)	N.A.	18.2	30.9	45.2	
Percent who are men	(6, 7, 8)	59.5	55.8	54.9	50.1	
Percent of all aged 14–34 college students who are aged 25 or more	(11)	17.1	22.3	25.5	26.2	
Percent of enrollment who are aged 35 or more	(12)	N.A.	8.8	10.9	11.7	
Number of nonimmigrant foreign students (000's)		121	151	179	264	
Total first-time students in higher education in fall (000's)		1,908	2,248	2,544	2,422	
Total full-time-equivalent fall enrollment, 50 states and DC (000's)	(9)	5,954	7,453	8,481	8,361	7,967
Percent of population enrolled in school or college in fall	(11)					
Aged 18–19		50.4	42.9	46.9	45.4	
Women		41.3	38.2	44.2	43.0	
Black*		45.4	37.8	47.1	46.2	
Aged 20–21		31.2	30.1	31.2	29.5	
Women		21.5	26.3	27.4	27.5	
Black		18.2	20.5	27.1	25.6	
Aged 22–24		13.8	14.5	16.2	16.3	
Women		8.3	10.2	12.6	13.6	
Black		7.9	12.4	14.2	15.0	
Aged 25–29		7.0	8.5	10.1	9.4	
Women		3.4	5.4	7.2	7.9	
Black		3.1	6.1	9.4	8.7	

*Of 18–19-year-olds in 1978 who are students, 54.9 percent of Blacks and 82 percent of

Table 1 *(continued)*

Item		1968	1973	1976	1978	Projected 1988
SOURCE						
Aged 30–34		3.9	4.5	6.6	6.4	
Women		2.9	3.6	5.6	6.2	
Black		3.3	5.0	7.1	7.9	
Aged 18–24 population (000's)		22,883	26,397	27,604	28,980	25,967
Percent who are nonwhite		12.4	13.7	14.2	14.9	17.3
Total high-school graduates (spring) (000's)		2,702	3,043	3,140	3,134	2,701
Number of higher education faculty in fall (instructor or above) (000's)	(9)	428	527	628	647	612
Full-time		332	389	440	445	416
Part-time		96	138	188	202	197
Percent who are part-time		22.4	26.2	29.9	31.2	32.2
Estimated demand for new full-time-equivalent faculty in higher education	(9)	48,000	46,000	81,000	25,000	21,000
Number of doctor's degree graduates of previous spring	(9)	23,089	34,777	34,083	32,131	28,630
Number of higher education institutions closing their doors during the previous five years		46	102		63	
Median income of college-educated workers as percent of median income of high-school graduates						
Four years of college	(10)					
Males		142.4ª			127.7	
Females		140.1ª			126.4	
Five or more years of college						
Males		151.5ª			143.8	
Females		175.4ª			156.7	
Percent of college graduates located in professional and managerial jobs	(10)					
Men		83.3			76.6	
Women		85.5			73.7	
Percent of college freshmen reporting the objective "be very well off financially" as essential or very important	(13)	41	56	49	60	

Whites are in college.   ª1969

of trends and characteristics of higher education during the
1970's. Information for 1975 is given for comparison—to report conditions when full-time-equivalent enrollments
reached a peak.

14   Following are some highlights from the Table:

- Total enrollment in higher education grew by 2.3 million (31.6 percent) in the five-year period between fall
  1968 and fall 1973, but by only 1.5 million (14.3 percent) over the subsequent five years. The 1988 fall enrollment projected for the 50 states and the District of
  Columbia shows a decline of 200,000 persons from the
  1978 figure.
- The two-year institutions captured a progressively
  larger percentage of higher education enrollments over
  the 10-year period from 1968 to 1978. Their enrollments grew from less than one-fourth to more than
  one-third of all students enrolled in higher education.
- Private institutions enrolled a decreasing percentage of
  higher education students in the years prior to 1975,
  but since then they have held their own.
- Federal financial aid to students probably has contributed to the growth of enrollments in higher education,
  with the proportion of students assisted rising dramati-
  cally beginning in 1975.
- The decline in the proportion of students who are men
  (from 3 in 5 students in 1968 to 1 in 2 students in 1978)
  reflects the rising rate of participation of women in
  higher education.
- The percentages of age groups being enrolled shows increased participation by students who are older than the
  traditional college age. Over the 10-year period, enrollment for the population aged 25–29 grew from 7.0 percent to 9.4 percent; and for the population aged 30–34,
  from 3.9 to 6.4 percent. The impact of older students
  on the campus is shown by the proportion of all students
  between ages 14 and 34 who are aged 25 or more,
  which grew from about 1 in 6 in 1968 to more than
  1 in 4 in 1978. Also, the percentage of all students enrolled who are aged 35 or more increased between
  1973 and 1978.

- Participation in higher education by members of subgroups other than White males has been increasing, while the percentage of White males aged 18–21 who are enrolled has decreased over the past 10 years (not shown). The increased percentages of Blacks and women in the age groups 20–21 and 22–24 who are enrolled reflect their improved staying power. Both of these subgroups also show increased enrollment of students over age 24.
- The number of nonimmigrant foreign students has risen from 1.6 percent of total enrollments in 1968 to 2.3 percent in 1978.
- The fact that the number of full-time-equivalent students peaked in about 1975–76 and is projected to stay below present levels at least through 1988 supports concern about the impact of total enrollments upon the number of faculty jobs.
- A similar harbinger of absence of faculty growth is the decline in the number of first-time students since 1975.
- The number of full-time faculty grew by 57,000 between 1968 and 1973 and by 56,000 between 1973 and 1978. It is projected to *decrease* by 29,000 by 1988. At the same time, the number of faculty members employed part-time increased by 42,000 between 1968 and 1973 and by 64,000 between 1973 and 1978; it is projected to decline by only 5,000 persons by 1988. The percentage of all faculty members who are employed part-time increased from 22.4 percent in 1968 to 31.2 percent in 1978 and is projected to reach 32.2 percent in 1988.
- The number of new faculty members needed in higher education was 48,000 in 1968 and 46,000 in 1973. The number dropped to 25,000 in 1978 and is projected to be only 21,000 in 1988. The number of doctor's degrees awarded rose from 23,000 in 1968 to 35,000 in 1973 but dropped to 32,000 in 1978. It is projected to be only 29,000 in 1988. Expectations of a continuing tight market in appropriate employment for doctor's degree graduates is supported by the trend in the ratio of such graduates to new full-time-equivalent faculty positions. That ratio rose from 48.1 percent in 1968 to

128.5 percent in 1978 and is projected to reach 136.3 percent in 1988.

- The decrease in the percentage of the population aged 18–21 enrolled in higher education during the middle 1970's may have resulted, in part, from reports of the decline in the monetary return on investment in higher education as well as from the termination of the draft. The outcome of the continuing tight market for jobs traditionally entered by college graduates is shown by the decrease in the ratio of the median income of workers who have completed college to the median income of workers who have graduated from high school as their highest level of education. The tight market is reflected also by the decrease in the percentage of employed college graduates whose jobs are classified in the professional and managerial category. The Department of Labor estimates that in the 1980's, 1 in 4 college graduates probably will have to enter an occupation not traditionally entered by college graduates (15).

- The continuing disappointment of many graduates in the value of higher education is shown by the increase in the percentage of freshmen indicating that improved financial status is an essential or very important personal objective.

15 ***What is Being Done.***   A primary approach that many colleges and universities will use in order to survive in the coming decades will be to keep enrollment steady or growing by appealing to segments of the population that perhaps are not within the traditional age range, are less well prepared than is traditional, or have goals outside the traditional purview of higher education. In other words, survival will probably necessitate institutional flexibility to meet changing demands. It is difficult even now, however, for institutions of higher education to obtain the financial resources necessary to maintain institutional quality. It will be even more difficult to obtain the financial support needed to make the changes necessary to serve a changing student population.

16 To maintain current quality, as well as to ensure survival of higher education, state agencies and national associations

are making the case for improved provisions in higher education funding formulas, increased levels of financial support from government and other sources, and some changes in the characteristics and services of higher education.

To obtain minimum support, as well as build the case for needed additional funding, institutions are increasingly being called upon to supply evidence of the viability and efficiency of their operations. As a result, faculty members are more likely than in the past to be involved in planning for enrollment change, and they are increasingly required to present evidence of their productivity.

Impact Upon Faculty. The following undermining influences will attack faculty morale:

- Fewer opportunities than before to move to new institutions to improve professional and financial status
- Continuing threats to job security
- Changes in the characteristics of the students in class and/or in the content of some classes
- Increased emphasis upon "productivity"
- Absence of clear indicators of institutional health
- Loss of institutional flexibility in many decisions affecting the institution
- The continued unfairness of systems for rewarding good job performance
- Conflicts about tenure status and tenure ratios
- The decline in the rate of growth of salary and benefits.

On the other hand, faculty morale may be supported somewhat by the expansion of faculty members' involvement in institutional planning of appropriate responses to the pressures the institution faces. It seems apparent that faculty members will be asked to assume greater roles in improving the attractiveness of the institution to present and future students, in building alumni and public support for higher education, and in improving the quality and efficiency of their own work.

Faculty Union Responses. Faculty associations have reason to strengthen their emphasis on the traditional concerns of economic status, academic freedom and due process, and job security. In addition, they will likely continue to direct increasing attention to newer concerns—institutional practices and criteria for evaluating faculty, assessment of institutional financial health, retrenchment planning, utilization of part-time faculty, opportunities for faculty development, components and limits of optimal faculty loads, faculty seniority issues, faculty retirement incentives, and most effective uses of institutional resources.

21 *Keys to Institutional Survival.* Institutions most likely to survive during the next two decades have been described as those having a favorable location, loyal alumni, competent trustees, and a high quality of institutional management (14). In addition, the surviving institutions will be able to develop and communicate a clear sense of institutional identity and purpose, which they will use to select and retain students and which they will evaluate continuously. The role of faculties will be critically important in establishing and evaluating institutional identities and purposes.

22 To ensure that their role is a vital one, the faculty of any college or university should examine the information, planning, communication, and management activities of the institution. In addition, they must examine their own attitudes to ensure that they remain positive in the face of discouraging developments.

- Information. The faculty needs to be familiar with the timing and severity of changes expected in the college-age population within the institution's service area. These changes will heavily influence both personal and institutional planning.
- Planning. The faculty should seek involvement in the departmental and institutional planning process.
- Communication. The faculty should insist upon accurate information on the informal and formal planning activities in their institutions. This applies to faculty-to-faculty as well as administration-to-faculty sharing of pertinent information. In many institutions, widespread involvement of faculty members will require conscious effort by the administration, faculty leaders, and the committees responsible for planning.

- Management. The success of an institution's response to its challenges will depend heavily upon the quality of the institution's leadership and management. Enlightened self-interest dictates that faculty members encourage, initiate if necessary, suggest, and/or support management activities that are in the best interests of the institution of higher learning.
- Positive attitude. The experience of little institutional growth or actual shrinkage, accompanied by increasing controls, constraints, and insecurity, is likely to contribute to reducing faculty creativity, flexibility, and effectiveness. Faculty members will need to guard against losing their vitality and positive outlook during the 1980's. The continued existence of any institution of higher education will depend heavily upon having robust, well-informed, and involved faculty members who share in the deliberations and actions of the institution.

Sources

1. U.S. Department of Commerce, Bureau of the Census. *Estimates of the Population of the United States, by Age, Sex, and Race: April 1, 1960, to July 1, 1973.* Current Population Reports, Series P-25, No. 519. Washington, DC: the Bureau, April 1974.

2. U.S. Department of Commerce, Bureau of the Census. *Estimates of the Population of the United States, by Age, Sex, and Race: 1970 to 1977.* Current Population Reports, Series P-25, No. 721. Washington, DC: the Bureau, April 1978.

3. U.S. Department of Commerce, Bureau of the Census. *Estimates of the Population of the United States, by Age, Sex, and Race: 1976 to 1979.* Current Population Reports, Series P-25, No. 870. Washington, DC: the Bureau, January 1980.

4. U.S. Department of Commerce, Bureau of the Census. *Projections of the Population of the United States: 1977 to 2050.* Current Population Reports, Series P-25, No. 704. Washington, DC: the Bureau, July 1977.

5. Western Interstate Commission for Higher Education. *High School Graduates: Projections for the Fifty States.* Boulder, CO: the Commission, 1979.

6. Pepin, Andrew J. *Fall Enrollment in Higher Education, 1978.* Washington, DC: U.S. Department of Health, Education, and Welfare, National Center for Education Statistics, 1979.

7. Wade, George H. *Fall Enrollment in Higher Education, 1973.* Washington, DC: U.S. Department of Health, Education, and Welfare, National Center for Education Statistics, 1975.

8. Wade, George H. *Fall Enrollment in Higher Education, 1970.* Washington, DC: U.S. Department of Health, Education, and Welfare, National Center for Education Statistics, 1971.

9. Frankel, Martin M., editor. *Projections of Education Statistics to 1986–87.* Washington, DC: U.S. Department of Health, Education, and Welfare, National Center for Education Statistics, 1978. Also includes updated tables for 1987–88 edition.

10. Dearman, Nancy B., and Plisko, Valena White. *The Condition of Education.* 1980 edition. Washington, DC: U.S. Department of Education, National Center for Education Statistics, 1980.

11. U.S. Department of Commerce, Bureau of the Census. *School Enrollment—Social and Economic Characteristics of Students: October 1978.* Current Population Reports, Series P-20, No. 346. Washington, DC: The Bureau, October 1979.

12. Frances, Carol. *College Enrollment Trends: Testing the Conventional Wisdom Against the Facts.* Washington, DC: American Council on Education, 1980. (Working Draft, page 9.)

13. Butler, James A. "Portrait of an Era." *Educational Record* 61: 73–75; Spring 1980.

14. Breneman, David. "Economic Trends: What Do They Imply for Higher Education?" *AAHE Bulletin* 32: 1–5; September 1979.

15. Norwood, Janet L. "The Job Outlook for College Graduates Through 1990." *Occupational Outlook Quarterly* 23: 2–7; Winter 1979.

Points for Discussion

1. Read the entire article carefully; then go back to the two introductory paragraphs and explain how they function to give the reader a clear statement of the writer's purpose and plan.

2. Using that introduction again, scan the article to discover its major divisions. Explain how those divisions are predicted in the introduction.

3. How does the writer develop the statement that the primary causes for enrollment changes "are demographic and economic" (par. 1)?

4. What were the writer's sources of information? Explain his method of documenting those sources. Why is such documentation important? Why is it essential that the writer give dates for sources?

5. Analyze the two figures and the table:

- Point out the relationship between the text of the article and those figures.
- Which paragraphs interpret the extensive table?
- What can you conclude about the type of material that the

author presents in the figures? What is the difference between Figure I—a bar graph—and Figure II—a diagram? What is the difference between both figures and the table?

6. Look closely at the arrangement of items under suggestions for "survival." Why do you think the writer placed those items in the order that he chose?

Suggestions for Writing

1. Here are several questions for you to investigate for a report related to the social sciences; you can modify these subjects and add others of your own. It is possible with many of them to use both primary and secondary research—with some you will find statistical methods useful; with others you may report your findings chiefly in words. Choose a method to suit your material.

- Do eighteen-year-olds vote? Why or why not?
- Does the eighteen-year-old vote make a difference? If so, where and how?
- Does television watching change reading habits?
- Does holding a job while in high school help or harm preparation (readiness) for college?
- How do high school dropouts (in your area or in other areas—generally) fare in the job markets?
- How have televised debates (other appearances—narrow the topic as you wish) influenced elections?
- What is the influence of car-ownership on teenagers?
- How does unemployment insurance affect some group of your choice?
- Is it really true that people are moving back to cities and deserting suburbs? Or are they moving to rural areas? What will be the results when and if such movements occur? (Choose one.)
- How do "support" groups such as Parents Without Partners, groups for families of alcoholics, and so on help?

2. Many topics about which you will write involve the handling of statistical evidence. From one of the broad areas listed below

choose a narrower focus; do some research to find statistics that apply to your topic, answer questions you have about it, and write a paper presenting your findings.

bilingualism	unemployment
women in the labor force	crime rates
	population growth
demography—e.g. migration to the Sun Belt	social security
	cost of college education
	distribution of wealth
imports and exports	medicare/medicaid
	welfare programs
taxation	sources of energy

An example of "narrowing" may help you get started: You might investigate the cost of college at the school you attend, changes in those costs over the last decade, and predictions about further change in the future. Or you might investigate the population change in a particular town, county, or state and show what has happened there to school population. Whatever you decide to study, see the section on Statistical Sources in the Guide to Reference Materials in the Social Sciences (Part IV). If a chart or graph helps convey your information, be sure to construct it carefully, introduce it clearly, and interpret any findings that need explanation.

Another form of sociological study is found in oral history such as that of *First-Person America,* a collection of reports that reflect people and situations from the years of the depression. The oral historian allows the interviewees—subjects—to speak for themselves, to tell their own stories and comment on the society and life around them. Such an historian-writer may collect information from the interview, take notes and transcribe them, or make tape recordings of those comments. In the writing itself, less of the question appears than in the usual interview article; less of the writer intrudes, although the writer is still there behind the work—collecting, selecting, and distilling to focus on the purpose, whether it be to reflect the life of the individual or to present a picture of a society. Usually, too, the writer introduces the subject by telling something about him or her, setting the scene in which the "life" story occurs, providing the focus for the work as a whole.

Eli Luster

It's too bad about them two submarines. They can experiment an everything, but they cain't go but so far. Then God steps in. Them fellows is trying to make something what'll stay down. They said they'd done it, but look what happened. Take back in 1912. They built a ship called the *Titanic.* Think they built it over in England; I think that was where it was built. Anyway, they said it couldn't sink. It was for all the big rich folks: John Jacob Astor—all the big aristocrats. Nothing the color of this could git on the boat. Naw suh! Didn't want nothing look like me on it. One girl went down to go with her madam and they told her she couldn't go. They didn't want nothing look like this on there. They told the madam, "You can go, but she cain't." The girl's madam got mad and told em if the girl didn't go she wasn't going. And she didn't neither. Yessuh, she stayed right here. 1

   Well, they got this big boat on the way over to England.[1] They said she couldn't sink—that was man talking. It was so big they tell me that was elevators in it like across yonder in that building. Had the richest folks in the world on it just hav- 2 ing a big tune. Got over near England, almost ready to dock, and ups an hits an iceberg, and sank! That was the boat they said was so big it couldn't sink. They didn't want nothing look like this on it, no sir! And don't you think that woman wasn't glad she stuck by that girl. She was plenty glad. Man can go only so far. Then God steps in. Sho, they can experiment around. They can do a heap. They can even make a man. But they cain't make him breathe. Why the other day I was down on 125th Street and Eighth Avenue. They got one of them malted milk places. Well, suh, they got a cow on the counter. It looks like a real cow. Got hair. I was standing there looking and the doggone thing moved its head and wagged its tail; man done even made a cow. But, they had to do it with electricity.

3   God's the only one can give life. God made all this, and he made it for everybody. And he made it equal. This breeze and these green leaves out here is for everybody. The same sun's shining down on everybody. This breeze comes from God and man can't do nothing about it. I breathe the same air old man Ford and old man Rockefeller breathe. They got all the money and I ain't got nothing, but they got to breathe the same air I do.

4   Man cain't make no man. Less see now: this heah's nineteen-hundred-and-twenty-nine.[2] For nineteen hundred years man's had things his way. He's been running the world to suit hisself. It's just like your father owned that building over there and told you you could live in it if you didn't do certain things. And then, you did what he told you not to. And he finds out and says, "Go on, you can have the whole building, I won't have nothing else to do with it. You can turn it upside-down if you want to." Well, that was the way it was in the world. Adam an Eve sinned in the Garden and God left the world to itself. Men been running it like they want to. They been running it like they want to for nineteen hundred years. Rich folks done took all the land. They got all the money. Men down to the City Hall making fifty thousand dollars a year and nothing like this cain't even scrub the marble floors or polish the brass what they got down there.

5   Old man Ford and J. P. Morgan got all the money and folks in this part cain't even get on relief. But you just watch:

the Lawd made all men equal and pretty soon now it's gonna be that way again. I'm a man. I breathe the same air old man Ford breathes cause God made man equal. God formed man in his own image. He made Adam out of the earth; not like this concrete we sitting on, but out of dirt, clay. Like you seen a kid making a snowman. He'll git him a stick and make the arms. And he'll git another stick and make for his neck; and so on, just like we got bones. That was the way God made man. Made him outa clay and in his own image: that was the way he made Adam. One drop of God's blood made all the nations in the world: Africans, Germans, Chinamen, Jews, Indians; all come from one drop of God's blood. God took something outa Adam and made woman, he made Eve. The preachers tell a lie and say it was his rib. But they have to lie, I guess. They didn't do nothing but sit back in the shed and let you do all the work anyway. But God went into Adam and took something out and made Eve. That's the Scriptures: it said he took *something.* I cain't remember the exact words, but it said he took *something* and it didn't say nothing bout no rib. Eve started having children. Some of em was black and some of em was white. But they was all equal. God didn't know no color; we all the same. All he want from man is this heart thumping the blood. Them what take advantage of skin like this got to come by God. They gonna pay.

They tell me bout George Washington. He was the first president this country ever had. First thing I heard was he said to keep us look like this down in the cornfield. He tole em, "Don't let em have no guns. You ain't to let em have no knife. Don't let em have nothing." He tole em if they wanted to have a strong nation to keep us down. He said if ever they git guns in they hands they'll rise up and take the land; don't let em have nothing. But he didn't say nothing about no pick and ax! 6

They been carrying out what he said. God didn't say nothing. That was just man's idea and here in this country they been carrying out what old man George Washington said. But God's time is coming. Today you hear all these folks got millions of dollars talking bout God. They ain't fooling nobody, though. They even got IN GOD WE TRUST on all the silver money. But it don't mean nothing. This sun and air is God's. 7

It don't belong to nobody and cain't no few get it all to theyself. People around this park can have all they want. But you wait. God's gonna straighten it all out.

8   Look at the dust blowing in the wind. That's the way all the money they got gonna be. You see things, folks they call white, but man ain't got no idea of how white God gon make things. Money won't be worth no more'n that dust blowing on the ground. Won't be no men down to Washington making fifty thousand dollars a week and folks cain't hardly make eighteen dollars a month. Everybody'll be equal, in God's time. Won't be no old man Rockefeller, no suh! Today you cain't even buy a job if you had the money to do it with. Won't be nothing like that then. He'll let loose and something'll slip down here and them what done took advantage of everything'll be floating down the river. You'll go over to the North River, and over to the East River, and you'll see em all floating along, and the river'll be full and they won't know what struck em. The Lawd's gonna have his day.

9   They'll be a war. But it won't be no more wars like the World War. It won't bother me and you. Won't really be no war. It'll be the wicked killing the wicked! The war like the World War'll never be again. They fooled now. They building navies and buying guns. But don't you worry, it'll be just the wicked killing out the wicked. It's coming; God's time is coming and it's coming soon!

Notes

1. The *Titanic* was sailing toward the United States when it sank.
2. It was 1939.

Points for Discussion

1. In recording oral history a writer usually attempts 1) to capture detail and language that give an impression of the personality and character of the speaker, and 2) to convey the overall significance of the speaker's message, its relationship to history (perhaps social, economic, cultural history).

From reading the account here, show what you know about the speaker's

- personal background, education, values;
- the society from which he comes;
- his representation of that social group;
- and the history of the period.

2. Ellison shows that certain things in Luster's life have become symbols to him. What does the Titanic represent? What do people like Astor, Ford, and Morgan represent in his life? Why does he reject the popular myth about George Washington?

3. What is Eli Luster's concept of ethnic and racial differences? What is portentous in his predictions in the last two paragraphs, epitomized in such a phrase as "look at the dust blowing in the wind. . . . God's time is coming . . ."? What does that final paragraph reveal about the "actuality" of the speaker versus the selectivity of the writer and his writing? Is oral history then "canned" or "planned"? In what ways?

4. Ann Banks comments in her introduction to *First-Person America* that the problem of dialect (how much to keep or to alter) was never fully resolved by the writers in the Federal Writers' Project. What dialect features do you find in Luster's account? What does the dialect add (or subtract) from the effect? Why is dialect a special problem for a writer of oral history?

Suggestions for Writing

1. Consider some widespread myth that has grown up around a prominent figure such as George Washington, Thomas Edison, John D. Rockefeller, Jane Addams, Henry Ford, Andrew Carnegie, Eleanor Roosevelt, Martin Luther King, Jr., Eva Peron, Marilyn Monroe, John Wayne, Elvis Presley. From reading you have done, attempt an "oral history" by writing a revealing speech for one of these figures. Try to capture what you think the person would say about society of the time and his or her personal life and attitudes.

2. The collectors of the material for the *Dictionary of American Regional English* (DARE), being made under the direction of Dr. Frederic G. Cassidy at the University of Wisconsin-Madison, used

extensive interviewing to gather regional words and dialect expressions. In the process they ran into many vivid stories told by a variety of persons. Try a similar technique by interviewing an "old timer" or someone who has recently gone through an unusual experience (such as a hijacking or accident, a catastrophe such as a flood or fire, the eruption of a volcano). Record the story, keeping it as much as possible in the storyteller's words. Try to show both the personality of the speaker and the significance of the event or events.

3. Countless narratives, many of them first-person stories by survivors, have been written about the Titanic, the ship mentioned (with some mistaken facts) by Eli Luster. Read one or more of these accounts and write a paper about the significance of the sinking. Why did it make such an impression? Why has the event become a national legend?

4. Recount the history of someone who is currently unemployed, and perhaps has been for a long period of time, giving his or her comments on the recession of the '80s; or write the oral history of someone who served in Vietnam, of someone involved in recent antinuclear marches, or a similar sociohistorical event.

4

PAPERS THAT CLARIFY AND DISCUSS ABSTRACTIONS

Writing about an abstraction—like democracy, freedom, truth, or whatever—requires special discipline. On the one hand is the temptation to be satisfied with vague generalizations; on the other is the trap of parading too many examples. If you use either technique exclusively, you do not explore and clarify the abstraction for yourself and your reader. The middle ground between the two extremes is careful examination of the concept, its meaning and implications, as well as the ways in which the abstraction appears in concrete situations.

The writers you find in this section actually use different methods or approaches to examine five different abstractions. As Hannah Arendt, one of the social scientists represented, says in a preface, they all attempt to apply a kind of thinking "to immediate, topical problems with which we are daily confronted, not, to be sure, in order to find definite solutions but in the hope of clarifying the issues and gaining some assurance in confronting specific questions." Some of the abstractions they deal with represent concepts that affect all our lives, that we struggle to understand for ourselves and explain to others;

others present ideas that are new or give us new ways of looking at a problem.

Abstraction	*Methods*
Lester Thurow on "the zero-sum game"	defines a term that is to be the basis for his view on the economy
Carl Becker on freedom of speech	traces historically the various uses of the term in order to arrive at a current definition
Philip Rhinelander on stereotypes	discusses theories that explain why we stereotype and follows this with two illustrations
Hannah Arendt on duty	analyzes one philosophical notion of duty (Kant's categorical imperative) to show how it provides the basis for another man's actions
Isaiah Berlin on ways of thinking	classifies great writers into major types to explain two ways of thinking

As you read these articles, consider using these approaches and strategies in your writing, especially when you are faced with the challenge of clarifying an abstraction.

LESTER THUROW

With this section early in his book Thurow sets up and defines a concept upon which his entire argument rests. Similarly, other writers clarify terms, especially those that they will use in a particular or new way, at the outset of speeches, articles, essays, or books.

"A Zero-Sum Game" from *The Zero-Sum Society*

. . . Our economic problems are solvable. For most of our problems there are several solutions. But all these solutions have the characteristic that someone must suffer large economic losses. No one wants to volunteer for this role, and we have a political process that is incapable of forcing anyone to shoulder this burden. Everyone wants someone else to suffer the necessary economic losses, and as a consequence none of the possible solutions can be adopted. 1

Basically we have created the world described in Robert Ardrey's *The Territorial Imperative.* To beat an animal of the same species on his home turf, the invader must be twice as strong as the defender. But no majority is twice as strong as the minority opposing it. Therefore we each veto the other's initiatives, but none of us has the ability to create successful initiatives ourselves. 2

Our political and economic structure simply isn't able to cope with an economy that has a substantial zero-sum element. A zero-sum game is any game where the losses exactly equal the winnings. All sporting events are zero-sum games. For every winner there is a loser, and winners can only exist if losers exist. What the winning gambler wins, the losing gambler must lose. 3

When there are large losses to be allocated, any economic decision has a large zero-sum element. The economic gains may exceed the economic losses, but the losses are so large as to negate a very substantial fraction of the gains. What is more important, the gains and losses are not allocated to the 4

same individuals or groups. On average, society may be better
off, but this average hides a large number of people who are
much better off and large numbers of people who are much
worse off. If you are among those who are worse off, the fact
that someone else's income has risen by more than your income has fallen is of little comfort.

5   To protect our own income, we will fight to stop economic
change from occurring or fight to prevent society from imposing the public policies that hurt us. From our perspective they
are not good public policies even if they do result in a larger
GNP. We want a solution to the problem, say the problem
of energy, that does not reduce our income, but all solutions
reduce someone's income. If the government chooses some
policy option that does not lower our income, it will have
made a supporter out of us, but it will have made an opponent
out of someone else, since someone else will now have to
shoulder the burden of large income reductions.

6   The problem with zero-sum games is that the essence of
problem solving is loss allocation. But this is precisely what
our political process is least capable of doing. When there are
economic gains to be allocated, our political process can allo-
cate them. When there are large economic losses to be allocated, our political process is paralyzed. And with political paralysis comes economic paralysis.

7   The importance of economic losers has also been magni-
fied by a change in the political structure. In the past, political
and economic power was distributed in such a way that substantial economic losses could be imposed on parts of the population if the establishment decided that it was in the general
interest. Economic losses were allocated to particular powerless groups rather than spread across the population. These
groups are no longer willing to accept losses and are able to
raise substantially the costs for those who wish to impose losses
upon them.

8   There are a number of reasons for this change. Vietnam
and the subsequent political scandals clearly lessened the population's willingness to accept their nominal leader's judgments that some project was in their general interest. With the
civil rights, poverty, black power, and women's liberation
movements, many of the groups that have in the past absorbed

economic losses have become militant. They are no longer willing to accept losses without a political fight. The success of their militancy and civil disobedience sets an example that spreads to other groups representing the environment, neighborhoods, and regions.

All minority groups have gone through a learning process. They have discovered that it is relatively easy with our legal system and a little militancy to delay anything for a very long period of time. To be able to delay a program is often to be able to kill it. Legal and administrative costs rise, but the delays and uncertainties are even more important. When the costs of delays and uncertainties are added into their calculations, both government and private industry often find that it pays to cancel projects that would otherwise be profitable. Costs are simply higher than benefits.

9

In one major environmental group, delays are such a major part of their strategy that they have a name for it—analysis paralysis. Laws are to be passed so that every project must meet a host of complicated time-consuming requirements. The idea is not to learn more about the costs and benefits of projects, but to kill them. If such requirements were to be useful in deciding whether a project should be undertaken, environmental-impact statements, for example, would have to be inexpensive, simple, and quick to complete. Then a firm might undertake the studies to help determine whether they should or should not start a project.

10

Instead, the studies are to be expensive and complex to serve as a financial deterrent to undertaking any project, to substantially lengthen the time necessary to complete any project, and to ensure that they can be challenged in court (another lengthy process). As a consequence, the developer will start the process only if he has already decided on other grounds to go ahead with the project. The result is an adversary situation where the developer cannot get his project underway—and where the environmentalists also cannot get existing plants (such as Reserve Mining) to clean up their current pollution. Where it helps them, both sides have learned the fine art of delay.

11

Consider the interstate highway system. Whatever one believes about the merits of completing the remaining intracity

12

portion of the system, it is clear that it gives the country an intercity transportation network that would be sorely missed had it not been built. Even those who argue against it do so on the grounds that if it had not been built, some better (non-auto) system would have been devised. Yet most observers would agree that the interstate highway system could not have been built if it had been proposed in the mid-1970s rather than in the mid-1950s.

13   Exactly the same factors that would prevent the initiation of an interstate highway system would also prevent the initiation of any alternative transportation system. A few years ago, when a high-speed rail system was being considered for the Boston-Washington corridor, a former governor of Connecticut announced that he would veto any relocation of the Boston-to-New York line on the grounds that it would be of prime benefit to those at either end of the line, but would tear up Connecticut homes. The groups opposing an intercity rail network would be slightly different from the groups opposing an intercity highway network, but they would be no less effective in stopping the project. Any transportation system demands that land be taken and homes be torn down. At one time, this was possible; at the moment, it is impossible.

14   The Balkanization of nations is a worldwide phenomenon that the United States has not escaped. Regions and localities are less and less willing to incur costs that will primarily help people in other parts of the same country. Consider the development of the coalfields of Wyoming and Montana. There is no question that most of the benefits will accrue to those living in urban areas in the rest of the country while most of the costs will be imposed on those living in that region. As a result, the local population objects. More coal mining might be good for the United States, but it will be bad for local constituents. Therefore they will impose as many delays and uncertainties as possible.

15   The same problem is visible in the location of nuclear power plants. Whatever one believes about the benefits of nuclear power, it is clear that lengthy delays in approving sites serve no purpose other than as a strategy for killing the projects. If the projects are undertaken anyway, the consumer will have to suffer the same risks and pay the higher costs associ-

ated with these delays. What is wanted is a quick yes or no answer; but this is just what we find impossible to do. The question of nuclear power sites also raises the Balkanization issue. Whatever the probabilities of accidents, the consequences of such failures are much less if the plants are located in remote areas. But those who live in remote areas do not want the plants, since they suffer all the potential hazards and do not need the project. Everyone wants power, but no one wants a power plant next to his own home.

Domestic problems also tend to have a much longer time horizon. In modern times, even long wars are won or lost in relatively short periods of time. In contrast, a project such as energy independence would take decades to achieve. The patience and foresight necessary for long-range plans is generally not an American virtue. Consequently, representatives seeking reelection every two, four, or six years want to support programs that will bring them votes. They do not want to stick their necks out for a good cause that may conflict with their careers. Even more fundamentally, domestic problems often involve long periods where costs accrue, with the benefits following much later. Think about energy independence. For a long time, sacrifices must be made to construct the necessary mines and plants. Benefits emerge only near the end of the process. The politician who must incur the costs (raise the necessary revenue and incur the anger of those who are hurt as the projects are constructed) is unlikely to be around to collect the credits when energy independence has been achieved.

16

Points for Discussion

1. Thurow opens his book with a brief statement of what he considers the current economic situation and immediately follows that with this explanation of "the zero-sum game." Explain why it is important for a writer to define new terms early in a paper or longer work.

2. In most definitions the "term" is placed in a larger genus, showing the general classification to which it belongs. In what class does Thurow place the zero-sum game? How then does he differenti-

ate between the zero-sum game and other items in that same general classification?

3. Divide the essay into (1) definition, (2) explanation of how zero-sums work, and (3) application of the zero-sum game to the economy today. Draw some conclusions about both the organization and the transitions that indicate that organization.

4. Thurow explains a second specialized term—"delays" as these are used by militant groups for their strategic purposes. Where does that explanation begin? How do examples serve to clarify "analysis paralysis"? Why are such examples important?

5. In what ways does the zero-sum game apply not only to the economy but to politics as well?

Suggestions for Writing

1. Choose a term that is used frequently in one of your courses, preferably one from a course in the social sciences. Write a short paper explaining that term as you find it used in the course. Perhaps your choice will be a term that your instructor has taken time to explain in class, one basic to further understanding in the course, as Thurow's "zero-sum" is for his book. Here are a few suggestions:

autism	behavior modification
ethnocentrism	indexing (applied to income
macroeconomics	tax)
GNP	cognition
electorate	closed shop
income transfer	balance of power
payments	cartel
open primary	selling short

As you can see, these terms come from a variety of subjects that you may be studying; you should be able to think of many others. You might also try explaining a term like "depression" as it applies to a particular context. For instance, how is it used by psychologists? by economists?

2. From class notes or in your reading find one or more explanations of terms, preferably an explanation that employs an example or two. Write a short paper (a paragraph or two will do) adding examples that you think of. Draw some conclusions about the value of exemplification in such explanatory material. How, for instance, does an example often lead the listener or reader to think of another illustration? If you can, add further examples to Thurow's definition of "analysis paralysis."

CARL L. BECKER

Writing in 1935, historian Carl L. Becker found that freedom of speech was a subject about which there was little agreement. When he says "one must be prepared to face the consequences" for what one says, he could be speaking of many controversial situations today. His clarification of a tenet to which we give at least lip service is a model of extended definition.

Freedom of Speech

The worth of men consists in their liability to persuasion.
—Whitehead

I

1   *The Nation* has recently reaffirmed its faith in freedom of speech. I suppose there has rarely been a time since the foundation of that distinguished journal when such a statement would not have been true. What is notable in the present instance is that the unashamed affirmation of the old doctrine called forth an unusual number of protests—all from persons who presumably accept the doctrine of free speech in principle. They protest, not against the principle, but against an unlimited application of it. Free speech, they seem to say, is a wholesome diet under normal conditions, but it should be taken in moderation when the community, being subject to unusual strain, is not feeling so good. A re-examination of the liberal doctrine is always in order, and never more so than now. The times are such that every liberal may well ask himself, not so much how far he is willing to carry the principle of free speech, but rather how far the principle is capable of carrying him.

2   It seems necessary to ask what we mean by freedom of speech, since people often have disconcerting ideas about it. A woman once asked me what all the bother was about. Weren't people always free to say what they thought? Of course one must be prepared to face the consequences. I didn't know the answer to that one. Last summer a Columbia Univer-

sity student explained to me that all governments, being based on force, were dictatorships, and that there was no more freedom of speech in the U.S.A. than in the U.S.S.R., the only difference being in the things one was permitted to say. I suggested that, supposing freedom of speech to be a good thing, a poor way of getting more of it than we already had would be to adopt a philosophy which denied that it was worth having. The editors of *The Nation* do not say that the laws guaranteeing freedom of speech are always effective. They say that freedom of speech, as defined in our fundamental law, is the foundation of free government, and should therefore never be denied to anyone—"even to the Nazis."

The fundamental law guaranteeing freedom of speech was 3 well formulated in the Virginia constitution of 1780: "Any person may speak, write, and publish his sentiments on any subject, being responsible for the abuse [as defined by law] of that liberty." As thus defined, freedom of speech was the principal tenet of the eighteenth-century doctrine of liberal democracy. Its validity, for those who formulated it, rested upon presuppositions which may be put in the form of a syllogism. *Major premise:* The sole method of arriving at truth is the application of human reason to the problems presented by the universe and the life of men in it. *Minor premise:* Men are rational creatures who can easily grasp and will gladly accept the truth once it is disclosed to them. *Conclusion:* By allowing men freedom of speech and the press, relevant knowledge will be made accessible, untrammeled discussion will reconcile divergent interests and opinions, and laws acceptable to all will be enacted. . . .

II

The major premise, with reservations as to "human rea- 4 son," we can accept—must do so in fact, since there is nothing else to cling to. Even if reason be not always Reason, even if, like Hitler, we have nothing better than our blood to think with, we must make the most of whatever thinking we can muster. "All our dignity," said Pascal, "consists in thought. Endeavor then to think well: that is the essence of morality." It was by taking thought that man first differentiated himself from the beasts; by taking more thought that he achieved whatever men have, by taking thought, judged worthy. What more he may achieve can be achieved, and whether it is worthy can be determined, only by taking still more thought. Since men must in any case think, and do what they think of doing, it seems axiomatic to say that they should be free to think and to express their thoughts as well as they can.

5   Nevertheless, the statement is not axiomatic—obviously not, since, if it were, *The Nation* would not bother to print articles about it. There is a catch somewhere. Perhaps we are too prone to think of freedom of speech in terms of Man and Speech. This was the way in which eighteenth-century liberals thought of it. Confronted with a social regime which hedged in the individual at every point, they found the obvious solution in the maximum of liberty for the individual—political liberty, economic liberty, liberty of speech and the press. Knowing little of these liberties in the concrete, they visualized them as ideal abstractions, so that all the spacious but unfurnished chambers in the Temple of Freedom could be brilliantly illuminated by turning on certain phrases—as, for example, Voltaire's epigram: "I disagree absolutely with what you say, but I will defend to the death your right to say it." Liberals still think of liberty somewhat too much in the eighteenth-century manner. Give us, in a mental test, the words: "free speech," and we are apt to recall Voltaire's epigram, which then fades into a picture of two amiable, elderly gentlemen engaged in a rational discussion of the existence of the Deity.

6   Voltaire's epigram expresses a profound truth in the ideal world of knowledge. It would be equally relevant to the world of practical activities if society were a debating club of well-intentioned and reasonable men in which speech, being the only form of action, issued in nothing more dangerous than abstract propositions about reality. Since the activities of men are diverse, the ideal of a debating club is sometimes nearly realized. Mathematical physicists, discussing the nature of the atom, enjoy (at least in this country) the utmost freedom of speech without having (as yet) to call upon *The Nation* for first aid. Economists, historians, even biologists are more likely to encounter obstacles, since their activities have a more direct bearing on practical affairs. Where the principle of free

speech has to fight for its life is in the realm of concrete politi-cal activities. Since the eighteenth century we have learned at least this much, that society is something more than a debat-ing club of reasonable men in search of the truth. We know what use men actually make of their liberties. We are there-fore in a position to estimate the principle of free speech in terms, not of Man and Speech, but of men and speeches—in terms of the best that has been thought and said by the Honor-able Members we have elected, the Attorney-Generals we have known, the Insults we have suffered, the fruity-throated announcers who, every day, for a profit, avail themselves of the Liberty of Lying.

Estimated in terms of its concrete manifestations, the prin-ciple of free speech is resolved into a diversity of oral and printed utterances, some of which need to be suppressed. No one has ever thought otherwise. Even the editors of *The Na-tion* do not approve of the freedom of speech that issues in slander and libel. Do they approve of the freedom of speech that issues in the lynching of Negroes? In the sale of poisoned cosmetics? The sale of worthless stock to honest but gullible people? They would say that of course there are, as the Vir-ginia constitution recognizes, "abuses" to be defined by law; but that unless the law is careful, the definition may be a greater abuse than the speech it suppresses. True enough: the law is always in danger of being "an ass." But as soon as abuses appear, the principle of free speech is merged in another and broader principle: "Liberty is the right of everyone to do whatever does not injure others"; and we are at once con-fronted with the fundamental practical problem of all govern-ment: What individual acts, including the act that is speech, do here and now injure others?

By no formulation of principles beforehand can answers to this question be provided for concrete situations. The an-swers must wait on experience. Experience has taught us, or surely will teach us, that the eighteenth-century solution for social ills will no longer serve. Economic liberty, which was to have brought in equality of conditions, has contrived, with the aid of machines, to bring about a monstrous inequality of conditions. That there are rich and poor is nothing new, nor even disastrous. What is disastrous is that a great part of social wealth is owned by the many who do not control it, and controlled by the few who do not own it. Having well learned this, liberals find the obvious solution for social ills not in extending but in restricting the economic liberty of the individual. What we have not learned, or not sufficiently, is that the economic liberty of the individual is intimately associated with his political liberty, and that both are associated with his liberty of speech and the press. It will prove extremely difficult to restrict the one without restricting the others.

9   The speech that is socially vicious, to the point of endangering all our liberties, functions chiefly as an instrument of the competitive "business" economy. Such an instrument it has always been, no doubt; but never before so important an instrument, for the reason that modern methods of communicating thought are more subtle and effective than any ever before known, while the verification of the truth or relevance of the thought so communicated is far more difficult. The result is that there issues daily from the press and the radio a deluge of statements that are false in fact or misleading in implication, that are made for no other purpose than to fool most of the people most of the time for the economic advantage of a few of the people all of the time. This steady stream of falsification is called by various names which smell, if not too sweet, at least not foul—"advertising," "propaganda," "selling the public." Selling the public is an exact description of what is essential to the "successful" conduct of "business"—so essential that it is itself a business; and not the least of its evil consequences is that it is creating a state of mind disposed to regard anything as O.K. if you can get by with it. This manifestation of free speech is a far greater menace to liberal democracy than the freest dissemination of an alien political philosophy by Nazis or Communists is ever likely to be; and the only defense for it is that to restrict it would endanger the principle of free speech.

III

10   The danger is chiefly verbal, since the practical problem carries us beyond the speech we condemn to the practical activities that occasion it. The evil cannot of course be cured by creating a board of censors pledged to exclude lies from oral

discourse and printed matter. But neither can it be cured by waiting while truth crushed to earth pulls itself up and assembles its battered armor. In the competitive business economy, as it now operates, those who largely control and extensively use the avenues of expression are not seeking truth but profits; and freedom of speech will not cease to be used for purposes that are socially vicious until it ceases to be profitable so to use it. It would seem, then, that the essential thing is either to abolish the profit motive or divert it into socially useful channels. Communists and Fascists confidently assert that neither of these objects can be attained through the liberal democratic political mechanism. They may be right. Liberals who think otherwise must at least take account of a disturbing fact: the liberal democratic political mechanism functions by enacting into law the common will that emerges from free discussion. Thus the circle seems completed: for curing the evil effects of free speech we must rely upon a public opinion formed in large part by the speech that is evil.

The editors of *The Nation* admit that the situation is full of "uncomfortable possibilities," but they hold to the traditional liberal method of meeting them—the promotion, by appealing from free speech drunk to free speech sober, of a "healthy movement to the left." The uncomfortable possibilities, as seen by *The Nation,* are that "continued economic decline," and the "demand of a despairing people for drastic action," may enable a "well-directed [Nazi] propaganda" [free speech] to bring about the "triumph of fascism . . . with all its attendant horrors." Another uncomfortable possibility, as I see it, is that the "healthy" movement to the left may become "unhealthy," and end in the triumph of Communism with all its attendant horrors. Among the attendant horrors, in either case, *The Nation* would no doubt include, as one of the drastic actions demanded by a despairing people, the drastic suppression of free speech as a political method. The logical dilemma involved in free speech for political objects is therefore this: if social ills cannot be alleviated by the democratic method of free speech, this very freedom of speech will be used by those whose avowed aim is the abolition of the democratic method, and free speech as a part of it. Am I expected to be loyal to the principle of free speech to the point of standing by while,

11

writhing in pain among its worshipers, it commits suicide? It is asking a lot.

12   It is asking too much only so long as we remain in the realm of logical discourse. In demanding the privilege of free speech from a liberal government in order to convince its citizens that free speech is a present evil, neither Nazis nor Communists have any standing in logic. Their programs, so far as the preliminaries of social reform are concerned at least, are based on an appeal to force rather than to persuasion. Very well, since that is their program, let us cease talking, resort to force, and see which is the stronger. Their own principles teach us that it is logical for them to resist oppression but merely impudent to resent it. Nevertheless, the logic of events is not very logical, and I see no practical virtue in a syllogistic solution of the problem presented by Nazi and Communist propaganda. The freedom of speech which by their own logic I deny them, I am therefore quite willing to concede them in fact.

13   I concede it because, for one thing, there is a bare chance that the Nazis, or the Communists, or both of them may be, as they seem to claim, true prophets whom the world would not willingly have stoned—agents of the God Woden or the Dialectic duly accredited and predestined to establish truth and justice by a ruthless suppression of oppressors. I should dislike very much to put myself in opposition to the forces, not of persuasion, that make for righteousness, apart from the fact that it would be futile to do so if they are in any case to triumph. But perhaps a better reason for conceding freedom of speech to Nazis and Communists is that freedom of speech can neither be suppressed by argument nor maintained by suppressing argument. The principle of free speech must justify itself or go under. The real danger, from the liberal point of view, is not that Nazis and Communists will destroy liberal democracy by free speaking, but that liberal democracy, through its own failure to cure social ills, will destroy itself by breeding Nazis and Communists. If liberal democracy can sufficiently alleviate social ills, freedom of speech will have sufficiently justified itself; if not, freedom of speech will in any case be lost in the shuffle.

Points for Discussion

1. Becker makes a direct reference to the situation in 1934–5, the situation that made freedom of speech a subject of controversy. Explain what that situation was. In what ways are there similar conditions in the world today?

2. Becker divides his "essay" into three parts; in your own words, explain what each section contributes to the overall development of his explanation.

3. Explain a *syllogism*. How does Becker use the syllogism to describe the thinking of the founders of American democracy? What is the "catch" to the syllogism as the founders set it up? Point out ways in which Becker uses this syllogism (and its basis in logic) as a way of unifying his essay.

4. Becker uses the terms "liberal" and "liberal democracy," apparently assuming that the reader understands and accepts them in the way he intends. Explain their meanings as they are used in the context of this article.

5. Identify Pascal and Voltaire. (The *Encyclopedia of Philosophy* is a good source to use.) What is the value of Becker's allusions to them? Also explain the value of the Whitehead quotation as an opener for this article.

6. What, in the long run, does Becker think will sustain the belief in free speech? Why is he not afraid to let opposing governments speak out?

Suggestions for Writing

1. In addition to freedom of speech, Becker considers other political principles such as the common good, liberty, and liberal democracy. Choose one of these or another political concept and write a position paper that the President of the United States might use in defining and explaining American policy today.

2. Becker says that the eighteenth-century liberals who founded this country felt hedged in; therefore they wanted "maximum liberty." Some people today think that maximum liberty has gone too far; others still defend it. Write your own definition of freedom of speech and freedom of access (one or the other, or both) as you think it should apply to government today.

3. Create a syllogism of your own (you can be serious or satiric) about some commonly-held belief—a freedom of another kind, if you wish. Then use that syllogism as the basis for explaining the abstraction you choose.

4. Arguments about freedom of speech and freedom of the press overlap. Highly controversial situations often arise over what the press has a right to publish. For instance, you might investigate the government intervention in a recent situation in which the *Progressive,* a magazine that deals with public issues, was about to publish an article on how to make an atom bomb. Or investigate one of the lawsuits brought against a tabloid publication that purports to "reveal all" about some celebrity or situation. Apply Becker's principles to your investigation of one of these or some similar situation and write a paper in defense of or against the "freedom" as you find it defined.

5. Becker says that "there issues daily from the press and the radio a deluge of statements that are false in fact or misleading in implication." He then finds fault with advertising especially and with other forms of "selling" for economic gain at the expense of truth. Write about the "stream of falsification" as you know it; limit your definition and examples to one area. For instance, does "falsification" ever invade the health food business? the cosmetic business? You will need to be cautious, as Becker is, not to write "unreasonably."

PHILIP RHINELANDER

Philip Rhinelander, Professor of Philosophy at Stanford
University, goes beyond definition to examine the applications
and implications of the over-generalizing that is involved in
stereotyping. His essay was first given as a speech and
reprinted in the Phi Beta Kappa *Key Reporter*.

Stereotypes—Their Use and Misuse

It is generally agreed that of all human capacities and accomplishments, the most significant and distinctive is the capacity to make and use symbolic systems, notably languages. However, like all human capacities—or at least most of them—this one is ambivalent. Language provides a vehicle for communication which is not otherwise available, but in so doing, it provides also an occasion for confusion and misunderstanding. As half-truths are often more dangerous than outright falsehoods since the error is less obvious and their surface plausibility lends them weight, so partial but incomplete communication can be more misleading than an outright failure. Where both parties know that they cannot understand, or have not understood, each other, neither is deceived, and, if they wish to proceed, new channels will be sought. But where there is an appearance of understanding, resting upon a merely verbal concurrence without any deeper comprehension, the misapprehension goes unnoticed, and uncorrected. If language is a form of currency—and I think the metaphor is useful—it is, like other currency, subject to Gresham's law: cheap and inflated currency drives out sound currency. Thus, the more we tend to rely in our thinking and talking upon catch-words, slogans, and popular jargon, the harder it becomes to deal thoughtfully, intelligently, and critically with our pressing problems.

Some thirty years ago, George Orwell wrote an essay on this point, entitled *Politics and the English Language.* His point was that the devaluation of language in our day and the increasing tendency in public discourse to substitute familiar but threadbare catch-words for critical inquiry signifies a similar devaluation on our basic political understanding. After arguing that "the present political chaos is connected with the decay of language" he went on to assert broadly that

> Political language—and with variations this is true of all political parties from Conservatives to Anarchists—is designed to make lies sound truthful and murder respectable, and to give an appearance of solidity to pure wind.

I would add merely that in the three decades since Orwell wrote, the situation has got considerably worse, and that the infection has spread from the political realm to virtually all other sectors, including ethics and morals.

3   Most philosophers today are aware of the difficulties caused by the vaguenesses and ambiguities of language and the need for clarification. But there are two difficulties. Unlike Socrates, they do not conduct discussions with ordinary citizens in the market-place challenging their accepted beliefs, but tend to treat questions of *meaning* as if they were technical matters to be grasped only by those having a specialized background. Thus the grosser popular errors remain untouched. Secondly, a substantial number of professional philosophers tend to direct their fire primarily against philosophical language (notably the language of metaphysics and theology) rather than against what is called "ordinary language." Thus, like the guns of Singapore, which faced the sea rather than the land, the most important frontier is left unguarded. While they are prepared to hold rival philosophical flotillas at bay, the rear is left open to infiltration from Madison Avenue and other specialists in the art of rhetorical manipulation.

4   This brings me to the matter of stereotypes—including stereotypes about stereotypes. Because the point has been drummed into us by repetition, we have come to accept the view that stereotypes are bad things; but very few of us have stopped to inquire why they are bad or what the remedy is. This lack of comprehension is shown clearly in the fact that most of the people who complain with the greatest justification that they have been victimized by stereotypes do not seek to eliminate stereotyping but set about creating new stereo-

types of their own to deploy against the old ones. This process clarifies nothing; it merely confronts one set of misconceptions with an opposite set, thus increasing the confusion, while obscuring the issues.

What is a stereotype? Why are stereotypes bad? The simple answer, I think, is that stereotypes are half-truths which (as I noted earlier) are often more dangerous than outright falsehoods because they have an aura of plausibility concealing their untruth. This is why they are persistent. The best analysis I know was made twenty years ago in Gordon Allport's book, *The Nature of Prejudice,* written in 1954, the year of the famous Supreme Court decision in *Brown* v. *Board of Education* where compulsory school segregation was held unconstitutional. Allport argued that prejudice (including race prejudice) rests on an over-generalization which is immune to evidence or criticism and which has the effect of reducing all individuals to pre-conceived types. There are three key elements: (1) an over-generalization (attached usually to a model of some sort), (2) which is false in some degree, and (3) which is immune to correction.

There are several points to notice. First, a prejudiced over-generalization can be positive as well as negative. That is to say, there can be blind and irrational prejudice in favor of some group or cause as well as against it. In fact, positive and negative prejudice often go together. Hitler's belief in the superiority of the Aryan race, for example, involved a complementary belief in the inferiority of all other races. These were, in effect, two sides of the same coin. But this need not always be true. One can have a disposition to favor or trust certain kinds of people without necessarily being hostile to others.

Second, the most serious practical effect of a prejudiced stereotype is that the individual person or the individual cause is not judged on his, her, or its individual merits but is categorized on a general basis without regard to the actual, particular circumstances. It is chiefly for this reason that stereotypes have worked injustice to minorities and women. If you assume, for example, that members of minority groups or women generally are unqualified for the higher positions in industry or the professions, the result is either to prevent those individuals who are qualified from obtaining entry and advancement or to put such obstacles in their way that it takes superhuman ability to surmount them. However, it must be remembered here, that this situation can occur on both sides of any issue. Thus the radical activist or the rhetorician who believes that all white males are 'sexist' or that all white Americans are 'racist' is engaged in prejudiced stereotyping just as much as the male chauvinist who proclaims the inferiority of women or the Mississippi redneck who believes that all blacks are lazy. In either case, the particularity of the individual is ignored: all members of a class are *typed* indiscriminately according to a model which might, perhaps, hold good in a few cases but which is false for many or most.

8   Third, and most important, what characterizes the prejudiced mind is a refusal to look at contrary evidence or to admit contrary argument, in short, a refusal to admit the possibility of error. Thus prejudice is not merely a matter of belief but of the way beliefs are held. It involves an attitude characterized by *arbitrary blindness* which may be willful or may be a matter of habit. But in either case, there is *irrationality* here.

9   I make this point because it seems to me crucial, yet it is often overlooked. If you believe that basic moral and political values are wholly irrational in any case—that our attitudes are shaped entirely by emotions, desires, or interests which are produced for us and in us by forces beyond our control and that they are immune to any kind of rational direction—then you *should have no objection to prejudiced* or stereotyped thinking. On the contrary, you should accept it and expect it. You should, if you wish to be consistent, line up squarely and firmly with Thrasymachus who argued in Plato's *Republic* that justice is nothing but the interest of the stronger. You should accept without qualms the view that, in the last analysis, only force counts in the real world—either physical force, or economic force, or the force of individual or class interest, or perhaps the force of history. You should conclude that all talk about justice or human rights or the intrinsic worth of the individual is merely a pious smoke screen—a kind of intellectual charade engaged in by academic types as a game played simply for their own amusement. And if you believed that, you ought not to be here at all, because universities like this one and an honor society like Phi Beta Kappa are committed to the belief

that rationality does count in the world, and not merely in the form of technological inventiveness but more importantly as casting light on the meaning and goals of human existence. I am not saying that rationality is everything, but only that it is a vital element, that the life of the mind is something that must be pursued and encouraged not as a mere cultural adornment but for the good of mankind.

It is this faith in the value of rationality that most clearly distinguishes what we call the Western tradition from other cultural traditions, many of whom do not share it. Moreover, it is intimately tied to our belief in the intrinsic value of the individual human being—which many other cultures do not subscribe to either. The connection lies in the fact that, just as it is the concrete human individual who is born, lives, breathes, struggles, loves, aspires, encounters triumph and tragedy, and finally dies, so it is the individual mind that *thinks.* I think it is correct to say that the whole long tradition of natural law and natural rights, upon which our own constitutional democracy is founded, reflects a persistent faith that there is—or that there can be found or devised—a system of laws which will commend themselves to thoughtful persons everywhere by their inherent *reasonableness* rather than by force. This faith presupposes that above and beyond immediate passions and interests, individual human beings also have a capacity for rational understanding.

Thus the vice of slogans and stereotypes lies chiefly in the fact that they are intrinsically *irrational,* regardless of the issues to which they relate or the particular causes which they may be designed to support. Of course, all of us are fallible, and all of us employ stereotypes on occasion. But the truly educated mind ought to oppose them resolutely and should be ready to amend its own thinking whenever it finds itself employing them for serious purposes.

My point is that we are quite ready to condemn slogans and stereotypes as prejudiced and irrational if and when they are used against us, or against causes we support, but we have got in the habit of tolerating them when they are invoked on our own side of the issue. Such conduct is plainly inconsistent. If we oppose blind irrationality as dangerous, we should oppose it everywhere. On the other hand, if we really suppose that *all* thinking on moral, political, or religious issues is *always* prejudiced and irrational, then we should accept it everywhere and give up attacking prejudice or irrationality altogether.

13   Before passing on to consider some examples of the kinds of slogans and stereotypes now current, it may be advisable to anticipate one objection. It may be argued that since human beings are not wholly rational, and indeed could never become so, and since feelings, emotions, desires, and aspirations determine most of our attitudes, too much preoccupation with rationality would be self-defeating. It could very easily inhibit action and become an excuse for apathy in the face of evil. As Bertrand Russell once observed, there is no way to demonstrate logically or scientifically that it is wrong to enjoy the infliction of cruelty. Thus, if we were to wait for this kind of demonstration, we should wait forever and allow manifest evils to go unchallenged for want of a fully rational proof that they were truly evil. The answer here is in two parts. First, the canons of scientific demonstration are not the sole measure of human rationality. As Aristotle pointed out long ago, it is a mistake to take the standards of proof appropriate to one particular field and to apply them as a universal standard for all other fields as well. "It is the mark of an educated mind," he wrote, "to expect that amount of exactness in each kind which the nature of the particular subject admits. It is equally unreasonable to accept merely probable conclusions from a mathematician and to demand strict demonstrations from an orator." (Nic. Eth., I, iii.) Secondly, although the ideal of rationality in practical affairs requires that we maintain open minds, an open mind need not be open at both ends. It is possible to commit oneself fully and whole-heartedly to a cause on the strength of one's present knowledge and convictions while still retaining the consciousness of fallibility. Gordon Allport (to whose study of prejudice I have already referred) argued in another paper that it is perfectly possible psychologically for the mature mind to combine *tentativeness* of outlook with firm *commitment* to chosen values. He wrote,

> . . . Since certainties are no longer certain, let all dogmas be fearlessly examined, especially those cultural idols that en-

gender a false sense of security: dogmas of race supremacy, of naive scientism, of unilinear evolutionary progress. Let one face the worst in oneself and in the world around him, so that one may correctly estimate the hazards.

Taken by itself such tentativeness, such insightfulness, might well lead to ontological despair. Yet acceptance of the worst does not prevent us from making the best of the worst. Up to now psychologists have not dealt with the remarkable ability of human beings to blend a tentative outlook with a firm commitment to chosen values . . .

A commitment is, as Pascal has said, a wager. . . . We have the freedom to commit ourselves to great causes with courage, even though we lack certainty. We can be at one and the same time half-sure and whole-hearted.

(*The Person in Psychology,* Essay 4, "Psychological Models for Guidance", pp. 74–75, Beacon Press, 1968.)

This is from a noted psychologist, whose chief concern was 14 with views of the human *person* as a functioning whole. I have always regarded it as one of the best summary descriptions of what a rational personality should be. He adds, incidentally, that where the attitudes of tentativeness and commitment are found together, one also finds another important attribute, namely a sense of humor. A sense of humor implies a sense of proportion, together with the ability to laugh at things you love while still loving them—including, of course, oneself. If this is true, it points, I think, to an important difference between a rational commitment and the kind of commitment we associate with fanaticism. The fanatic is humorless; he cannot laugh either at his cause or at himself. To do so might imply uncertainty, and the "true believer" (in Eric Hoffer's sense of the term) cannot admit to himself any possibility of error. A rational conviction, religious or otherwise, is one which can admit uncertainty without being paralyzed by the admission.

I turn now to consider briefly some specific illustrations 15 of the way in which popular slogans and stereotypes can become substitutes for understanding. They appear, because of vague associations, to have meaning—at least what is called emotive meaning—but in fact even this turns out to be elusive.

1. "Liberation."   We hear a great deal today about "libera- 16 tion" in a variety of contexts. There is talk about the "liberated" female, the "liberated" male, the "liberated" worker, the "liberated" artist, the "liberated" writer, and, of course, the "liberated" homosexual. Obviously *liberation* is taken to be a Good Thing, and, of course, in many contexts it is. But liberation is not a quality, like height, or weight, or a condition, like happiness or peace of mind. Liberation is a *relational* term. It has meaning only if you specify (a) who is liberated, (b) in what respect, (c) from what, and (d) for what. Now in some contexts, these factors are quite clear, as when we talk about the abolition of slavery or freeing nations or peoples from colonialism. But as the term gets extended metaphorically, the meaning gets increasingly vague until, like Lewis Carroll's smiling Cheshire cat, the face has vanished leaving behind only the fading aura of the original expression. In this situation, "liberation" can be invoked equally well on both sides of many issues, thus cancelling itself out.

17   The question of sexual freedom is a case in point. Sexual freedom—including freedom for homosexuals—is seen by its advocates as required in the interests of personal "liberation"—in this case liberation from restrictions imposed by the culture and especially by the Church. Yet the argument upon which these supposedly "repressive" views were founded was itself based on the need for personal "liberation"—in this case (as Max Scheler described it) "a liberation of the highest powers of personality from blockage by the automatism of the lower drives." I shall not stop to argue here which view is right. My point is simply that talking abstractly about *liberation* proves nothing either way, since the concept can be (and has been) invoked on both sides. So also when Spinoza talked of "human bondage," he referred to men's bondage to their own passions, from which he believed rational men should always endeavor to free themselves. Today what Spinoza condemned as bondage is praised as the true measure of personal autonomy. As the context shifts, the concepts of "liberation" and "bondage" reverse their polarity.

18   I am not suggesting, of course, that liberation or being liberated is bad. I am saying only that if such terms are to have any ascertainable significance, one needs to look beyond them. Otherwise they function simply as ritual incantations,

employed to avoid the need for addressing the underlying problems.

In this connection, I might note a further assumption which can add to confusions on this point. Many writers today either assert or assume that all socially imposed rules or norms are essentially repressive. This view stems in part, I think, from a tendency to take the criminal law as a model for all law (which involves, incidentally, a kind of stereotyping). This leads to the belief that the essential function of law is to impose restrictions upon individual conduct, supported by penalties forcibly imposed by government agents. Given the increasing spread of government operations, coupled with a serious distrust of governmental authority generally—a distrust which was nourished by the Watergate scandals and other evidences of malfeasance—it has come to be assumed that the law is not merely restrictive but seriously oppressive. This view is reinforced by the position of some existential philosophers who have claimed that it is a breach of personal authenticity—a kind of "bad faith" in Sartre's terminology—for the individual to accept any general norms of conduct imposed externally by society. Although this point of view has some plausibility because it can be justified in certain cases, it leaves out of account the fact that some norms and laws can be enabling rather than restrictive, and the more basic fact that no community can exist at all without norms and standards of some kind, distinguishing acceptable from unacceptable behavior. The reason, as put succinctly by Dorothy Emmet, is that

> . . . in social life people sometimes compete and sometimes, for whatever reason, cooperate, and . . . they could do neither effectively unless they could count up to a point on what others would do. These fairly stable mutual expectations, which are the conditions of purposive action in any society, are only fulfilled where there are some generally accepted ways of behaving . . . (*Rules, Roles and Relations,* 11.)

If this fact is borne in mind, it may help to off-set the current feeling that society *as such,* and perhaps our own society in particular, is essentially repressive and that problems of individual self-restraint and self-control are of only secondary importance. In any case, where the older moralists and the Church stressed the primary importance for individuals of internal self-discipline as necessary to achieving personal *integrity,* many current writers (mistakenly in my opinion) equate integrity with *autonomy* and are thus led to suppose that personal integrity requires "liberation" from externally imposed standards and rules. In this context, of course, personal responsibility is devalued, while society or government becomes, at the same time, responsible for most injustices yet an instrument of oppression if it endeavors to increase its control so as to cope with them.

20   *2. "Discrimination."*   Because certain types of discrimination are unjust—notably discrimination against racial minorities—many people have come to speak and write as if all forms of discrimination were unjust. Thus the word "discrimination" has come to be used, not only in the news media but by some serious writers, as if discrimination were wrong in itself. To call something "discriminatory" is a way of condemning it.

21   This is a very serious and dangerous error, because all knowledge, all understanding, and all virtue, including justice itself, involve discrimination. Imagine, if you can, a person lacking all ability to discriminate. Such a person could not distinguish anything from anything else; experience, if we could call it such, would be a mere blur—what William James called a buzzing blooming confusion. He could not tell light from dark, up from down, future from past, friend from foe, truth from falsity or good from bad. He would be worse off than most animals, since, as Justice Holmes remarked in connection with the important distinction we make in law and morals between intentional and unintentional acts, even a dog distinguishes between being stumbled over and being kicked. (*Common Law,* p. 3) Many distinctions can, of course, be questioned, but if we make none at all, we can not discriminate between justice and injustice.

22   More specifically, the first requirement of any system of justice is that it should discriminate between the innocent and the guilty. To treat an innocent person like a guilty person is not to serve the interests of justice and equality, but to deny

them. Again, all laws and rules of any kind discriminate among different kinds of conduct. A law against stealing discriminates against thieves. A law against drunken driving discriminates in favor of those who are sober. Thus it is obvious that the question in all cases of alleged "discrimination" is whether the discrimination can be *justified,* i.e., whether there are reasonable and acceptable grounds for making it. Consider, for example, the case of *Bakke* vs. *Regents of the University of California* decided last September by the Supreme Court of California and now pending before the U.S. Supreme Court. That well known case involves what is called "reverse discrimination." The issues are complex and extremely important. This evening I want to call attention only to one point. If a college or university has more applicants than it can accept—in the Bakke case there were more than 2000 applicants for 100 places—it is going to have to discriminate among them on some basis, since some will be taken while others are refused. So the question is not whether you will discriminate, but what *grounds* may properly be used in making the selection.

Notice that several grounds might be used. One might go on the principle of first come, first served, accepting applications in the order of receipt without any regard to qualifications. This would be normal and reasonable if one were, say, assigning hotel rooms or theatre tickets. But I think most of us would think this method unreasonable for university admissions. Again, one might make the choice by lot, among all applications received by a certain date. Here every applicant would have an equal chance. And this method would be appropriate, for example, in administering a draft law for military service. But again, one would hesitate to think this method of discrimination was suitable for university admissions. Why? Because most of us feel, I think, that academic qualifications ought to be relevant. Indeed, Bakke's claim seems to be that priorities should be determined *primarily* on that basis. But this claim would, of course, result in discriminating against those with poorer academic qualifications regardless of other merits.

What emerges is the fact that discrimination is not wrong *per se.* It becomes wrong when, as, and if it is arbitrary, unreasonable or unjust. And this depends upon the circumstances and the context. Decisions here may be difficult, and much depends on wise judgment. But this brings us back to the initial point: there is no substitute for careful and prayerful rational inquiry, weighing all relevant factors. Invoking slogans and stereotypes serves only to cloud the issues.

25   I could go on indefinitely, discussing other important words which have been so worn out or skewed by current usage that they have become substitutes for thinking rather than aids to inquiry. And there are many new verbal coinages, too, which are vague and evocative rather than helpful: terms like *racism, sexism, elitism.*

26   But I have said enough to suggest that the first task of rational inquiry is either to avoid such terms altogether, or to make sure that they be clarified. This requires looking behind the labels and the stereotypes to the issues. The main difficulty is that the more complex our problems become, the more pressure there seems to be to find simplistic solutions. Let us do our best to avoid yielding to that pressure.

Points for Discussion

1. We often accuse someone (or we are accused) of stereotyping. What does Rhinelander find dangerous in that practice? Locate a sentence or two that might be called a statement of the writer's purpose in this essay.

2. Show how Rhinelander's definition of *stereotype* as a "prejudiced over-generalization" (par. 6) follows the system of logical definition: *term—genus—differentia.* What does he do to develop differentia further?

3. Summarize both Gordon Allport's analysis of prejudice and Rhinelander's three points about this analysis. What then is the chief problem, according to Rhinelander, with slogans and stereotypes?

4. In what sense might this article be called a plea for better defining of abstractions?

5. What is the effect of organizing this article around the two illustrations (par. 15, ff.) that follow the opening discussion and definition?

6. Identify the persons (authorities) Rhinelander refers to and comment on the suitability of these references.

7. Paragraph 5 opens with two "rhetorical" questions. What is their effect on the reader? In what sense do they provide a transition?

8. Rhinelander, like Carl Becker, deplores "infiltration from Madison Avenue and other specialists in the art of rhetorical manipulation" (par. 3). Find other ideas about which the two agree; for instance, what do both say about the importance of rationality?

9. Notice a number of "pointing" words with which Rhinelander opens paragraphs: "First" and "Second" from paragraphs 6 and 7 are examples. Find other such connectives and directions to the reader and comment on their importance in definition.

Suggestions for Writing

1. Choose one of the many general terms that Rhinelander uses to explain his views about stereotypes and write an essay of your own around that term. Define the term by considering various meanings attached to it; if you can, explain dangers that arise from the fact that it might be "skewed by current usage," as Rhinelander says in paragraph 25. Try to show that you have looked seriously at different views, and that you are not being "undiscriminating" in the broad sense of that term. Here are a few suggestions:

- catch-words and slogans: their power, danger, usefulness
- prejudice (as it affects the lives of people you know)
- irrationality/rationality
- a sense of humor (see par. 14)
- "academic types" (par. 9)
- commitment (as you see it; you need not agree with Rhinelander, of course)

- tentativeness (as a human attribute)
- the Western tradition (par. 10)
- liberation
- rules or norms
- personal authenticity (par. 19)

There are many others in the essay or suggested by it. Be sure to explain clearly how you use the term by giving differentia in the form of suitable examples.

2. Choosing the right number and variety of illustrations is always important. Though Rhinelander selects only two—liberation and discrimination—he also comments on others he might have chosen:

> I could go on indefinitely, discussing other important words which have been so worn out or skewed by current usage that they have become substitutes for thinking rather than aids to inquiry. And there are many new verbal coinages, too, which are vague and evocative rather than helpful: terms like *racism, sexism, elitism.*

This is a common and effective technique: to consider, in detail, one or two illustrations, while showing that these are representative of many other examples that might also be examined. That way the writer demonstrates both depth and breadth of thought.

Using this same technique, write an article about the way language, in Rhinelander's words, can be "an occasion for confusion and misunderstanding." Some topics you might explore are

- current "isms" (e.g., racism, sexism, elitism, ageism)
- White House-ese (i.e., gobbldygook from elected and appointed office holders)
- computer language (e.g., input, output, feedback, impact)
- euphemism (e.g., "pre-owned" for "used"; "termination with extreme prejudice" for "liquidation")

3. Consider how the advertising industry creates stereotypes with brand names—brand names as selling factors, as deception, as distinction, as powerful *economic* factors, and as *social* factors. Write an essay considering such "brand" stereotyping, choosing your illustrations to carry whatever views you have about the sub-

ject. Keep Rhinelander's cautious approach in mind. For instance, you may wish to consider the possible selling power or feeling of distinction we sometimes attach to the term "generic."

Or, if you prefer, think of another form of labeling that is used and misused, another illustration of the power of using language as a form of currency.

HANNAH ARENDT

In these paragraphs Hannah Arendt probes the thinking about duty that led the Germans under Hitler to the awful deeds of the holocaust. As Arendt points out, both legal and moral questions are involved in different definitions of the abstract term *duty.*

"Duties of a Law Abiding Citizen" from *Eichmann in Jerusalem*

1 So Eichmann's opportunities for feeling like Pontius Pilate were many, and as the months and the years went by, he lost the need to feel anything at all. This was the way things were, this was the new law of the land, based on the Führer's order; whatever he did he did, as far as he could see, as a law-abiding citizen. He did his *duty,* as he told the police and the court over and over again; he not only obeyed *orders,* he also obeyed the *law.* Eichmann had a muddled inkling that this could be an important distinction, but neither the defense nor the judges ever took him up on it. The well-worn coins of "superior orders" versus "acts of state" were handed back and forth; they had governed the whole discussion of these matters during the Nuremberg Trials, for no other reason than that they gave the illusion that the altogether unprecedented could be judged according to precedents and the standards that went with them. Eichmann, with his rather modest mental gifts, was certainly the last man in the courtroom to be expected to challenge these notions and to strike out on his own. Since, in addition to performing what he conceived to be the duties of a law-abiding citizen, he had also acted upon orders—always so careful to be "covered"—he became completely muddled, and ended by stressing alternately the virtues and the vices of blind obedience, or the "obedience of corpses," *Kadavergehorsam,* as he himself called it.

The first indication of Eichmann's vague notion that there   2
was more involved in this whole business than the question
of the soldier's carrying out orders that are clearly criminal
in nature and intent appeared during the police examination,
when he suddenly declared with great emphasis that he had
lived his whole life according to Kant's moral precepts, and
especially according to a Kantian definition of duty. This was
outrageous, on the face of it, and also incomprehensible, since
Kant's moral philosophy is so closely bound up with man's faculty of judgment, which rules out blind obedience. The examining officer did not press the point, but Judge Raveh, either
out of curiosity or out of indignation at Eichmann's having
dared to invoke Kant's name in connection with his crimes,
decided to question the accused. And, to the surprise of everybody, Eichmann came up with an approximately correct definition of the categorical imperative: "I meant by my remark
about Kant that the principle of my will must always be such
that it can become the principle of general laws" (which is not
the case with theft or murder, for instance, because the thief
or the murderer cannot conceivably wish to live under a legal
system that would give others the right to rob or murder him).
Upon further questioning, he added that he had read Kant's
Critique of Practical Reason. He then proceeded to explain that
from the moment he was charged with carrying out the Final
Solution he had ceased to live according to Kantian principles,
that he had known it, and that he had consoled himself with
the thought that he no longer "was master of his own deeds,"
that he was unable "to change anything." What he failed to
point out in court was that in this "period of crimes legalized
by the state," as he himself now called it, he had not simply
dismissed the Kantian formula as no longer applicable, he had
distorted it to read: Act as if the principle of your actions were
the same as that of the legislator or of the law of the land—or,
in Hans Frank's formulation of "the categorical imperative in
the Third Reich," which Eichmann might have known: "Act
in such a way that the Führer, if he knew your action, would
approve it" (*Die Technik des Staates,* 1942, pp. 15–16). Kant,
to be sure, had never intended to say anything of the sort; on
the contrary, to him every man was a legislator the moment

he started to act: by using his "practical reason" man found the principles that could and should be the principles of law. But it is true that Eichmann's unconscious distortion agrees with what he himself called the version of Kant "for the household use of the little man." In this household use, all that is left of Kant's spirit is the demand that a man do more than obey the law, that he go beyond the mere call of obedience and identify his own will with the principle behind the law—the source from which the law sprang. In Kant's philosophy, that source was practical reason; in Eichmann's household use of him, it was the will of the Führer. Much of the horribly painstaking thoroughness in the execution of the Final Solution—a thoroughness that usually strikes the observer as typically German, or else as characteristic of the perfect bureaucrat—can be traced to the odd notion, indeed very common in Germany, that to be law-abiding means not merely to obey the laws but to act as though one were the legislator of the laws that one obeys. Hence the conviction that nothing less than going beyond the call of duty will do.

3   Whatever Kant's role in the formation of "the little man's" mentality in Germany may have been, there is not the slightest doubt that in one respect Eichmann did indeed follow Kant's precepts: a law was a law, there could be no exceptions. In Jerusalem, he admitted only two such exceptions during the time when "eighty million Germans" had each had "his decent Jew": he had helped a half-Jewish cousin, and a Jewish couple in Vienna for whom his uncle had intervened. This inconsistency still made him feel somewhat uncomfortable, and when he was questioned about it during cross-examination, he became openly apologetic: he had "confessed his sins" to his superiors. This uncompromising attitude toward the performance of his murderous duties damned him in the eyes of the judges more than anything else, which was comprehensible, but in his own eyes it was precisely what justified him, as it had once silenced whatever conscience he might have had left. No exceptions—this was the proof that he had always acted against his "inclinations," whether they were sentimental or inspired by interest, that he had always done his "duty."

4   Doing his "duty" finally brought him into open conflict

with orders from his superiors. During the last year of the war, more than two years after the Wannsee Conference, he experienced his last crisis of conscience. As the defeat approached, he was confronted by men from his own ranks who fought more and more insistently for exceptions and, eventually, for the cessation of the Final Solution. That was the moment when his caution broke down and he began, once more, taking initiatives—for instance, he organized the foot marches of Jews from Budapest to the Austrian border after Allied bombing had knocked out the transportation system. It now was the fall of 1944, and Eichmann knew that Himmler had ordered the dismantling of the extermination facilities in Auschwitz and that the game was up. Around this time, Eichmann had one of his very few personal interviews with Himmler, in the course of which the latter allegedly shouted at him, "If up to now you have been busy liquidating Jews, you will from now on, since I order it, take good care of Jews, act as their nursemaid. I remind you that it was I—and neither Gruppenführer Müller nor you—who founded the R.S.H.A. in 1933; I am the one who gives orders here." Sole witness to substantiate these words was the very dubious Mr. Kurt Becher; Eichmann denied that Himmler had shouted at him, but he did not deny that such an interview had taken place. Himmler cannot have spoken in precisely these words, he surely knew that the R.S.H.A. was founded in 1939, not in 1933, and not simply by himself but by Heydrich, with his endorsement. Still, something of the sort must have occurred. Himmler was then giving orders right and left that the Jews be treated well—they were his "soundest investment"—and it must have been a shattering experience for Eichmann.

Points for Discussion

1. Examine, paragraph by paragraph, the way Arendt develops the notion of duty. What is the purpose of saying that Eichmann had opportunities for "feeling like Pontius Pilate" (par. 1)? In what way does that phrase lead to summarizing his ideas about duty later in the paragraph? Why are the words *duty, orders,* and *law* italicized?

2. From commenting on Eichmann's idea of duty, Arendt leads you to know how she defines the term. Express that definition as clearly as you can in your own words.

3. Referring to the *Encyclopedia of Philosophy* or another source, further explain Kant's categorical imperative. How did Eichmann distort the theory to justify his actions? Why, according to Arendt, did helping any Jews make him uncomfortable? How did doing his "duty" finally bring him into conflict with superiors?

4. Arendt's style is appealing because she uses variety in sentence structure. Analyze the pattern and length of several of her sentences to show that variety. The last two sentences in paragraph 2 might serve as good examples.

5. Notice how Arendt weaves Eichmann's words into her sentences. What is the purpose (and effect) of using so many direct quotations?

6. Echoes, or reiteration of an idea in different words, often are a way of linking ideas. For instance, the phrase "go beyond the mere call of obedience" in paragraph 2 is echoed three sentences later with "going beyond the call of duty." Find other echo links and explain how they contribute to style.

Suggestions for Writing

1. Conflicts over duty are always critical, but they have particular significance for many young people today. Situations such as the My Lai, Watergate, and Jonestown incidents, and attitudes toward groups like the Moonies, to name a few, force thinkers to examine just what the word "duty" means. Select a recent event or situation and explore it as a crisis over the idea of duty. You might build in purpose and audience by writing to a friend or group involved in such a conflict—joining an organization to which parents object; holding to party affiliation over objections to chosen candidates; continuing financial contribution to a cause that has changed leadership but is still a worthy cause; and so on. Or you might center your paper on an individual faced with some crisis in government or soci-

ety—a mayor who knows that the only way to get a city park is to seek financial favor from a special-interest group; a teacher who knows that a student leader or star athlete is cheating; a social worker who becomes aware that someone not entitled to a benefit is nevertheless "milking the system." Use that person's words and construct a line of reasoning to show what he or she considers duty.

2. Later in *Eichmann in Jerusalem* Hannah Arendt speaks of the "larger issue at stake" as the "assumption current in all modern legal systems that intent to do wrong is necessary for the commission of a crime." There she develops the idea of "justice," and rejects the notion that "where all, or almost all, are guilty, nobody is," at least in the case of Eichmann and similar criminals. She considers the problem of "intent" and the idea that there is no crime when "the ability to distinguish right from wrong is impaired." Write a paper dealing with this problem as it is demonstrated in some current legal or political situation.

3. When is it a "duty" to defy the law, to demonstrate or act against a government or some decision thereof, to act against *orders?* Can the word "duty" be applied in such cases of individual decision? Write a paper about someone or some group that has used or now uses the word duty to cover some action (or inaction). Develop the definition of duty that this person or group might hold.

ISAIAH BERLIN

Sir Isaiah Berlin, born in Latvia over seventy years ago, has had a varied career as critic and scholar. His essays, many of them dealing with figures famous for their contributions to the world of ideas, are complex but clear. One of the best known is the model of definition and classification, "The Hedgehog and the Fox."

The Hedgehog and the Fox

1   There is a line among the fragments of the Greek poet Archilochus [fl. 720–680 B.C.] which says: 'The fox knows many things, but the hedgehog knows one big thing.' Scholars have differed about the correct interpretation of these dark words, which may mean no more than that the fox, for all his cunning, is defeated by the hedgehog's one defence. But, taken figuratively, the words can be made to yield a sense in which they mark one of the deepest differences which divide writers and thinkers, and, it may be, human beings in general. For there exists a great chasm between those, on one side, who relate everything to a single central vision, one system less or more coherent or articulate, in terms of which they understand, think and feel—a single, universal, organizing principle in terms of which alone all that they are and say has significance—and, on the other side, those who pursue many ends, often unrelated and even contradictory, connected, if at all, only in some *de facto* way, for some psychological or physiological cause, related by no moral or aesthetic principle; these last lead lives, perform acts, and entertain ideas that are centrifugal rather than centripetal, their thought is scattered or diffused, moving on many levels, seizing upon the essence of a vast variety of experiences and objects for what they are in themselves, without, consciously or unconsciously, seeking to fit them into, or exclude them from, any one unchanging, all-embracing, sometimes self-contradictory and incomplete, at times fanatical, unitary inner vision. The first kind of intellectual and artistic personality belongs to the hedgehogs, the second to the foxes; and without insisting on a rigid classifica-

tion, we may, without too much fear of contradiction, say that, in this sense, Dante belongs to the first category, Shakespeare to the second; Plato, Lucretius, Pascal, Hegel, Dostoevsky, Nietzsche, Ibsen, Proust are, in varying degrees, hedgehogs; Herodotus, Aristotle, Montaigne, Erasmus, Molière, Goethe, Pushkin, Balzac, Joyce are foxes.

Of course, like all over-simple classifications of this type, the dichotomy becomes, if pressed, artificial, scholastic, and ultimately absurd. But if it is not an aid to serious criticism, neither should it be rejected as being merely superficial or frivolous; like all distinctions which embody any degree of truth, it offers a point of view from which to look and compare, a starting-point for genuine investigation. Thus we have no doubt about the violence of the contrast between Pushkin and Dostoevsky; and Dostoevsky's celebrated speech about Pushkin has, for all its eloquence and depth of feeling, seldom been considered by any perceptive reader to cast light on the genius of Pushkin, but rather on that of Dostoevsky himself, precisely because it perversely represents Pushkin—an arch-fox, the greatest in the nineteenth century—as a being similar to Dostoevsky who is nothing if not a hedgehog; and thereby transforms, indeed distorts, Pushkin into a dedicated prophet, a bearer of a single, universal message which was indeed the centre of Dostoevsky's own universe, but exceedingly remote from the many varied provinces of Pushkin's protean genius. Indeed, it would not be absurd to say that Russian literature is spanned by these gigantic figures—at one pole Pushkin, at the other Dostoevsky; and that the characteristics of other Russian writers can, by those who find it useful or enjoyable to ask that kind of question, to some degree be determined in relation to these great opposites. To ask of Gogol, Turgenev, Chekhov, Blok how they stand in relation to Pushkin and to Dostoevsky leads—or, at any rate, has led—to fruitful and illuminating criticism. But when we come to Count Lev Nikolaevich Tolstoy, and ask this of him—ask whether he belongs to the first category or the second, whether he is a monist or a pluralist, whether his vision is of one or of many, whether he is of a single substance or compounded of heterogeneous elements, there is no clear or immediate answer. The question does not, somehow, seem wholly appropriate; it seems to breed more darkness than it dispels. Yet it is not lack of information that makes us pause: Tolstoy has told us more about himself and his views and attitudes than any other Russian, more, almost, than any other European writer; nor can his art be called obscure in any normal sense: his universe has no dark corners, his stories are luminous with the light of day; he has explained them and himself, and argued about them and the methods by which they are constructed, more articulately and with greater force and sanity and lucidity than any other writer. Is he a fox or a hedgehog? What are we to say? Why is the answer so curiously difficult to find? Does he resemble Shakespeare or Pushkin more than Dante or Dostoevsky? Or is he wholly unlike either, and is the question therefore unanswerable because it is absurd? What is the mysterious obstacle with which our inquiry seems faced?

3   I do not propose in this essay to formulate a reply to this question, since this would involve nothing less than a critical examination of the art and thought of Tolstoy as a whole. I shall confine myself to suggesting that the difficulty may be, at least in part, due to the fact that Tolstoy was himself not unaware of the problem, and did his best to falsify the answer. The hypothesis I wish to offer is that Tolstoy was by nature a fox, but believed in being a hedgehog; that his gifts and achievement are one thing, and his beliefs, and consequently his interpretation of his own achievement, another; and that consequently his ideals have led him, and those whom his genius for persuasion has taken in, into a systematic misinterpretation of what he and others were doing or should be doing. No one can complain that he has left his readers in any doubt as to what he thought about this topic: his views on this subject permeate all his discursive writings—diaries, recorded *obiter dicta,* autobiographical essays and stories, social and religious tracts, literary criticism, letters to private and public correspondents. . . .

4   The unresolved conflict between Tolstoy's belief that the attributes of personal life alone were real and his doctrine that analysis of them is insufficient to explain the course of history (i.e. the behaviour of societies) is paralleled, at a profounder

and more personal level, by the conflict between, on the one hand, his own gifts both as a writer and as a man and, on the other, his ideals—that which he sometimes believed himself to be, and at all times profoundly believed in, and wished to be.

If we may recall once again our division of artists into   5
foxes and hedgehogs: Tolstoy perceived reality in its multiplicity, as a collection of separate entities round and into which he saw with a clarity and penetration scarcely ever equalled, but he believed only in one vast, unitary whole. No author who has ever lived has shown such powers of insight into the variety of life—the differences, the contrasts, the collisions of persons and things and situations, each apprehended in its absolute uniqueness and conveyed with a degree of directness and a precision of concrete imagery to be found in no other writer. No one has ever excelled Tolstoy in expressing the specific flavour, the exact quality of a feeling—the degree of its "oscillation," the ebb and flow, the minute movements (which Turgenev mocked as a mere trick on his part)—the inner and outer texture and "feel" of a look, a thought, a pang of sentiment, no less than that of the specific pattern of a situation, or an entire period, continuous segments of lives of individuals, families, communities, entire nations. The celebrated life-likeness of every object and every person in his world derives from this astonishing capacity of presenting every ingredient of it in its fullest individual essence, in all its many dimensions, as it were; never as a mere datum, however vivid, within some stream of consciousness, with blurred edges, an outline, a shadow, an impressionistic representation: nor yet calling for, and dependent on, some process of reasoning in the mind of the reader; but always as a solid object, seen simultaneously from near and far, in natural, unaltering daylight, from all possible angles of vision, set in an absolutely specific context in time and space—an event fully present to the senses or the imagination in all its facets, with every nuance sharply and firmly articulated.

Yet what he believed in was the opposite. He advocated   6
a single embracing vision; he preached not variety but simplicity, not many levels of consciousness but reduction to some

single level—in *War and Peace* to the standard of the good man, the single, spontaneous, open soul: as later to that of the peasants, or of a simple Christian ethic divorced from any complex theology or metaphysic, some simple, quasi-utilitarian criterion, whereby everything is interrelated directly, and all the items can be assessed in terms of one another by some simple measuring rod. Tolstoy's genius lies in a capacity for marvellously accurate reproduction of the irreproducible, the almost miraculous evocation of the full, untranslatable individuality of the individual, which induces in the reader an acute awareness of the presence of the object itself, and not of a mere description of it, employing for this purpose metaphors which fix the quality of a particular experience as such, and avoiding those general terms which relate it to similar instances by ignoring individual differences—"the oscillations of feeling"—in favour of what is common to them all. But then this same writer pleads for, indeed preaches with great fury, particularly in his last, religious phase, the exact opposite: the necessity of expelling everything that does not submit to some very general, very simple standard: say, what peasants like or dislike, or what the gospels declare to be good.

7   This violent contradiction between the data of experience from which he could not liberate himself, and which, of course, all his life he knew alone to be real, and his deeply metaphysical belief in the existence of a system to which they *must* belong, whether they appear to do so or not, this conflict between instinctive judgment and theoretical conviction—between his gifts and his opinions—mirrors the unresolved conflict between the reality of the moral life with its sense of responsibility, joys, sorrows, sense of guilt and sense of achievement—all of which is nevertheless illusion; and the laws which govern everything, although we cannot know more than a negligible portion of them—so that all scientists and historians who say that they do know them and are guided by them are lying and deceiving—but which nevertheless alone are real. Beside Tolstoy, Gogol and Dostoevsky, whose abnormality is so often contrasted with Tolstoy's "sanity," are well-integrated personalities, with a coherent outlook and a single vision. Yet out of this violent conflict grew *War and*

Peace: its marvellous solidity should not blind us to the deep cleavage which yawns open whenever Tolstoy remembers, or rather reminds himself—fails to forget—what he is doing, and why. . . .

. . . . Tolstoy began with a view of human life and history which contradicted all his knowledge, all his gifts, all his inclinations, and which, in consequence, he could scarcely be said to have embraced in the sense of practising it, either as a writer or as a man. From this, in his old age, he passed into a form of life in which he tried to resolve the glaring contradiction between what he believed about men and events, and what he thought he believed, or ought to believe, by behaving, in the end, as if factual questions of this kind were not the fundamental issues at all, only the trivial preoccupations of an idle, ill-conducted life, while the real questions were quite different. But it was of no use: the Muse cannot be cheated. Tolstoy was the least superficial of men: he could not swim with the tide without being drawn irresistibly beneath the surface to investigate the darker depths below; and he could not avoid seeing what he saw and doubting even that; he could close his eyes but not forget that he was doing so; his appalling, destructive, sense of what was false frustrated this final effort at self-deception as it did all the earlier ones; and he died in agony, oppressed by the burden of his intellectual infallibility and his sense of perpetual moral error, the greatest of those who can neither reconcile, nor leave unreconciled, the conflict of what there is with what there ought to be. Tolstoy's sense of reality was until the end too devastating to be compatible with any moral ideal which he was able to construct out of the fragments into which his intellect shivered the world, and he dedicated all of his vast strength of mind and will to the life-long denial of this fact. At once insanely proud and filled with self-hatred, omniscient and doubting everything, cold and violently passionate, contemptuous and self-abasing, tormented and detached, surrounded by an adoring family, by devoted followers, by the admiration of the entire civilized world, and yet almost wholly isolated, he is the most tragic of the great writers, a desperate old man, beyond human aid, wandering self-blinded at Colonus.

Points for Discussion

1. Into what two groups does Berlin divide thinkers? How does he explain each of the groups?

2. How does the initial division of thinkers into two groups lead to the focus on Tolstoy? Why is Tolstoy especially interesting to Berlin?

3. Writers often make a clear opening statement of both their content and structure. Explain the value of Berlin's opening paragraph in contributing to both purposes.

4. Berlin first exemplifies the two kinds of thinkers in two famous names—Dante and Shakespeare—and then goes on to provide a list of other important figures. What is the function of this catalog of names?

5. What is the significance of this sentence from paragraph 3? "The hypothesis I wish to offer is that Tolstoy was by nature a fox, but believed in being a hedgehog . . ." How does the sentence relate to the rest of the essay?

6. Writers often reiterate an idea for emphasis or for purposes of developing clear links or for both. Show that the opening sentence of paragraph 5 serves one or both of these functions.

7. In paragraphs 5 and 6 Berlin draws several conclusions about Tolstoy's work and place in literature, but cites supporting examples only briefly. What elements in Berlin's writing make you as a reader trust his judgment?

8. Point out some phrases and words that Berlin employs to make smooth connections between paragraphs and between sentences within paragraphs. For instance, the opening sentence of paragraph 7 starts this way: "This violent contradiction between the data of experience . . ." The closing sentence of that paragraph reads: "Yet out of this violent conflict grew *War and Peace*. . . ."

Suggestions for Writing

1. To classify items—as Berlin does in his division of thinkers into hedgehogs and foxes—writers first analyze a collection of examples to determine what connects and separates them. Then they group these examples according to discovered similarities, thus arranging the items in a classification system. If the material is to be used in an explanatory paper, this system provides the structure or framework for presenting the examples.

Use this method in handling one of the following topics:

1. Welfare programs take several forms: _____, _____, _____. . . .
2. Teenagers conform to society in a number of ways.
3. The American Indian before Columbus used various types of tools.
4. Taxes may be classified according to _____, _____, _____. . . .

You may, of course, formulate a similar topic of your own.

2. Conflicting theories or views about ways to meet current crises—social, economic, political—often center on two key figures or two opposing groups (political parties, divisions within parties, leaders of some movement, economists with differing opinions about interest rates, and so forth). Modeling your paper on Berlin's essay, formulate a thesis about such a division and write an analytical essay in which you consider several leaders who fall into different "camps" regarding some current issue.

5

PAPERS THAT ANALYZE EVENTS AND THEIR CAUSES

Historians constantly both trace events and analyze the forces that contribute to bringing them about; writers in other areas of social science use similar processes in showing the development or decline of an institution, an aspect of the economy or culture, an attitude or commonly-held belief. Whenever you trace a process, you must, of course, keep events or items in a clear order, usually in a time sequence, although your chief purpose in tracing is not merely to show chronology but to explain how one event relates to another. In such writing, words indicating time and those showing causal relationships are often the links between various parts of the organization. Words like *first, second, then,* and *next* are used as time indicators; and sometimes dates are used to indicate time exactly. Words and phrases like *thus, therefore, consequently, a major reason* and *as a result* are useful in pointing to causes.

In reporting a history of any kind, you will want to be selective, enlarging where items are significant or interesting, avoiding the clutter of unnecessary distraction from details that are not very important. Being certain that you have valid analysis of causes requires careful research and reflection; that is, you must weigh the various factors you analyze and determine the difference between those that are major and those that are less important. Above all, keep in mind that you as the writer are the determiner of what to include, what to omit, and how to organize your well-chosen material to achieve the effect or make the points you want to get across.

You will discover such careful tracing of events and thoughtful analysis of why they happened in the three selections that follow.

DANIEL J. BOORSTIN

Education has been part of the American dream—the way to a better life, the way "up." Here author Daniel J. Boorstin, winner of the Pulitzer prize and Librarian of Congress, analyzes why American education and our notions of it are different.

Experimenting with Education

1   Of all a nation's institutions, its colleges and universities—next to its churches—are the most easily petrified. In England, for example, before the end of the nineteenth century the political system had been liberalized, the franchise broadened, the economy industrialized. But Oxford and Cambridge, the centers of academic prestige and power, remained relics whose customs could be understood only by a sympathy for the Middle Ages. The Old School Tie and the college blazer remain remnants of class snobbery. Long after Americans had ceased to study Latin, and the language was employed only by medical doctors writing their prescriptions, Latin continued to be the language of college diplomas.

2   In view of this worldwide phenomenon of academic stasis, the story of higher education in the United States is remarkable, perhaps unique. While our colleges and universities have not failed to be citadels of the status quo, here, more than in most other nations, these institutions have been frequently and liberally irrigated by the currents of change. They have even become some of the more conspicuous areas for democratic experiment.

3   Needless to say, the American phenomenon has not been the product mainly of the desire of professors to dissolve the ancient categories of their revered expertise or to enter the risky competitive marketplace. Rather it has been a by-product of characteristically American circumstances. In the United States we offer a spectacle—unfamiliar on the world scene—of the endless fluidity of the categories of knowledge, and the intimate entanglement of the so-called higher learning with the changing needs and desires—even the whims—of the larger community.

In the United States, by 1977, there were some 10 million   4
students in about 3,000 institutions of higher learning. The
faculties of these institutions numbered some 700,000. During most of our history, excepting certain periods of war and
depression, all these figures have been steadily increasing. The
G.I. Bill of 1944 and its successor programs (1952; 1966) offered unprecedented opportunities and inducements for vet-
erans of World War II, the Korean War, and the Vietnam War
to enter colleges and universities. During much of our recent
history, the absolute numbers, the proportion of the American
population in such institutions, and the rate of increase of
these numbers have been significantly higher than those in
other industrially developed countries. At the same time,
American education (including higher education) has been
characterized by the lack of any national *system.* In most places,
and certainly in Europe, the system was built like a pyramid.
Elementary schools prepared vast numbers of people to read
and write, then smaller numbers were selected for secondary
schools, and finally a tiny proportion of these were sent on
to colleges and universities. This elite group at the top tended
to come, of course, from the wealthy and the wellborn.

Our arrangement—it should not be called a system—grew   5
quite differently. American democracy gave a bizarre shape
to our educational institutions. Instead of being a pyramid
wide at the bottom, these institutions are very much like an
inverted pyramid—top-heavy at the upper levels. From the
traditional European point of view, our educational structure
is upside down.

In place of an educational system we have had a widely   6
diffused national program of educational experiment. Despite, even because of, this lack of a system, certain features
have emerged in American education as a whole:

Community Emphasis and Community Control.   American   7
institutions of higher education have tended to be founded
by communities and to be supported by communities for particular purposes. They have been expected to justify themselves to the communities which founded them (commonly
defined geographically or by religious denomination). For example, Harvard College, the oldest institution of higher edu-

cation in the United States, was set up in 1636 by the Massachusetts Bay Colony for a communal purpose, to provide a learned ministry. It was founded by an Act of the colony, was established with a gift from John Harvard, and then was supported by the whole colony through public appropriations and private gifts. The governing body did not consist of the scholars teaching there (as in Oxford or Cambridge colleges), but of a lay, nonacademic board which was the ancestor of all the boards of trustees that control American universities today. A continuing community emphasis has kept these American institutions under the control of community representatives, and has created and confirmed the pressure to satisfy the expectations of the community which has supported the institutions by municipal or state funds or by private donations. The spectacular growth of community colleges after World War II expressed this additional emphasis anew and helped expand opportunities for higher education under local control.

8 *Adaptability of Institutions and Fluidity of Subject Matters.* Such institutions—founded by a particular community—have tended to be willing, or even eager, to adapt themselves to whatever at the moment has been considered to be their sponsoring community's urgent needs. Just as Harvard College aimed to provide a learned ministry for the Massachusetts Bay community, so land-grant institutions (many of which were originally called agricultural and mechanical colleges) aimed to train farmers and their wives for rural America, and normal colleges aimed to train teachers. The host of law schools, business schools, engineering schools, schools of journalism, schools of nursing, and their descendants have aimed to provide qualified practitioners.

9 Traditional distinctions between high culture and low culture, between the "liberal arts" and the practical arts, and other time-hallowed distinctions have tended to dissolve. As new schools and new "programs" and projects for degrees and certificates have been freely added, the boundaries of traditional disciplines have been befogged. In England, for example, there has been a tendency to define history as what is taught or examined in the Honours School at Oxford or in the Tripos at Cambridge. But in the United States, where we

have had no Oxford or Cambridge to dominate the scene, people supply their own definitions. Sometimes these are crazy, often they are faddish, but often, too, they are fertile and suggestive. New subjects enter the curriculum casually. "No Trespassing" signs are harder for professors to erect. Sociology, anthropology, psychology, economics, and statistics become more easily interfused with history, or begin to be taught in a regular curriculum. One man's sociology is another man's history.

There come to be nearly as many definitions of subjects   10
as there are institutions; institutions compete in their definitions of subject matter and in their invention of subject matters. This fluidity has, of course, encouraged fashionable, "newsworthy," and up-to-the-minute subject matters and those which seem to have some instant vocational use. The prestige pool—for both students and faculty—is indefinitely expanded. Just as German and French officers serving with the American Revolutionary Army were astounded at the omnipresence of Americans who bore the title of captain, so European visitors nowadays are understandably puzzled at the range of subjects for which Americans can be awarded the B.A. degree and at the countless American "professors."

Competition Among Institutions.   In countries with orga-   11
nized, centralized systems of higher education, there tend to be a hierarchy of institutions, a uniform salary scale, and roughly uniform conditions of employment. In the United States the rule is diversity. An instructor in one institution may receive a salary as high as that of a full professor in another; he may have a smaller teaching load and greater freedom to define his job. Institutions compete for faculty, faculty members compete for positions elsewhere. The variations in the conditions of student life, in academic standards, and in extracurricular facilities produce a widespread competition for students. The diversity can increase opportunities for self-fulfillment for both faculty and student. A student who has been disadvantaged in family or in early education can enter an easy institution and transfer to a more difficult institution with higher standards. While each institution has an incentive to be "with it" in curriculum and living conditions, and to em-

ploy the full apparatus of advertising and public relations, it also has an incentive to excel.

12   These characteristics of American higher education are all found in some form or other in American elementary and secondary education. Community emphasis and community control are ensured by locally elected school boards. Adaptability of programs and fluidity of subject matters come from community pressures. And even the competition among institutions is expressed in the competition between parochial and public schools, between private academies and public schools, and in an increasingly mobile American population in which families with children often choose their place of residence by the character and quality of the local public schools.

13   All these history-rooted characteristics have been modified and confused by certain developments that have climaxed in the later twentieth-century America. These have tended to remove or reduce the benefits of our traditional experimentation and to substitute dogmatic central purpose—or the demands of a homogeneous populism—for the plural experimental spirit. Most of these recent developments have tended to encourage or enforce a greater uniformity in American educational institutions:

a. The interpretation of the federal Constitution, and numerous federal laws, to ensure the constitutional right of students to nondiscrimination in educational opportunities. The landmark here, of course, is the desegregation decision of the Supreme Court, *Brown* v. *Board of Education* (1954). One consequence has been a general reduction in the differences between institutions, even where their differences showed a variety of interest rather than an intention to discriminate. Thus there are fewer all-male or all-female institutions.

b. Increasing sources of federal funding for education, e.g., funds for buildings, books, audiovisual aids, and numerous special programs (Head Start, et cetera), the founding of and increasing appropriations for the National Endowments for the Arts and Humanities.

c. Increasing federal support of scientific and technological research and development, using university faculties and facilities. An obvious example is the federal support of the research climaxing in the first nuclear chain reaction at the University of Chicago. As much as half of the budget of some "private" institutions consists of federally funded projects. The National Institute of Health has become a potent influence.

d. Increasing foundation support for education, research, and publication. The Ford Foundation, the Rockefeller Foundation, the Guggenheim Foundation, and a host of other foundations, large and small, operate in the national arena.

e. Increasing strength of professional organizations for teachers and specialized groups of scholars and of accrediting organizations. For example, the American Association of University Professors (which has its rules of tenure and has blacklisted institutions) and the American Federation of Teachers and other unions. Accrediting organizations for colleges and professional schools (e.g., the North Central Association, the Association of American Law Schools) increase in power as their accreditation can affect the eligibility of an institution for sizable federal aid.

f. Increasing influence of students dominated by one or another current national political or reformist dogma.

g. Increasing pressure for sexual, racial, and other "minority" quotas for teachers and students. Often these pressures take the form of special federal and state programs, enforced by administrative or quasi-judicial bodies, and by the threats of federal agencies to withdraw aid.

Despite these and other pressures toward uniform standards, uniform conditions, and uniform opportunities in American educational institutions, American higher education retains many of its historic strengths and weaknesses. At best, the American situation has offered a national opportunity for creative chaos, endless variety, and open opportunity. At worst the American situation has been anarchy and philistinism. 14

One notable consequence of this maelstrom has been the peculiar difficulty we Americans find in agreeing on the definition of an educated person. We become increasingly wary of 15 traditional humanistic definitions of a liberal education, and dangerously reluctant to make literacy, much less literariness, a necessary ingredient of the highly educated.

16   The American experience—a federal experience with a strong tradition of community variety and local control—suggests that any effort to provide a more feasible, more precise definition of the "educated person" is not apt to succeed here through the proclamation or enforcement of national norms. Efforts to establish national standards in education have not been spectacularly successful. Where they have been somewhat effective it has been in a negative way—by finding means to prevent the violation of the rights of all citizens to equal treatment and equal opportunity. Or in the enforcement of minimum requirements (such as library facilities, numbers of Ph.D.s on the faculty, faculty freedom from interference by boards of trustees).

17   The American preoccupation with the future—to which the past and present are considered only a clue—has always made it difficult here to instill a decent respect for the body of traditional learning, and the vocabulary required for that acquisition. Perhaps the closest approach to a universally acceptable American definition is Alice Freeman Palmer's "That's what education means, to be able to do what you've never done before."

18   This experimental spirit, which had made the new nation politically possible, would explain much that would be distinctive of the nation's life in the following two centuries. The American limbo—a borderland between experience and idea, where old absolutes were dissolved and new opportunities discovered—would puzzle thinkers from abroad. With their time-honored distinction between fact and idea, between materialism and idealism, they labeled a people who had so little respect for absolutes as vulgar "materialists." In the gloriously filigreed cultures of the Old World it was not easy to think of life as experiment. But American life *was* experiment, and experiment was a technique for testing and revising ideas. In this American limbo all sorts of novelties might emerge. What to men of the Old World seemed a no-man's-land was the Americans' native land.

The experimentalism which had worked on the land, and   19
would test the varied possibilities of fifty states, had found new
arenas in the course of the nineteenth century. What federalism was in the world of politics, technology would be in the
minutiae of everyday life. While ideology fenced in, federalism—and technology—tried out. Just as federalism would test
still unimagined possibilities in government, so technology
would test unimagined possibilities in the modes of experience.

It was not surprising that the United States would become   20
noted—some would even say notorious—as a land of technology. The Swiss writer Max Frisch once described technology
as "the knack of so arranging the world that we don't have
to experience it." But in American history technology could
equally well be described as "the knack of so arranging the
world as to produce new experiences." In America the
time-honored antithesis between materialism and idealism
would become as obsolete as that old petrified absolute of
"sovereignty," which had made the British Empire come
apart, and then made the American Revolution necessary.
American experimentalism—in its older political form of
American federalism and in its more modern generalized form
of American technology—would become the leitmotif of
American civilization.

Points for Discussion

1. What basic difference does Boorstin say makes American education unique? What are the reasons contributing to its difference?

2. Boorstin's organization here is very clear. After the initial explanation of the difference between American and European education, he considers "certain features [that] have emerged in American
education as a whole" (par. 6.)

   a. What is the advantage of using a sub-head to name each of
   these factors?
   b. Construct a brief outline of the overall pattern.

3. All parts of this essay interlock. Examine the first sentences of paragraph 7 to show how ideas there relate to the preceding ones in paragraph 6. Point out other links, especially those achieved by repetition and echoes.

4. What is the special function of paragraph 12?

5. What are the advantages of diversity (par. 11)? What is the relationship between community and diversity? What developments in the twentieth century does Boorstin think work for uniformity and against the tradition of diversity?

6. Paragraph 13 is a clearly structured list. What are the advantages of itemizing as Boorstin itemizes the influences against diversity? What is the effect of the repetition of the word "increasing"?

7. Why does America have trouble defining "an educated person"? To what degree can standards be defined or achieved? How does preoccupation with the future influence attitudes toward education?

Suggestions for Writing

1. Write a paper analyzing the cause/effect relationships in some area of education; these topics are suggestions:

- What have been the results of increasing "diversity"?
- Why should (or shouldn't) every student take a stipulated subject? (examples: driver education, physical education, American government, certain English courses)
- Why are there objections to certain kinds of government funding in research? (defense funding for math or physics, for instance) In turn, what have been the results of such funding?
- What has led to (and been the result of) such programs as bilingual education, mainstreaming, or other "special" classes (at any level)?
- What led to the extensive student loan programs and what has been the effect of these programs on education?

With any of these topics, or a similar one of your choosing, you may want to begin by tracing its history and then "itemizing" causes and results as Boorstin did.

2. What will be the effect on education of the increasing emphasis upon "computer literacy"? Write a paper in which you consider reasons for increasing emphasis upon computer education and the possible effects of learning by this method. Or broaden the topic and consider the effects of technology in general: "The Machine at School" is a possible title.

3. Write a paper in which you define what you mean by an "educated person." Be sure to develop your definition by using illustrations. Or write a paper explaining *why* it is so difficult to define such a person, why we cannot agree on what it means to be educated. Is such disagreement good or bad?

DANIEL T. RODGERS

In these nine paragraphs from a widely known work of history, Professor Rodgers traces the role of labor unions in their effort to gain the eight-hour day.

"The Working Day" from *The Work Ethic in Industrial America, 1850–1920*

1   How much of a man's life should work consume? No work-related question is more central than this, and none in the nineteenth and early twentieth centuries divided workers and employers more sharply. The early factory masters took over the traditional sun-to-sun workday, stretched it to between twelve and fourteen hours of labor winter and summer alike with the introduction of gas lighting in the 1830s and 1840s, and brought the full weight of generations of moralizing to bear in justification. "Labor is *not* a curse," they insisted; "it is not the hours per day that a person *works* that breaks him down, but the hours spent in dissipation." Give men "plenty to do, and a long while to do it in, and you will find them physically and morally better."[1]

2   But among workingmen, the drive to shorten the hours of labor was a long and fervent struggle. The campaign began early in the nineteenth century with the appearance of the first self-conscious workingmen's organizations. By the 1840s the ten-hour movement had moved into the New England textile mills, producing a massive flood of shorter-hours petitions, the largest, from Lowell in 1846, containing signatures equivalent to almost two-thirds of the city's cotton mill operatives.[2] After 1850 the shorter-hours demand—now typically put in terms of the eight-hour day—was at the forefront of every organized labor effort. The National Labor Union at its first convention in 1866 declared a federal eight-hour law "the first and grand desideratum of the hour," and, though the organization drifted shortly thereafter toward rival programs of coopera-

tives and currency reform, many of its member unions clung firmly to the original platform. P. J. McGuire of the Carpenters, for example, told a congressional committee in 1883 that the reduction of working hours was the "primary object" of the union he headed. The American Federation of Labor under Samuel Gompers was a still more persistent champion of the shorter workday—"eight hours to-day, fewer to-morrow," as Gompers defined the cause. The shorter workday was "the question of questions," the only one which "reaches the very root of society," Gompers declared in the 1880s, and over the next twenty years he labored tirelessly to promote strikes over the issue. Nor did the labor left disagree. For Bill Haywood of the IWW, the only fit motto for the working class was "the less work the better."[3]

"However much they may differ upon other matters, . . . all men of labor . . . can unite upon this," Samuel Gompers wrote in defense of the eight-hour issue in 1889.[4] If the unions, particularly the nonfactory building trades unions, led the agitation for the shorter workday, there was more than Gompers's testimony to indicate that the shorter-hours dream had a strong hold on the larger number of nonunionized workers as well. For three decades after 1869, until they turned to the neutral and duller task of compiling purely statistical data, many of the new state bureaus of labor statistics took upon themselves the task of canvassing the opinions of the workingmen they took to be their constituents. Who these often nameless workers were and how their opinions found their way into print is not clear, but, taking opinion samples as they come, none more closely approaches the rank and file of labor than these. And when they posed the working-hours question, the surveys repeatedly turned up strong, often overwhelming support for the shorter-hours demand.[5] "We go into the factory too young and work too hard afterwards," a New Jersey glass blower put the recurrent complaint in the mid-1880s. A decade and a half later, Thomas Jones, a nonunion Chicago machinist, interrupted his testimony on the un-American and anti-Christian policies of trade unions to interject that "we nonunion men are not opposed to more pay and shorter hours; not at all."[6]

Twice in the nineteenth century, moreover, the

shorter-hours demand mushroomed into popular crusades un-
surpassed in their intensity by any other of the era's labor issues. The first wave of enthusiasm began quietly in 1865 with
the organization of the Grand Eight-Hour League of Massachusetts by a small group of Boston workingmen. Three years
later workingmen's Eight-Hour Leagues had proliferated
throughout the Northern states and, together with the trade
unions, had succeeded in writing the eight-hour day in the
statute books of seven states and forcing an eight-hour law for
federal employees through Congress. Riddled with loopholes,
the legislation proved a hollow victory, and workers angrily
turned to more aggressive tactics. In Chicago some 6,000 to
10,000 workers walked off their jobs on 1 May 1867 in a massive demonstration to demand enforcement of the new Illinois
eight-hour law, and strikes, rioting, and some machine breaking followed in its wake. A year later in the anthracite coalfields of Pennsylvania, similarly angered workers abandoned
the coal pits and, marching from mine to mine, shut down virtually all operations in the state's leading coal-producing
county in a bitter three-month strike. Only in the building
trades did the first eight-hour campaign bear fruit, and many
of those gains evaporated in the depression of the 1870s. But
the experience suggested something of the emotional reserves
behind the shorter-hours issue.[7]

5   The second eight-hour crusade of the mid-1880s was still
larger and more spontaneous than the first. When in 1884 the
Federation of Organized Trades and Labor Unions issued a
call for a general eight-hour demonstration to take place on
1 May 1886, it was a quixotic gesture on the part of a weak
and barely solvent organization. But the call fell on unexpectedly fertile ground. Over the next two years, workers flocked
into the labor unions filled with hopes for a shorter working
day. The Knights of Labor, the chief recipient of the influx,
ballooned from 104,066 members in July 1885 to 702,924
members a year later, and the newcomers threatened to over-
whelm the organization. Grand Master Workman Terence
Powderly waged a vigorous fight to dampen the strike fever
of the local Knights assemblies. In place of a general strike,
Powderly proposed an educational campaign and a nation-
wide essay contest on the eight-hour question and, that failing,

championed a less than realistic scheme to shorten the working day through a cooperative agreement between the Knights and a yet unformed general association of the nation's manufacturers. A month before the day set for the demonstration, P.M. Arthur of the strongly organized locomotive engineers denounced the whole affair as a demand for "two hours more loafing about the corners and two hours more for drink." Yet notwithstanding such foot-dragging at the top, 190,000 workers struck for the eight-hour day in the first week of May. In Milwaukee, according to the Wisconsin Bureau of Labor and Industrial Statistics, the shorter hours issue was *"the* topic of conversation in the shop, on the street, at the family table, at the bar, [and] in the counting room." Beginning with a monster picnic on 2 May, the crusade turned grim and bloody as police opened fire on workers intent on shutting down the city's iron and steel works. In Chicago, the center of the movement, May opened with police and worker battles, some five hundred individual strikes, and still more imposing demonstrations.[8]

Despite Samuel Gompers's best efforts over the next decade and a half, the general strike of 1886 was never repeated. Most workers who walked off their jobs in the late nineteenth and early twentieth centuries struck over wage-related issues, not working hours; and where the wage question pressed most heavily or where hours reduction meant a cut in pay, hours demands generally made little headway. Yet, larger on the average than wage strikes, shorter-hours walkouts possessed a peculiar intensity.[9] And in the massive garment workers' strikes of 1910–11, the IWW-led silk workers' walkout in Paterson, New Jersey, in 1913, the great steel strike of 1919, and elsewhere, the shorter-hours issue smoldered under the surface of many of the era's most famous labor disputes long after the experience of 1886 had faded from memory.

Where rank-and-file workers divided from union leaders was not over the desirability of shorter working hours—whose appeal cut across lines of ideology and unionization—but over rationale. For most union spokesmen the eight-hour day was essentially a link in a complex economic equation whose upshot was wages. A large number of the late nineteenth century's most influential labor leaders—Gompers, George E. Mc-

Neill of the Knights, and Adolph Strasser of the Cigarmakers among them—learned the eight-hour creed in the 1860s from a self-educated Boston machinist, Ira Steward. In Steward's argument, wages fell to the minimum standard of living workers would tolerate, and leisure was the one effective means of raising both. Let "the ragged—the unwashed—the ignorant and ill-mannered" have time "to become ashamed of themselves," to raise their expenses and desires, and the demand for higher wages would no longer be resistible. "The *idea* of eight hours isn't eight hours," Steward insisted; "it is *less poverty!*"[10] As late as 1915, Steward's jingle

> Whether you work by the piece
> Or work by the day
> Decreasing the hours
> Increases the pay

could still be found in the pages of the *American Federationist.* And if this was by then a remnant of an increasingly old-fashioned idea, the argument that pushed Steward's aside in labor circles in the 1890s took an equally instrumental attitude toward leisure. Shorter working hours were a means of spreading the work being relentlessly whittled down by machinery, ironing out the boom and bust cycles of the economy, or employing the unemployed.[11]

8   One can find appeal to all of these arguments among the respondents of the state bureaus of labor statistics; but far more often than union leaders, the men whose ideas were preserved there demanded leisure not as a means but as an end in itself. "I do not believe that God ever created man in order to spend his life in work and sleep, without any time to enjoy the pleasures of the world," a New Jersey miner wrote in 1881. A Pennsylvania workingman reiterated the theme; to know "nothing but work, eat and sleep" was to strip a man of his humanity, to make him "little better than a horse." In an argument particularly appealing to the middle-class moralists, some workingmen proposed to turn the time set free from work into labors of self-education, but in the records of the bureaus of labor statistics such men are few. In 1880 the Massachusetts bureau tried to find out what textile mill operatives would do with more leisure. Most proposed to rest, read the

newspaper, visit, look around "to see what is going on," and spend time with their families.[12] For all the complex intellectual rationale behind the eight-hour campaigns, the essential appeal of the shorter day was the obvious one: the promise of relief from toil.

It is the privilege of moralists, as vigorously exercised in the mid-twentieth century as in the nineteenth, to point to decay. But the chasm between the work ideals of those who stood inside and outside the new work forms and employee relations was present virtually from the very beginning. "Toil, toil, toil, unending," the sweatshop poet Morris Rosenfeld protested in the plaint that echoed deeply through the most vocal segment of those caught in the new half-free, time-pressed labor of the factories. While the middle-class moralists, torn between the allure and the apparent dangers of leisure, wrestled with questions of pleasure and duty, industrial workers crossed far fewer inner compunctions as they struggled to pare down the looming place of labor in their lives. "Eight Hours for Work. Eight Hours for Rest. Eight Hours for What We Will." To Samuel Gompers, the persuasively symmetrical rallying cry of the eight-hour crusade was the workers' "fling-back" at the ethic of all-consuming industry.[13]

9

Notes

1. Massachusetts Bureau of Statistics of Labor (MBLS), *Tenth Annual Report* (Boston, 1879), p. 149; MBLS, *Report* (Boston, 1870), p. 221; Ohio Bureau of Labor Statistics, *Second Annual Report* (Columbus, 1879), p. 281.

2. Norman Ware, *The Industrial Worker,* 1840–1860 (Boston: Houghton Mifflin, 1924), chaps. 8, 10.

3. Marion C. Cahill, *Shorter Hours: A Study of the Movement since the Civil War* (New York: Columbia University Press, 1932), p. 35; U.S. Senate, Committee on Education and Labor, *Report upon the Relations between Labor and Capital,* 4 vols. (Washington, D.C., 1885), 1:315, 299, 294; *Twentieth Century Illustrated History of Rhode Island and the Rhode Island Central Trades and Labor Union* (Providence: Rhode Island Central Trades and Labor Union, 1901), p. 143; William D. Haywood and Frank Bohn, *Industrial Socialism* (Chicago: Charles H. Kerr, 1911), p. 62.

4. Gerald N. Grob, *Workers and Utopia: A Study of Ideological Conflict in the American Labor Movement, 1865–1900* (Evanston, Ill.: Northwestern University Press, 1961), p. 149.

5. MBLS, *Report* (Boston, 1870), pp. 287–98; New Jersey Bureau of Statistics of Labor and Industries (NJBLS), *Seventh Annual Report* (Trenton, 1885), pp. 237–56; Pennsylvania, *Annual Report of the Secretary of Internal Affairs, Part III: Industrial Statistics* (hereafter *Pennsylvania Industrial Statistics*), 15 (Harrisburg, 1888): 16H-28H;

Michigan Bureau of Labor and Industrial Statistics (MichBLS), *Fourteenth Annual Report* (Lansing, 1897), pp. 195–96.

6. NJBLS, *Seventh Annual Report,* p. 239; U.S. Industrial Commission, *Reports,* 19 vols. (Washington, D.C., 1900–1902), 8:196.

7. David Montgomery, *Beyond Equality: Labor and the Radical Republicans, 1862–1872* (New York: Alfred A. Knopf, 1967), chaps. 6–8; Robert Ozanne, *A Century of Labor-Management Relations at McCormick and International Harvester* (Madison: University of Wisconsin Press, 1967), pp. 6–7; Clifton K. Yearley, *Enterprise and Anthracite: Economics and Democracy in Schuylkill County, 1820–1875* (Baltimore: Johns Hopkins University Press, 1961), p. 182.

8. John R. Commons and Associates, *History of Labour in the United States,* 4 vols. (New York: Macmillan, 1918–35), 2:375–86; Donald L. Kemmerer and Edward D. Wickersham, "Reasons for the Growth of the Knights of Labor in 1885–1886," *Industrial and Labor Relations Review* 3 (1950): 213–20; Terence V. Powderly, *Thirty Years of Labor, 1859 to 1889* (Columbus, Ohio: Excelsior Publishing House, 1889), pp. 471–525; Henry David, *The History of the Haymarket Affair* (New York: Farrar and Rinehart, 1936), chaps. 7–8; Wisconsin Bureau of Labor and Industrial Statistics, *Second Biennial Report* (Madison, 1886), pp. 314–71.

9. U.S. Commissioner of Labor, *Twenty-first Annual Report, 1906: Strikes and Lockouts* (Washington, D.C., 1907).

10. Ira Steward, "A Reduction of Hours an Increase of Wages" (1865), in *A Documentary History of American Industrial Society,* ed. John R. Commons et al., 10 vols. (Cleveland: Arthur H. Clark, 1910–11), 9:290; Montgomery, *Beyond Equality,* pp. 252–53.

11. Sidney Fine, "The Eight-Hour Day Movement in the United States, 1888–1891," *Mississippi Valley Historical Review* 40 (1953): 441–62.

12. NJBLS, *Fourth Annual Report* (Somerville, 1881), p. 90; *Pennsylvania Industrial Statistics,* 17 (Harrisburg, 1890): 32E; MBLS, *Twelfth Annual Report* (Boston, 1881), pp. 450–53.

13. Philip S. Foner, *American Labor Songs of the Nineteenth Century* (Urbana: University of Illinois Press, 1975), p. 288; Samuel Gompers, *Seventy Years of Life and Labor,* 2 vols. (New York: E. P. Dutton, 1925), 1:54.

Points for Discussion

1. This selection opens with a question, one that Rodgers says is "central." Relate that question and the answers given in the following paragraphs to the idea that the struggle for an eight-hour day has "moral" ramifications as well as financial ones.

2. What is the importance of the dates cited in helping organize this selection? Where the material is not arranged in strict chronological sequence, what is the organizing principle?

3. Point out the links, both in idea and in words and phrases, between paragraphs 4 and 5.

4. This selection and its accompanying notes are taken from a longer selection. Why does Rodgers offer such thorough documentation?

5. Rodgers does not use the pronoun *I* as viewpoint here; only once does he resort to the pronoun *one* (par. 8). What is the effect of "keeping to the subject" without the author's intruding? Did you actually notice the absence of an author's personal voice? Explain your answer. From a selection of this kind, what conclusions can you draw about the author? about the audience for which he is writing?

6. A writer about labor unions and labor problems might sometimes be accused of bias for or against, even when that writer wants to remain analytical. What then is the role of documentation and the impersonal approach in writing such as Rodgers does here?

7. What is the relationship between the eight-hour day and wages as Rodgers explains it in paragraph 7 and following?

Suggestions for Writing

1. The IWW was sometimes labeled the "I won't work" group. Look up the name of this organization and write a paper tracing its history. Include a record of its goals, leadership, and achievements as Rodgers did in his analysis.

2. Choose an important labor leader (one mentioned in the article or another of your choice) and write a paper about the rise and, perhaps, fall of that person's career or influence. Analyze the reasons—personal, social, and political—for the person's achievements.

3. Many questions of cause/effect may be asked concerning the relationships between business and labor, and between labor and the public. How much does the presence of a union cause a business to grow, change, or move? What accounts for some efforts to prevent a union from organizing? How have benefits been achieved in a particular industry? Choose one of these or a similar question and write a paper about an aspect of business or union change. Or write about the causes and effects of public opinion about union organiza-

tion and organizers; for instance, how do attitudes affect unions among public workers such as teachers, health care professionals, and so on.

4. Study the history of some strike—local or national, little known or widely publicized—and write a paper about the causes of that strike and results it has obtained or failed to obtain.

5. Do some research about plans for job sharing or the four-day work-week, and write a paper analyzing what might be the results of such a practice. You may wish to limit your analysis to a particular area or industry.

6. Write a paper about the results of union efforts to achieve greater safety in a field such as mining or lumbering.

HENRY STEELE COMMAGER

Henry Steele Commager, a noted historian and author of many books, analyzes some changes in the American presidency and explains why they have occurred.

Presidents Then and Now

Almost a century ago, George Bryce, in his classic "American Commonwealth," asked, "Why are Great Men not elected to the Presidency?"

1

His question, reasonable enough when Grover Cleveland was in the White House (and about to be succeeded by the forgotten Benjamin Harrison), was nevertheless premature. After all, Bryce himself lived to see both Theodore Roosevelt and Woodrow Wilson elected. But clearly the question he asked in 1888 is relevant today; within the last 50 years, only one man of world stature—Franklin Delano Roosevelt—has occupied the Presidency.

2

It is sobering to compare the first six American Presidents with recent American Presidents. When the United States was a new nation, it had from four to ten million inhabitants scattered over an immense territory, with no major cities, no great universities, no national newspapers or journals, and, as Henry James observed, with barely a national capital. Yet its voters (at a time when only adult white males had the vote) had the wisdom and good fortune to elect Washington, John Adams, Jefferson, Madison, Monroe, and John Quincy Adams to the Presidency.

3

Now we are a great world power of some 225 million persons, with a dozen major cities and a genuine world capital, scores of great universities and research institutions, the most elaborate system of communications extant, and the longest tradition of participatory democracy of any people. Yet in recent years our leaders were Harry Truman, Dwight Eisenhower, John Kennedy, Lyndon Johnson, Richard Nixon, and Gerald Ford—estimable men all (except one), but not one of world stature.

4

5   How can we explain the decline of the American Presidency?

6   First, this decline in leadership is not a phenomenon singular to politics: It afflicts almost every segment of our increasingly anonymous society. Where are the national leaders in the military, in banking, in industry and transportation, in education and religion?

7   Politics and politicians reflect the society they represent; now, more than ever before, they reflect not society as a whole but those who function as "imagemakers." Increasingly our political leaders have abandoned Madison for Madison Avenue. Increasingly we can say of them what Emerson said back in the 1840s: that "things are in the saddle and ride mankind." The "things" are computers and pollsters and packaging; imagine a Washington, a Jefferson, a Lincoln, submitting to the indignities of an image maker or a speech writer.

8   The absence of great Presidents reflects social, rather than individual, change. There is no decline in the pool of talent. Talent remains the same from generation to generation. In every 100,000 people, there are potentially the same number of scientists, poets, musicians, philosophers and statesmen.

9   In the early years of our Republic talent generally went into the public arena. What outlets for talent were there? Few certainly in the military, the church, business, or scholarship. It was politics and public service that offered the most glittering rewards and that attracted, therefore, the best and most honorable talent.

10   But in our own day it is the other way around. It is business, industry, finance, science, and the arts, not public service, that attract the best.

11   Nor can we find an explanation of the decline of leadership in the absence of experience. There is no discernible correlation between political experience and statesmanship in the history of the American Presidency.

12   Washington had no political experience, nor, for that matter, had Lincoln. Theodore Roosevelt had brief experience as governor of New York and Wilson as one-term governor of New Jersey. Buchanan, Harding, and Nixon, the worst failures in American Presidential history, all had long and varied experience in public life. Experience is no substitute for judgment, or integrity.

It cannot even be said that the problems of our day are   13
more difficult or baffling than those that challenged earlier
Presidents. The notion that the problems we face are of unprecedented complexity and intransigence is an expression of
private and collective vanity, for it excuses our failures.

The task of writing a Constitution and creating a nation   14
that confronted Washington, the task of holding the Union
together and ending slavery that confronted Lincoln, the task
of overcoming the greatest of depressions, transforming the
nation from a private enterprise to a welfare state, and fighting
a global war that confronted Franklin Roosevelt—these were
graver and more difficult than any problems now facing us.

The kind of self-indulgence that ceaselessly bleats about   15
our towering problems is similar to the self-indulgence that
persuades millions of amateur psychologists that the problems
of love and sex are more profound today than they were when
Homer wrote of Penelope or Virgil, of Dido or Dante, of Be-
atrice. It also convinces us that the problems of old age are
more grievous than when Shakespeare wrote of King Lear or
Goethe, of Faust.

The problem of the Presidency today is not a matter of   16
personal talent, or of mounting difficulties. It is a matter of
popular attitudes, habits, and expectations, of policies, laws,
and administration. It can and should be remedied by changing the policies, the laws, and the administration.

Here are some of the changes that might give us better   17
Presidents:

1. Either abolish the cumbersome and illogical Electoral   18
College and provide for election by simple national majorities
(or pluralities) or restore the Electoral College to its original
character.

The first solution would recognize that we are one people,   19
not 50, with common interests and objectives, and that the
President is indeed a *national* leader. The second, which, after
all, gave us Washington and Adams and (after some complexities) Jefferson, would at least free electors from being robots
and put a premium on electors who had minds of their own.

2. Abolish primaries and go back to the system of national   20
party caucuses, which served us pretty well in the early years
of the Republic. If that is too "undemocratic" (as if our present system can be called democratic!), we might provide for

national primaries, all on the same day (or days), so we could avoid the misleading competition for attention that now obtains.

21   The spectacle of far-reaching decisions made by the chance of primaries in a little state like New Hampshire is almost as vulgar as the conduct of those primaries, the amount of money spent on them, and the excessive notoriety they command in television and press.

22   3. Shorten the election process. The British allow three to four weeks for the choice of a new government. Why should it take us a year or more? There was some excuse for long-drawn-out campaigns in the early years of the Republic when distances were great, communication slow, and candidates often known only regionally. At a time when television brings every candidate into every household, it is ironic that we take three or four times as long to select candidates and conduct campaigns as we did before we had such technology.

23   4. Perhaps most important of all, eliminate money from Presidential campaigns and elections. This is not in itself a very astonishing proposal; after all, William Jennings Bryan made it back in the 1890s, and Theodore Roosevelt endorsed it when he was President. Yet we still take for granted that it is proper for candidates to spend millions getting themselves nominated and elected. Clearly the costs of campaigns and elections are monstrously excessive.

24   Those costs have three pernicious consequences: First, they shift the center of gravity in campaigns from issues to money-raising; second, they put successful candidates in debt, perhaps even in hock, to those who finance their campaigns and thus open the doors to a form of blackmail; third, they discourage those without access to money from entering politics at all.

25   The solution to this problem is elementary: the costs of Presidential (and doubtless of Congressional as well) campaigns should be strictly regulated, and financed by the Congress. The Congress has, in recent years, made some half-hearted gestures towards controlling campaign expenditures.

26   What is odd is that most criticism of Congressional legislation charges that it is too restrictive, rather than that it is not

restrictive enough. But, after all, campaigns were not expensive in the 19th century; there is no reason why they should cost millions today.

The chief expense, now, is for television. The American   27
people own the air and could require networks to provide free television time to legitimate candidates. That seems to work in other countries. Why not here?

5. We should restore—and rehabilitate—the original char-   28
acter of the Vice Presidency. The framers of the Constitution assumed that the Presidents and Vice Presidents were constitutionally equal. George Washington and John Adams, as Justice Story observed in his "Commentaries on the Constitution," both "were candidates deemed equally worthy and fit for the Presidency."

But the office of Vice President soon came to be looked   29
upon as an exercise in futility. Parties persist in naming to that exalted office men who are justly forgotten, like William Wheeler or Garret Hobart (or Thomas R. Marshall, whose only memorable contribution was his observation that "what this country needs is a good five-cent cigar"), or men we should like to forget like Richard Nixon and Spiro Agnew. Considering that eight Vice Presidents have succeeded their Presidents, that office scarcely deserves the insignificance that has been imposed upon it.

6. A political rather than a legal or administrative change.   30
Restore the Cabinet to its former position as not only a body of advisors to the President, but as effective departmental administrators. We did better when Presidents had, and used, strong Cabinets than we have done since Presidents have largely ignored them.

We have an economy today more elaborately committed   31
to banking, finance, and business than any other nation. Why is it impossible for us to find an Alexander Hamilton or an Albert Gallatin to head the Treasury? We have a government more deeply involved in foreign affairs than at any time in our history. Why do we not have a Thomas Jefferson, a James Madison, a John Quincy Adams to head the State Department?

7. Much could be done to overcome and remedy the prob-   32
lem of nonvoting and to increase participatory democracy.

Slightly more than half of those entitled to vote in Presidential elections do so. In Congressional elections, it's less than half. Voting in Britain, Germany and Scandinavia generally attracts some 80 to 90 percent of the electorate: In Zimbabwe (formerly Rhodesia), over 90 percent of potential voters took part in the first national elections.

33   Registration could be simplified and made permanent, absentee voting facilitated, and residency requirements (meaningless in national elections) abolished.

34   8. Finally, the American people must somehow be brought to a realization that the American Presidency is a world office, not just a national one. Presidents should be selected for their ability to understand world, not just national, affairs. Presidents, required to devote most of their attention to global problems (and most of our national problems are merely part of larger global problems), must be relieved of the burden of politics, the burden of day-by-day administrative decisions, the burden of excessive ceremonial activities and gestures.

35   What is called for are just those talents of statesmanship that Americans found and celebrated in Washington and Jefferson. What is called for are leaders who meet those qualifications that Justice Story set forth almost a century and a half ago:

> A statesman must be master of the past, present and future. He must see what is behind as well as what is before. He must learn to separate the accidental in human experience from that which constitutes the cause or the effect of measures. He must legislate for the future when it is, as yet, but dimly seen, and he must put aside much which might win public favor in order to found systems of solid utility whose results will require ages to develop but . . . are indispensable for the safety, the glory and the happiness of the country.

Points for Discussion

1. Comment on Commager's estimate of recent American presidents. What does he mean by "world stature" (par. 4)?

2. Point out several general statements that Commager apparently expects a reader to take on faith. What audience will accept these statements without further proof? If you are not among those who accept, explain why not.

3. This essay can be divided into three major parts. Identify these parts and formulate a sentence summary to show what each of those divisions contributes to the whole. What transitions or signals let you recognize the divisions easily?

4. Of what two parts does each of the eight proposals consist? Insofar as possible, explain the relationship of the two parts and the paragraphing within each proposal.

Suggestions for Writing

1. Write a comparison/contrast paper about two of the presidents Commager uses as examples of "world stature" and "lack of world stature." Draw some conclusions about requirements for such stature. Or argue against Commager's thesis by showing how "times make the man," perhaps using Wilson and Roosevelt as examples of wartime presidents.

2. Choose one of Commager's proposals for an analytical paper of your own; explain in more detail why and how that proposal should be (or should not be) carried out and show clearly what the results of that change would be.

3. Commager says that we cannot argue that a president needs a base of political experience, yet we hear that argument advanced by people campaigning for office and those in opposition: "He has a lot of political know-how," or "He lacks any political background—he won't be able to handle the more experienced politicians." Using examples of elected officials (at any level) that you know, argue this point, pro or con.

4. What are the qualities that make for great leadership? Using examples of your own, show what you think the qualities of great leaders in public office or other areas should be. Explain as well as

you can the reasons for your "list" of special assets a leader should have.

5. Commager seems to be looking back nostalgically to a time when he thinks presidents were greater than they now are, and he scorns the idea that early presidents needed an "image maker." Write a paper dealing with the role of image makers in present-day political life. What are the reasons for having such functions? What are the effects? Are they all bad, all good, or a mixture?

6

PAPERS THAT ARGUE AND PERSUADE

The writing you do to support a thesis is always to some extent *argument,* but some papers you write will be more strongly persuasive in purpose than others. In such papers you may use a variety of means to win the reader's agreement with a definite position or to change the reader's ideas or attitudes. The rhetoric of argument and persuasion includes many directives, suggestions for what to do and what to avoid, and you can discover many of these practices by reading the essays in this section.

First, perhaps obviously, anyone who wishes to persuade must take a definite stand or make some specific proposal, not just examine various sides of an issue in order to encourage thinking about a subject. Consequently, when you wish to persuade, you must know where you stand in regard to a subject that is potentially controversial. Second, if you are to persuade, you must establish yourself by letting your reader know that you argue from a position of authority that comes from knowing the subject. Such knowledge, of course, becomes evident in the collection of examples, facts, statistics, and data of all types that you use for proof, but you may also tell the reader directly about your experience or research: "After traveling 10,000 miles on European trains, I think I can speak about the advantages of a Eurail pass."

Another major responsibility in persuasion involves recognizing the present knowledge, interests, and attitudes of the audience you wish to reach. That audience may be general—anyone who happens to read the article you write; or it may be specific—a well-identified group of people who already partially agree or who strongly disagree with you. For instance, Henry Steele Commager, in his article on page 189, assumes his intended audience already pretty well agrees with him. When that agreement is not a "given," however, you must decide not only on the kinds and amount of proof to provide but on the tone to take, with its implications for choice of language. Overdoing (the "hard sell") may offend; belittling ("talking down") may insult; emotional appeals ("loaded language") may be detected and assumed false, even in a good cause. It is usually safest to regard the reader as an intelligent thinker who will respond to well-considered proof and careful logic, as one who shares your concern but has not previously shared the convictions or facts you can offer.

While persuasion often depends heavily on stirring the reader's feelings with emotive language or moving examples, it depends primarily on logic. The reader must be certain that the conclusions you draw come logically from the line of reasoning and the facts behind it that you present. In the essays here you will find both *inductive* reasoning and *deductive* reasoning. If induction is sound, the particulars lead logically to the generalization. Deduction, on the other hand, is characterized by the application of the general to the specific, by moving from a general statement to further instances, similar cases, or comparable situations. The logician refers to this type of reasoning as a syllogism.

Major premise:	Drivers who have accidents pay higher insurance rates.
Minor premise:	Tom recently had two accidents.
Conclusion:	Tom will now pay higher insurance rates.

At times, one premise is omitted to express the logic in a single sentence enthymeme: Because Tom has had two accidents, his

automobile insurance will cost him more. The logic represented in a carefully worked out syllogism often becomes the
basis for a thesis: It is only fair that drivers who have accidents
pay higher insurance rates because . . ." Even though a syllogism is seldom specifically stated in your papers, you may at
times test your reasoning by describing your argument in that
form.

The essays here represent various kinds and degrees of
persuasion and offer examples of skills that you too can acquire
and practice in persuading your readers.

AMITAI ETZIONI

Amitai Etzioni, a professor of sociology at Columbia University, wrote this article while he was a guest scholar at the Brookings Institution in Washington, D.C. Etzioni argues here for a resolution to differences between policymakers and social scientists.

Social Science vs. Government: Standoff at Policy Gap

1   The first credit goes to Plato, who worried that the thinkers who specialized in reflecting on society were not communicating effectively with those whose job involved guiding it—the elected officials, their civil servants, and, ultimately, the electorate. His solution was to make the philosophers kings. Recently, both the scientific community and the U.S. Congress have become concerned with the same issue. Congress, amid rising criticism of social programs, has intensified its questioning of what national policymakers get out of the $1.8 billion the federal government spends each year on social science research. At the same time, the social science community seems to feel increasingly hassled by the demands for practical "results." A flurry of recent reports has documented the gulf between the camps; the most recent, by the National Academy of Sciences, is aptly titled *Knowledge and Policy: The Uncertain Connection*.

2   Most of the federal money invested in social science research (about 60 percent) is spent by the Department of Health, Education, and Welfare; most of the rest is disbursed by the National Science Foundation, the Department of Labor, the Agency for International Development, and the Defense Department. About a third of the money goes for social statistics that keep track of such issues as changing employment opportunities for women, desegregation of schools, and compensatory education for minorities. Public-opinion sur-

veys and evaluations of federal programs, from welfare to housing subsidies, cost another few hundred million (exact figures seem to be unavailable). Only a fraction of the funds is invested in basic research, from psychological experiments to mathematical modeling of social data.

"Too much of this money has gone into poorly conceived   3
projects; too few of the results have been rigorously assessed," Elliot Richardson is quoted in the NAS report as saying when he was still secretary of HEW. Comments by his staff were not much more charitable: "There probably are no hidden jewels coming out of our R&D that are waiting to be discovered." And the NAS report says the Department of Defense and the Bureau of the Budget believe government-funded research is largely a subsidy for academicians and a source of difficulty with Congress, which objects to it for being too soft, impractical, or laced with liberal biases.

The investigative arm of Congress, the Government Ac-   4
counting Office, has also looked into the matter, in a 1977 report dourly titled "Social Research and Development of Limited Use to Policymakers." The GAO interviewed top federal officers and found that only 4 percent thought social R&D had a "substantial effect." Thirty-one percent allowed that its consequences might be "moderate," but 54 percent scored it as *less* than moderately effective and 11 percent saw it as having little or no effect.

The GAO put a good deal of blame on the people commis-   5
sioning the research. The report said studies have been ordered in "broad" categories that are of limited use to policymakers facing specific issues; research management is fragmented among numerous federal agencies and not related to a coordinated national policy; monitoring (i.e., supervision) is poor; dissemination of the findings is inadequate. Clearly, the GAO believes the weak connections between social science and policymakers can be fixed by tighter government management of research—but this is the kind of management, I should add, that we rarely achieve in other areas, from welfare to Medicaid, and that is anathema to researchers, who seek to follow where the data—not federal bureaucrats—lead them.

Social science researchers quoted in the NAS report addi-   6 tionally charge that policymakers do not listen, that when they "use social science at all, it will be on an ad hoc, improvised, quick-and-dirty basis," that pressures to be relevant lead to "shoddy products" and trendy research.

7   As in any decent circle of philosophers, there are heretics in this debate who maintain that we are all the *beneficiaries* of the communication gap. Social sciences are still so nascent, in this view, that usually they are best left to develop a while longer, before anybody leans on them too readily.

8   As I see it, much social research indeed is still rather weak, with some of the weakest mass-produced by the fly-by-night profit-making firms that have mushroomed in recent years to compete for government research contracts. Yet, social science studies have produced some solid and potentially useful results. They have shown, for example, that it is possible to provide the poor with a secure income without killing their motivation to work, suggesting that a "negative income tax" or "income maintenance" system could be a viable policy. They have warned against excessive reliance on formal communication as a means of changing people's health habits, a warning whose validity is made clearer every day by the ineffectiveness of efforts to advertise and mail pamphlets to curb smoking, alcoholism, and the abuse of other drugs. A large body of research has shown that for many mental patients and children with learning disabilities, being placed in a special institution creates more problems than it solves.

9   The findings about institutions have been a major factor in creating the Community Mental Health Centers, and in advancing "deinstitutionalization" and "mainstreaming" of pupils. But the research on income supports and health habits has had less impact—as has sound research in many other areas. Policymakers, often understandably hard put to tell the social science wheat from the chaff, tend to end up avoiding both.

10   At the same time, policymakers who proceed in the face of well-established evidence that their favorite schema will not work are often playing to the galleries or giving in to narrow political considerations. Thus, the death penalty is paraded again and again as a solution to crime, despite the fact that there is precious little evidence that it would even make a dent

in the problem. Welfare clients are urged to go to work, though most of them are not able-bodied, or are mothers of young children (who might be all too happy to work if proper child-care centers were provided—which they often are not).

There is no simple answer to the Platonic problem. But it seems safe to conclude that at least two developments would help. If the public became better informed about research findings, policymakers who concoct programs that sound good but do not work might be more frequently booted out of office. The policymakers might then be more inclined to seek out the advice of social scientists. (The NAS report suggests a need for more "research brokers" able to translate social science terminology into language that policymakers can comprehend.) Another way to advance the cause is for social scientists to make it their business to publicize data policymakers have repeatedly ignored. Social scientists could also help by being less tolerant of the quacks and con artists in their ranks. They can crack down through their professional boards, which review research contracts.

Such developments will not make philosophers kings or kings philosophers, but they could make for public policy that is more "reality-tested" and for a social science that is more useful.

Points for Discussion

1. Although a writer may not always make an outline before writing a paper, a finished article or essay is almost always tightly organized around a carefully constructed plan. That plan, of course, makes it easy to follow the writer's meaning. Divide Etzioni's article into sections, determining what each section contributes to the whole:

   a. How much of the article introduces the situation between government granters and social scientists?
   b. How many paragraphs explain the critical attitude of the "policymakers"?
   c. Which section (again, how many paragraphs) cites the side of the social scientists, giving their answers to outside criticism?

d. What is the special function of paragraph 10? Point out a key line from that paragraph.

e. If paragraphs 11–12 together form a conclusion, what does each paragraph contribute? How does the writer relate beginning and ending?

2. When you compare or contrast two situations, persons, or ideas, you may deal with one and then the other, treating them as *units,* or you may list several points and examine each subject under those *points* (see p. 6). Show which method Etzioni uses by referring to the article itself.

3. What in this article convinces you that Etzioni knows his subject thoroughly? Why is that conviction of the writer's knowledge persuasive?

4. How would you characterize the *tone* of this article? Why is tone of great importance in persuasive writing?

Suggestions for Writing

1. Write an answer to some critic of a particular "funded" research project. You might look up the "Golden Fleece" award created by Senator Proxmire of Wisconsin for suggestions of projects that have been under fire; or you may find a project that has come in for criticism on your own campus. You might agree with the critic, or you might defend the research against the attack.

2. Write an "objection" to some grant or research that you have heard about, one you think is wasteful perhaps of both time and energy.

3. In recent years, various parts of the United States' space program have been sharply criticized, and many expenditures for military-related research have been and currently are under attack. Write a persuasive letter to some person in government telling why you think a particular program of this kind should or should not be continued.

4. Investigate an area in which research seems to reveal controversial results, or where two pieces of research come up with quite

different findings. Present your findings in an oral report or in a well-documented paper. Use statistics, case studies, interviews, or any other method that lets you show exactly what the researchers have accomplished; you may, of course, decide that one side or another is right, or that both or neither is "on target." Here are a few subjects on which researchers have differed widely:

- the effects of some drugs—of tobacco, marijuana, certain prescription drugs, even aspirin or vitamin C
- the need to take vitamins regularly
- some substance or other cause that produces cancer
- the reasons for or against studying grammar
- the value of speed reading
- the relationship of speed to automobile accidents
- the value of certain types of exercise (jogging, for instance)
- the value of a particular food or diet
- the causes of certain types of crime—or the best ways of preventing crime (narrow to a particular crime as you wish)

CAROLINE BIRD

Sometimes persuaders tell us what they are against, rather than
make suggestions for reform. Here Caroline Bird attempts to
persuade by attacking what she sets up as the common beliefs
about "a liberal education." From what she opposes, you can
probably infer the qualities that she values.

"The Liberal Arts Religion" from *The Case Against College*

1   The academic dean of a famous old college lowered her voice,
glanced apprehensively around her office, and confessed: "I
just wish I had the guts to tell parents that when you get out
of this place you aren't prepared to *do anything.*"

2   Actually, it did not take much guts. The "best" colleges
are the liberal arts schools which are the most "academic"—they don't teach students anything useful in particular.
Even after they have to face the world, alumni expect no more.
In a study intended to probe what graduates seven years out
of college thought their colleges should have given them, the
Carnegie Commission found overwhelming preference for
"liberal" over "vocational" goals.[1]

3   What does anyone mean by "a liberal education"? People
shift their ground when they try to explain what it is and why
it is so important. It's hard to tell whether they're talking about
subjects that can be studied in school, such as philosophy and
literature; a *process* of learning or thinking; or a *personal transformation* ("college opened my eyes"); or a *value system* to
which the wise and honest can repair.

4   The *subject matter* of the liberal arts used to be the classics.
If not the ancients, then newer books on history, sociology,
economics, science, and other products of the minds of men.
As we near the twenty-first century, however, most educators
have given up the attempt to pass on the "great tradition of
Western man" in a four-year core curriculum. It's not *what*
you study, they say, it's *how* you study it.

"A liberal education is an experience that is philosophical   5
in the broadest sense," David Truman, dean of Columbia and
later president of Mount Holyoke, has said. "The particular
subjects do not so much contain this quality as provide jointly
a possible means of approaching it. The liberal arts, then, include those subjects that can most readily be taught so as to
produce an understanding of the modes of thought, the
grounds of knowledge, and their interrelations, established
and to be discovered."

In plainer language alumni say, "College taught me how   6
to think for myself." If you ask people what they mean by
thinking and how college teaches it, they recoil from the implication that the kind of thinking they mean is a specific skill,
such as the art of rhetoric, but start talking about a "whole
new way of looking at the world"—a personal transformation.

Personal transformation, not only in how one's mind   7
works but in how one views the world and oneself, is the most
cherished expectation—and sometimes it is achieved. "College changed me inside," one alumnus told us. Some wax poetic. "The liberal arts education aspires to expand the imaginative space and time in which a person lives." Others talk about
the "broadening" that occurs when a young woman from a
Midwest farming town encounters adults who don't regret the
fact that MacArthur was not elected President, or when the
son of a city plumber learns that the police are not always right
and that some people on welfare aren't cheating. Discoveries
like this are valuable, alumni say, because they force students
to "formulate the values and goals of my life," as the Carnegie
Commission puts it.

And this turns out to be the hidden agenda of a liberal   8
arts education. A value system, a standard, a set of ideals to
keep you pointed in the right direction, even if you can't get
there. "Like Christianity, the liberal arts are seldom practiced
and would probably be hated by the majority of the populace
if they were," said one defender.

The analogy is apt. The fact is, of course, that the liberal   9
arts are a religion in every sense of that term. When people
talk about them, their language becomes elevated, metaphori-
cal, extravagant, theoretical, and reverent.

In answering a black student who charged the Kirkland   10
College curriculum with "irrelevance," President Samuel F.

Babbitt remonstrated that her liberal arts education aimed to expose her "to the values, the successes, the failures of great minds, great men and women engaged in every conceivable endeavor through the study of history and literature and art and the other disciplines that man has formed in order to understand where he has been and how to order his world."

11   "The purpose of the liberal arts is not to teach businessmen business," Alfred Whitney Griswold, former president of Yale told an alumni gathering. Rather, he went on, it is to "awaken and develop the intellectual and spiritual powers in the individual before he enters upon his chosen career, so that he may bring to that career the greatest possible assets of intelligence, resourcefulness, judgment, and character."

12   These thickets of verbal foliage are embarrassing to the more sensitive spokesmen for higher education. John T. Retalliata, president of the Illinois Institute of Technology, told an audience of parents in 1973, "I suppose a generalized goal is to have your sons and daughters, somehow, become 'educated' and, with that education, become well-employed and happy." Clark Kerr, notable as the embattled president of the University of California during the 1960s, told a 1972 television audience that "generally, the studies show that people who've been to college, oh, enjoy life more, they have more varied interests, they participate more in community activities." On another occasion, he told Alan Pifer, president of the Carnegie Corporation, that "with all that has happened in the world of knowledge in recent years, it is really impossible for people in higher education to come to agreement on what constitutes a liberal education."

13   Intellectuals have trouble describing the benefits of a liberal education because the liberal arts are a religion, the established religion of the ruling class. The exalted language, the universal setting, the ultimate value, the inability to define, the appeal to personal witness, the indirectness, the aphorisms—these are all the familiar modes of religious discourse.

14   As with religion, no proof is required, only faith. You don't have to prove the existence of God. You don't have to understand the Virgin Birth. You don't have to prove that Camus is better than Jacqueline Susann. Camus is sacred, so Camus is better and so are the people who dig him. If you don't dig Camus, the trouble is not with Camus, but with you.

Faith in personal salvation by the liberal arts is professed   15
in a creed intoned on ceremonial occasions such as commencements. It is blasphemy to take the promises literally, and if you
don't understand what the words mean, you are only admit-
ting your lack of grace.

Take, for instance, the goal of college most fervently   16
sought by the alumni queried by the Carnegie Commission,
"development of my abilities to think and express myself."
Only the captious dare to ask, "What do you mean by your
ability to think?" If you inquire, it very quickly develops that
those who value this objective aren't talking about what the
Swiss educator Jean Piaget, the semanticist Noam Chomsky,
or the Harvard psychologist Jerome Bruner mean when they
talk about "thinking."[2] The kind of "thinking" the cognitive
psychologists are talking about has to be acquired long before
you are old enough to go to college, and if Piaget is right,
most of it has to be learned before a child is old enough to
go to school. What the alumni and employers expect college
to teach is the habit of logical analysis and the conventions of
rhetoric that make it possible to resolve differences of view
on human affairs by debate and discussion. Colleges with very
small classes try to give their students practice in the art of dia-
logue, but the students who speak up in class are usually the
ones who have already learned how at the dinner table at
home and in bull sessions with friends.

If the liberal arts are a religious faith, the professors are   17
its priests. Professors are not accountable to the laity they
serve. They themselves define the boundaries of their authority and choose their own successors. Their authority is unas-
sailable, because by definition they know best. As such, they
are invulnerable to lay criticism. One of the educators with
whom I talked dismissed the doubts of students out of hand.
"I am not convinced that eighteen-year-olds can or should be
expected to know what college will ultimately do for them."

The professors disclaim arbitrary personal power. They go   18
by rules. They contend that right is not what they think but
what the sacred scriptures or the ecclesiastical courts decree.
Professors say that truth is what comes out when you subject
data to a process called the scientific method, and it is this process, rather than its product, that is written in the stars. But
the process itself, this very scientific method, is also a product

of the mind of man, and it may not be the only process the mind of man can devise. Other processes may produce other kinds of truth. No one, for instance, would suggest that the visions of William Blake could be "disproved" by the scientific method.

19   Colleges govern themselves by their own rules and sometimes confront civil authority. Only during the 1960s, when the students were out of control, did college administrators admit the right of the local police to "invade" the campus. And, like the church, American colleges have used their credibility to exercise political, economic, and social power in an irresponsible way. Along with access to heaven, they don't mind controlling access to the good things of this world. So long as the diploma is a credential for good jobs, giving or withholding it determines the fate of students here on earth. The colleges do not claim that they are preparing candidates for executive work, for instance, but they do not renounce their role as gatekeeper of the best jobs. As one professor told us, "We can't help it that the big companies like to hire our graduates."

20   To be blunt, the colleges have been as willing as the church to grab the power the faithful thrust upon them. Through their power to issue the diploma, they decide the fate of individuals. Through their power to determine who shall be admitted to college, they select as "naturally better" those who manipulate abstract symbols and unwittingly consign to the damnation of dead-end, second-class roles, those whose intelligence is manual, visual, or artistic. The power we allow them to have makes our society more vulnerable to words and abstractions than it would otherwise be, and it is not necessary to have a settled opinion on whether this is good or bad to recognize the danger of subjecting young people during their formative years to control by authorities who are pursuing objectives that leave most of the population cold. We think they are benign, therefore we accept their rule over our young. Imagine the outcry at the very idea of turning our surplus young people over to the military for safekeeping!

21   Americans have always been sensitive to the attempts of their armed forces to use military competence as a basis for exercising political power. But we do not distrust the same

kind of bid when it comes from the professoriate. Through their control of research, they decide what frontiers of knowledge shall be pushed back. Through their interpretation of the scientific method, if not the sacred writings of "the great Western tradition," they decide what shall be accepted as good, or true, or even beautiful.

But just as technical progress threatened the various monopolies of the church at the end of the Middle Ages, so the information explosion today threatens the monopoly of college over knowledge.   22

Of all the forms in which ideas are disseminated, the college professor lecturing his class is the slowest and the most expensive. The culturally deprived for whom college is supposedly so broadening are in the best position to see this. "I can read a book just as good as the man can talk," a black woman student told us. "Nine chances out of ten that's all you get—a professor who's just reading out of the book."   23

A better college experience would, no doubt, have provided more stimulation than students encountered in the overloaded colleges of the 1960s. But this begs the issue.   24

Today you don't have to go to college to read the great books. You don't have to go to college to learn about the great ideas of Western man. If you want to learn about Milton, or Camus, or even Margaret Mead, you can find them. In paperbacks. In the public library. In museum talks. In the public lectures most colleges offer for free. In adult education courses given by local high schools. People don't storm these sources because they aren't interested, and there's no particular reason why they should be. Forcing people to "learn" about them by all sorts of social and economic carrots and sticks implies that those who have had contact with "high culture" are somehow better than other people.   25

And if you do want to learn, it isn't always necessary to go to the original source. I say this knowing that I am stamping myself as an academic heretic. But the culture consumer should be able to decide for himself exactly why, when, how much, and in what form he would like to partake of Daniel Defoe's *Robinson Crusoe,* or Milton's *Areopagitica,* or Simone de Beauvoir's *The Second Sex.* When I was in high school during the 1920s, the whole English class took a month to read   26

Ivanhoe, Sir Walter Scott's novel about the crusades. In 1969 my eight-year-old son zipped through a Classic Comic version in fifteen minutes, and I don't think the original warranted the extra time it would have taken him. If you are not interested in the development of the English novel, *Robinson Crusoe* can be an exasperating, slow-moving yarn, significant only because the name has become a symbol of lone adventure and one of the passwords recognized by all men who consider themselves educated. Milton's *Areopagitica* is another password, important for what it says and when it was said. There's a benefit in knowing about these works, but the benefit to any particular person at a particular time may not justify the cost of taking them raw. For many people, and many purposes, it makes more sense to read a summary, an abstract, or even listen to a television critic.

27   The problem is no longer how to provide access to the broadening ideas of the great cultural tradition, nor even how to liberate young people so that they can adopt a different life-style than the one in which they were reared. The problem is the other way around: how to choose among the many courses of action proposed to us, how to edit the stimulations that pour into our eyes and ears every waking hour. A college experience that piles option on option and stimulation on stimulation merely adds to the contemporary nightmare. Increasingly, overloaded undergraduates give up the attempt to reason and flirt, half seriously, with the occult, which leaves vexing decisions to fate.

28   In order to deal with options, you need values. When Morris Keeton and Conrad Hilberry attempted to define a liberal education in their book *Struggle and Promise: A Future for Colleges,* they found that one of the recurrent themes was that it provides "an integrated view of the world which can serve as an inner guide,"[3] and more than four-fifths of the alumni queried by the Carnegie Commission said they expected that their college should have "helped me to formulate values and goals of my life." The formation of values may not be the first goal mentioned in discussions of a liberal education, but it tends to be the final ground on which hard-pressed defenders take their stand.

29   How does a student acquire a standard of values? The lib-

erally educated are forbidden, by their own creed, from any procedure so simple as telling students what is right and good. In theory a student is taught how to decide for himself, but in practice it doesn't work quite that way. All but the wayward and the saints take their values of the good, the true, and the beautiful from the people around them. When we speak of students acquiring "values" in college, we often mean that they will acquire the values—and sometimes we mean only the tastes—of their professors.

The values of professors may well be "higher" than many   30
students can expect to encounter elsewhere, but often those values aren't relevant to the situations in which students find themselves in college or later. Too many academics systematically overvalue symbols and abstractions. Historians will recall that it was a professor of history, President Woodrow Wilson, who sent American soldiers abroad to "make the world safe for democracy."

In addition to a distressing confusion of symbol and thing,   31
professors are sometimes painfully ignorant of many essential facts of life. A lot of them know very little about the economic structure of the United States, and their notions of what goes on inside major corporations are based on books written forty years ago about conditions prevailing fifty years ago. And they may also be partially responsible for some of the "alienation" of the young because they have encouraged the belief that transactions of power and money are to be avoided as a dirty business.

In so doing, of course, they are intuitively defending the   32
legitimacy of their own power. A poor boy who wanted to make good in the Middle Ages had to become a priest and at least profess to see the world in spiritual terms. A poor boy who wants to make good in twentieth-century America has to get a liberal education and at least profess to see the world in intellectual terms.

The academic elite are the self-proclaimed guardians of   33
what's right. Who's to tell them when they are wrong? Academics pride themselves on introducing students to a free marketplace of ideas, but they are the ones who make the rules, and the rules themselves can perpetuate dangerous distortions of reality. Not so long ago, for instance, no painter who drew

pubic hair on a nude figure could expect to be taken seriously
as an artist. It would have been vulgar to see it. The oversight
is amusing now, but it was not trivial. Victorian prudery was
hard to combat because it was a convention of the "best people." It's easy to laugh, but harder to be sure that we are not
overlooking some other facts of life today.

34   A liberal arts education does, of course, transmit standards
of value, and those in charge assume, almost as self-confidently
as that great Victorian, Matthew Arnold, that "the best that
has been known and thought in the world" is what they say
it is. Intellectual leaders today worry about sounding snob-
bish, but they are just as sure as the great eighteenth-century
English essayist Richard Steele that "it is the great aim of education to raise ourselves above the vulgar." And those who
have been so educated are happy to accept the distinction. At
Harvard commencements there is an audible sigh of emotion
when the president, as he has done for 300 years, welcomes
the new graduates into "the fellowship of educated men."
(Since 1970, it has been "the fellowship of educated men and
women.")

Notes

1. "When alumni were forced to choose between a general education and a ca-
reer-oriented education, they overwhelmingly endorsed the idea of a general education," Joe L. Spaeth and Andrew M. Greeley reported in *Recent Alumni and Higher
Education,* a Carnegie Commission study published by McGraw-Hill, New York, in
1970. The study queried 40,000 graduates of the class of 1961 in 135 colleges in
1961, 1962, 1963, 1964, and 1968.

2. For a quick introduction to the slippery concepts involved in thinking about thinking, see the section "The Elements and Vehicles of Thought," pp. 188–237, in Berel-
son & Steiner, *Human Behavior, An Inventory of Scientific Findings,* Harcourt Brace, New
York, 1964.

3. A dogged attempt to cope with the verbal foliage surrounding definitions of a liberal education, appears in Morris Keeton and Conrad Hilberry's *Struggle and Promise:
A Future for Colleges,* McGraw-Hill, New York, 1969, p. 260. They identify several
common elements including cultivation of the intellect; encouragement of "independent judgment" or "critical thought"; liberating the individual so that he can see the
world in perspectives other than his own; evoking an integrated view of the world
which can serve as an inner guide; equipping the individual to serve his society.

Points for Discussion

1. In paragraph 3 Bird declares that people vacillate between
four definitions of a liberal education. After reading the entire essay,

show how she uses these definitions in the overall structure.

2. Relate what you think Bird's purpose is to her statements in
paragraph 13: ". . . the liberal arts are a religion, the established religion of the ruling class."

3. In much persuasive writing "names" are used as authorities
to support the writer's stand. How does Bird use names in paragraphs
10–12? How does she use them in paragraph 16? Look up the meaning of the *ad hominem* argument (or fallacy) and determine how
fully you find Bird's argument succeeds.

4. Much of the essay from paragraph 17 on is an attack on professors as "priests" of a liberal education. What proof does Bird offer
for her statements about professors? Which does she expect you to
take on faith, as she says professors expect students to take their
teaching?

a. Is it your experience that professors think truth comes only
from subjecting data to the scientific process (par. 18)? Explain.
b. How much of Bird's argument depends on emotive language?
What, for instance, is the force of saying colleges "decide the
fate of individuals" and that their "objectives . . . leave most of
the population cold" (par. 20)?
c. Bird says in paragraph 29 that "we often mean that [students]
will acquire the values . . . of their professors." Test this statement against your experience. Are there other means by which
college-aged students acquire values? What influences do you
find strongest?

5. What is meant by the statement that "academics systematically overvalue symbols and abstractions" (par. 30)? What other
shortsightedness does Bird find characteristic of professors?

6. What do you think is the "reality" that Bird thinks a liberal
education obscures or ignores?

7. Attempt to construct a syllogism or an enthymeme summing
up Bird's argument. Or break her argument into parts and construct
two or three syllogisms summing up those parts. Discuss the logic
(or lack of it) you find in her argument.

Suggestions for Writing

1. Write your own paper under the title "The Case Against College" or "The Case for College." Or narrow the topic and write an argument for or against a certain type of curriculum (e.g. a general language requirement, a free elective system) or the advisability or error in choosing a particular major (such as political science rather than engineering).

2. Write a paper attacking or defending the "rule" of the professors. For instance, have you had professors who simply read the book? Have you felt your teachers ignored or did not understand reality? Or has your situation been different?

3. Since *The Case Against College* was written, many people have come to believe that education in general, and the liberal arts in particular, have lost credibility. Write a paper explaining why this shift has occurred. You may choose to persuade your reader that the loss is beneficial, that education did enjoy too much power over people's lives; or you may show that the diminishing respect for education (or the liberal arts alone, if you wish) is regrettable.

DAVID COHEN

Common Cause is the name of a group of citizens organized for
lobbying, promotion of policies to improve government and
living conditions, and representing voters on various issues.
The following letter was one of the group's appeals for
membership. In it the writer uses many methods of persuasion.

A Letter from Common Cause

Common Cause
2030 M Street, N.W.
Washington, D.C. 20036

Dear Citizen-Taxpayer:
Even though you may have known it for some time, more and   1
more Americans are just waking up to the plain and simple
truth:

> The reason the United States Government cannot solve the ur-
> gent problems that are plaguing our country, is because *the gov-*
> *ernment is the problem.*

Our government has become our most critical problem *be-*   2
cause our government has become incapable of solving the momentous
problems we face—runaway inflation shattering the dreams of
millions of our citizens, higher-than-ever taxes overburdening
our workers, and the constant threat of a crippling energy crisis hanging over our heads.

Our government in Washington cannot even begin to   3
solve these problems because it has allowed itself to become
paralyzed, held captive like a colossal Gulliver, bound by the
money-enforced ties of special interests, ensnared in miles of
red tape and overregulation, and immobilized by its own bureaucratic obesity.

Yes, today our federal government—the most powerful   4
government in the world—is unable to move, unable to work
for us as it should.

AND . . . only you and I and all concerned American citi-   5 zen-taxpayers, men and women who are fed up with a non-working government, can get it back on its feet.

6   How?

We must change the United States Government without destroying it. Because unless we do, our government will destroy itself.

7   STOP RIGHT HERE! Don't throw up your hands and say, "It can't be done!"

8   *It can be done—it must be done. We have no other choice.*

9   Whether or not you approve of its approach, you cannot fail to acknowledge the tremendous significance of the passage of the now famous Proposition 13. What California voters proved is that when citizens get mad enough they can make themselves heard. And most observers agree, Californians were not just angry about property taxes, dealt with in Proposition 13: they were mad at Washington as well as their state government, mad at "politics as usual," and mad at government that eats up their taxes and doesn't perform. So they spoke!

10   Now, please do not misunderstand me. I am not advocating that measures such as Proposition 13 be applied to our federal government. No, not at all. First of all, Proposition 13 was aimed solely at property tax relief. Secondly, and more importantly, while measures like Proposition 13 may give citizens a fleeting feeling of power in forcing their taxes lower, it stops there. It does not get to the basic decay in government. And that is what must be removed if our federal government is to get on its feet again. No, the most significant thing about Proposition 13 is that it proves the power of citizens to raise hell, if they get mad enough. It proves ordinary citizens *can* change government!

11   And that is why I am writing to you. I want to impress upon you the critical need for citizens to unite to change our government before its paralysis is fatal. I want to ask you to join us in Common Cause, as we fight to change our government without destroying it. Right now, I want to invite you to fill in the enclosed Membership Application and join me and over 200,000 other Americans in a citizens' movement that has directly brought about some of the most historic

changes in American government, and is now fighting hard for equally radical—*but reasoned*—changes to get our government back to work for all citizens.

When you join us in Common Cause, your membership will help us . . .   12

- *break the "big-money" bonds which hold our Congress the captive* of the AMA, the Teamsters' Union, the Dairy Lobby, "Big Oil" and hundreds of other powerful special-interest groups. Only by outlawing their big corruption-inducing campaign contributions and providing public financing for Congressional elections—as we did for Presidential campaigns—will we ever take Congress off the special-interest "auction block" and get it back to work for us!
- *cut the reams of red tape and overregulation* which actually add to inflation instead of fighting it. We must force our government into a massive housecleaning. We must strip from the books archaic, competition-hindering restrictions, like those of the ICC which are the direct cause of scandalous energy waste and cost you and all consumers between $1.4 and $1.9 *billion* annually!
- *pare off the bureaucratic fat* by demanding "Sunset Legislation" which will require every government program and agency to be terminated unless it is specifically reauthorized after periodic and thorough reexamination of its worth.
- *eliminate unjustified tax advantages and loopholes* that enable giant corporations to pay *less* federal income tax than you do by forcing periodic Congressional review of the tax system. A secretary, married to a school teacher, gave vent to her frustration in a *New York Times* article with what has become a national complaint, "We're both working because we have to, not because we want to, but when you turn around, they (the government) stab you in the back and take out all those taxes." Perhaps she might feel even more outraged if she were aware that *many of our largest corporations do not pay a single penny in U.S. federal income tax!*
- *put an end to the downright fraud and theft in government.*

No matter how you cut taxes, you and all taxpayers are
still being cheated until we pass laws that will take firm
action to halt rip-offs by dishonest government employees and will create new protection for those who expose
waste and mismanagement.

13   In the enclosed folder, you will find more information on
Common Cause's proposals to achieve these radical but rea-
soned changes . . . along with some specific changes Common
Cause has already brought about.

14   You see, Common Cause has been working for
change—change for the better—since 1970. Then, we were
up front in the fight to turn our government away from the
war in Vietnam and its senseless waste of lives and resources.
We helped win that fight, and we went on to others—
President Nixon's election finances, Congressional reform,
ethics in government, etc.

15   Common Cause's nonpartisan commitment to fairness and
honesty, to getting our government to work for all the people,
has made us the recognized voice of over 200,000 Americans—Democrats, Republicans and independents alike—from
all walks of life, from every state. This strong united voice of
ordinary citizens, people like yourself, who want to make certain they are getting a fair shake and a fair chance at achieving
their personal hopes and dreams, is augmented by a professional lobbying staff in Washington, D.C. and in many state
capitals.

16   When Common Cause's lobbyists swing into action, fully
armed with carefully researched facts substantiating our positions, Senators and Representatives listen. They listen because
they know that we represent over 200,000 vocal Americans.

17   And while our professional staff and volunteers are at
work in Washington, individual Common Cause members can
also help, if they wish, by becoming "citizen-lobbyists" at
home. In a handy informative booklet, *Citizen's Action Guide,*
you will see exactly what you can do, if you wish to join our
activists. We will also keep you posted on our progress—and
our setbacks, too—with *In Common* (published 4 times a year)
and *FrontLine* (published 6 times a year).

18   It is this unique combination of professional lobbying

know-how and the impact of over 200,000 citizens that has made Common Cause a citizens' action lobby *with clout.* And we believe we have the clout to get our government back on its feet.

Of course, to effect these sweeping reforms in government would be almost an impossible task for any outside organization were it not for the many members of Congress, of both parties, who also want to see our government back in shape. Yet, all too often these forward-looking men and women find themselves frustrated and held powerless by the special-interest state in which they must work. They need the voice and the power of the people behind them, so that they can work for the same changes we seek. For example, here are the words of just one representative: 19

> . . . the real message of Proposition 13 is that people are resisting bad programs, inefficient and ineffective government, that all too often has come about because we have listened to the voice of the special pleaders, who by virtue of their special interest contributions have gotten the ears of Members of Congress and the committee chairmen, and as a result we have passed poorly designed legislation. I think that is the message of Proposition 13.

We, at Common Cause, wholeheartedly agree. We also believe that you and taxpaying citizens like you are fed up with a government that cannot solve our problems because it is powerless against special-interest pressure, and immobilized by its own bureaucratic fat. Therefore, we also hope that you are fed up enough to want to do something about it right now. Join us in Common Cause and help get our government back to work for us.   20

Sincerely,

David Cohen
President

P.S. When you glance at the enclosed Common Cause membership application, you will notice the basic annual dues is only $15. Despite inflation-caused increases in costs, we have maintained this low figure since our inception in 1970. At Common Cause, we practice what we preach.   21

Points for Discussion

1. Point out the ways in which the writer of the letter personalizes the appeal. What is his attitude toward the reader? Be particularly aware of his use of the personal pronouns—*I, we,* and *you.*

2. How does the writer attempt to dramatize the situation he finds in government? What does format contribute to emphasis?

3. Emotive words give force to the goals in paragraph 12. For instance, "Big-money bonds" that hold Congress "captive" and "cut reams of red tape" are phrases that have emotional appeal. Find other words and phrases that are used for this effect.

4. What is the value of listing successes in paragraph 14?

5. Point out the abstract words in paragraph 15 and explain their appeal.

6. What is Proposition 13? What use does the writer make of it even though he says the group does not support the proposition itself?

7. Characterize the level of language in the letter. Overall, how would you describe the writer's tone?

Suggestions for Writing

1. Write a paper protesting a situation in which you see government (national, state, local) as "non-working" or as paralyzed by red tape. If you wish, put your paper in the form of a letter to the agencies you wish to address, or make it an open letter to other citizens you think need persuading of the same problem.

2. When a government agency or service is terminated or when a new one is proposed, the public is often aroused to protest: "Employees will be thrown out of work" or "This will just increase the bureaucracy and cost too much"; "People really need that service"

or "The whole program invites graft and interference by big-brother." Write a paper convincing your readers (define that group for yourself) of the advisability of discontinuing or establishing some special government office or service.

3. Write an answer to David Cohen of Common Cause explaining why his letter would or would not persuade you to join the group.

LAURA NADER

Laura Nader, a professor of anthropology at the University of
California at Berkeley, is the author of *The Disputing Process:
Law in Ten Societies.* She directs this short persuasive essay to
her fellow social scientists.

Studying Up

1   Look at social science literature in the United States and you
will find abundant research on ethnic groups, the poor, and
the disadvantaged, but very little on the middle class and
scarcely any on the upper classes. There are well over 600
journals in the behavioral sciences alone—psychology, anthropology, and sociology—spewing forth new findings each year,
yet over 90 percent of the funding for social science research
is allocated for studies of lower economic classes. Social scientists should examine the consequences of this bias, which pre-
fers that the subject of study be socially inferior to the researcher.

2   Studying "up" as well as "down" would force us to rephrase many "common sense" questions. Instead of asking
why some people are poor, we would ask why some people
are so greedy. We would have to explain the fantastic resistance to change among those whose options are so many—the
universities, the auto industry, the professions. We might understand the ghetto better if we examined the people and institutions with which ghetto residents must deal. We could, for
example, study the banking and insurance industries that mark
out areas of the city to which they will not extend credit or
sell insurance—so-called "red-lining." We could study the
landlords who in violation of the law pay off municipal officials
so that building codes are not enforced.

3   Just look at the consequences of existing social science research on crime. By virtue of our concentration on lower-class
crimes, we have aided in the public's definition of the
"law-and-order problem" as lower-class or street crime. Yet
wasn't it a "law-and-order" problem when 76 workers in
Hopewell, Virginia, were infected by the pesticide Kepone

and dangerous chemical wastes were pumped into the James River? This kind of white-collar crime, as hazardous to life as the street variety, gets short shrift by justice organizations.

A fresh perspective on white-collar crime might change   4 our focus for study. In developing new theories about slum gangs, we might ask whether it is sufficient to see gangs as products of their subculture's value system alone. We would study the marketing or transportation systems that, as in Watts, make virtual islands of some ghetto areas. We would examine the degree to which red-lining, plea bargaining, corrupt judicial appointments, or the often shoddy quality of legal services for the poor contribute to cynicism about the law in the ghetto.

We are not dealing with an either/or proposition. We sim-   5 ply need to recognize when it is useful to study up, down, or sideways. By studying a problem across class, we could test whether certain upper- or lower-class problems are due to a particular kind of family pattern or to the context in which that family is operating: how, for example, an executive or blue-collar worker's job affects the entire family's health, safety, and lifestyle. At the least, setting the problems in a comparative frame would help us trace the forces that generate excessive poverty or affluence and perhaps learn whether they come from the larger society or are transmitted within each group.

Studying up as well as down would force us to revise our   6 social science books, whose indexes barely mention the advertising, insurance, banking, realty, or energy industries— institutions and network systems that affect millions of lives. For such work to become central in social science, we need to rethink why it is that social scientists are trained to relate down while lawyers in general are trained to relate up.

Points for Discussion

1. Nader accuses social scientists of "bias" in "studying down" only (par. 1). Point out ways that she attempts to protect herself against this same charge of bias. If you wish, begin with the word "might," which occurs in several sentences.

2. Of what special persuasive value are the statistics concerning grants and "journals in the behavioral sciences" in paragraph 1?

3. Study paragraphs 2, 3, and 4 to decide how many sentences make a general statement and how many offer specifics to illustrate those generalizations.

4. What assumption lies behind a statement such as this: "Instead of asking why some people are poor, we would ask why some people are so greedy" (par. 2)? Select another sentence or two and explain the assumptions behind the statements.

5. How much of Nader's essay depends on analysis of cause/effect relationships? Which causes are proven and which are implied? Why is that difference significant?

6. Only once—in the first sentence—Nader addresses her audience directly as "you." (*You* is, of course, implied in the imperative of the first sentence in paragraph 3.) What is the effect of the use of first person pronouns—*we, our, us*—throughout the essay?

Suggestions for Writing

1. Write a short persuasive paper appealing to some well-defined group to make a change, major or minor, in their area of study or methods of working. For instance, you might address tax consultants with an appeal for clarification of tax forms; lawyers or doctors with an appeal about fee setting; publishers or journalists regarding practices in covering political events; educators or educational administrators suggesting changes in curriculum or admissions policies. This illustration may help you get started:

> High schools should add a free reading period three times each week, balancing the emphasis now placed on required physical education. If we placed more emphasis on reading for enjoyment. . . .

2. Choose a group project in which you have been involved—a class project, a committee, a number of friends who attempted some joint effort. Write a persuasive essay suggesting a different approach from that you took. Or if you are persuaded the one you did take

is the only right way, show why you advocate that choice. Address your group as audience, showing them how things would be different (or right) from following your suggestions.

3. Write to a teacher concerning an assignment, telling that instructor how directions might have been clearer and easier to follow, offering reasons for the suggestion, and explaining the results you expect from it.

4. Study two or three issues of journals in the behavioral sciences that Nader mentions. Report on evidences of bias that you find there to determine if she is right in her assessment in paragraph 1.

5. Choose one of the practices Nader considers prevalent among middle and upper classes and write a paper persuading your reader that study should be made of that practice. Examples: the refusal to change some practice in a university, the auto industry, or a particular profession (par. 2); "red-lining" (par. 2); a particular white-collar crime (par. 3). Be sure you show persuasively why the study should be undertaken and what the possible results might be.

RENÉ DUBOS

René Dubos, professor emeritus of Rockefeller University
whose long and distinguished career spanned several
disciplines, died in 1982. His column "The Despairing
Optimist" appeared for several years in *The American Scholar.*
In this essay from that journal, Dubos deals persuasively with a
problem much discussed today—what age is too young and
what too old in considering a person for a particular job.

From "The Despairing Optimist"

1   Shortly after I joined the staff of Harvard University Medical
School in 1942, I was asked to serve on a search committee
for a new chairman of the department of physiology. The
problem was to find a successor for Walter Bradford Cannon,
long the most illustrious American physiologist, who had finally decided to retire at the age of seventy-one. The members
of the committee soon agreed that the candidate with the best
scientific qualifications was Homer W. Smith, formerly of Cannon's department at Harvard and at that time professor of
physiology at New York University. His name was rejected,
however, on the grounds that his age might not give him
enough time to create a strong department during his tenure
of office. The new rules at Harvard made retirement compulsory at age sixty-five, and he was then forty-eight years old!
The second candidate to be considered was a brilliant young
physiologist then working independently as a recipient of a
special fellowship. But his name also was discarded because
he was only thirty years old and therefore not mature
enough—so the committee felt—to be entrusted with large
decision-making responsibilities affecting the future of a famous medical school department.

2   Walter B. Cannon was still a creative scholar and a forceful
administrator in 1942, even though he was then past the official retirement age. Furthermore, he had become known as
a creative scientist early in his life, during his mid-twenties,

and was under thirty-five when he was appointed full professor of physiology at Harvard. These facts gave rise to my doubts about the significance of chronological age as a measure of scientists' ability to engage in creative work and to shoulder administrative responsibilities. These doubts were reinforced when I came to realize that Louis Pasteur made his first great scientific discovery at the age of twenty-two, and had proven a very effective dean of a new school of science at thirty-one. He was past sixty-three, as well as partially paralyzed, when he began to work out the theoretical principles and practical aspects of vaccination. I have since learned that many artists, politicians, and businessmen likewise became known for their achievements before the age of thirty, and continued to be productive long past middle age, both in their fields of specialization and in other social roles.

I do not see much evidence, therefore, that people between the ages of thirty and sixty are any more capable of creative work or of holding responsible positions than are younger or older adults. Yet there has been a trend in Western countries to postpone the age at which young people are allowed to play responsible and creative roles in important social activities—and simultaneously another trend to hasten the age of retirement. In my opinion, both these trends are biologically unjustified and socially destructive. They are an expression, not of the influence of chronological age on ability to function creatively and responsibly, but of the fact that our society does not know how to create enough adult roles for able people. 3

One unfortunate consequence of this state of affairs has been an artificial, nonbiological prolongation of adolescence, resulting in the creation of a post-teen-age, pre-adult phase of life for which there is no useful role in society as currently organized. Another deplorable consequence has been to deny a chance for creative social activities to older people who are still vigorous and capable of productive tasks but are compelled to accept retirement from active life, simply for reasons of bad social planning. I shall discuss later how our present social structures are thus responsible for wasting human potentialities at both ends of the life span—on the one hand, among young people who are fully developed and, on the other, 4 among older people who are still potentially capable of productive activities.

5   Unemployment among teen-agers, especially in the black population, is one of the greatest tragedies of present-day life in the United States. It causes much human misery now, and will certainly aggravate social problems in the future. The reason I do not discuss this problem here is that its determinants are purely ethnic and economic, and therefore somewhat outside my theme, which is the relationship between chronological age and intellectual development.

6   In most parts of the world, especially in prosperous countries, most children and teen-agers are now developing biologically faster than they did several decades ago. This phenomenon is most obvious with regard to body size and sexual maturity. For example, most teen-agers are taller than their grandparents and parents: the age of first menstruation has been advanced by probably more than three to five years since the beginning of the century. It would be surprising if this acceleration of biological maturity were not accompanied by acceleration in the development of mental attributes. From many points of view, in any case, chronological age now has physiological and psychological connotations quite different from those it had in the past.

7   There is a painful paradox in the fact that, while young people are now developing faster than they used to, society tends to treat them as dependent children for a longer and longer time. Gone are the days when, in Europe and even more in this country, children were entrusted with chores at home, on the farm, or in the shop and thus had a chance to acquire early, by practice and observation, the confidence and the skills of adult life. In theory, teen-agers are now glorified, but in practice they are given little if any opportunity to act as responsible members of the adult community. Whereas in the past many persons in their twenties occupied positions of leadership in all walks of life, people are now regarded as still somewhat immature, and hence not quite dependable, almost until they have reached their thirties. This is just as true for plumbers as for lawyers and doctors; if present trends continue, the period of training will be longer than the period of performance and creativity.

The justification commonly given for prolonging the   8
schooling and training period in our times is the greater complexity of the modern world: a person needs more knowledge
and more experience than in the past in order to become really
creative and socially responsible. I can only outline here some
of my reasons for questioning the validity of this assumption.

While it is obvious that the amount of information has in-   9
creased, most of it is now codified in the form of organized
structures and of general laws that make knowledge more
readily available and easier to comprehend. Furthermore,
only a few people do not reach full development of their intellectual capabilities by the end of their teen years. From then
on, most of them are as able as they will ever be to acquire
the specific kinds of knowledge they will need to deal with
particular problems. History shows ad nauseam that, in the
arts, in the sciences, as well as in all other walks of life, innova-
tive advances are just as likely to come from people in their
early twenties, or even younger, as from people who have
been active in particular fields for a long time.

The attributes denoted by the vague word *wisdom* are un-   10
questionably an expression of experience, but there is no evidence that they are correlated with chronological age. In my
opinion, they are acquired largely through the practice of taking responsibility, and in particular as a result of having to
weigh the multiple factors that need to be considered in any
choice or decision. One does not acquire experience by living
longer, but by having to deal with complex situations. If
young adults lack experience, it is not because they suffer from
a kind of biologically determined immaturity, but chiefly because they have been denied occasions to acquire experience
through the exercise of responsibility.

In the past, many great prophets and political rulers, many   11
conquerors and legislators, as well as many artistic and scientific creators, were people in their twenties who would now
be considered too young to hold responsible positions.

All events leave a practically permanent imprint on the bo-   12
dies and minds of the participants; experience is made up of
these lasting memories. Until recent times, most societies recognized a social value in such accumulated experience and
gave moral authority to their elderly members. The wisdom

associated with age was regarded as a valuable social asset. Modern societies, in contrast, no longer regard the wisdom acquired through the experiences of a long life as an asset of permanent value. The conditions of life change so rapidly, it is said, that the experience of the father is of little use to his son because the problems of the modern world are fundamentally unlike those of the past from which this experience was derived.

13   Although the opinion that experience gained in the past is not applicable to the present has been defended by eminent scholars, I question its validity. That ways of life are changing is obvious, but it is also obvious that the fundamental needs, limitations, potentialities, and aspirations of human beings remain much the same as they have been for thousands of years. The experience of the father may not be of much use to his son in designing new kinds of engines for aircraft, but it is very relevant to the reasons why people want to travel by aircraft and to the kind of service they demand. Experience is still a valuable asset in our society wherever human behavior is involved—which means in most of what we do and what we experience.

14   In the course of the aging process under various social conditions, certain biological and psychological factors clearly affect the quality and usefulness of experience. Aging inevitably brings about organic and behavioral changes, some of which are obvious and others hidden; in particular, it progressively weakens the physiological drive that motivates and activates people during early adulthood. Indolence commonly develops—along with an indisposition, and perhaps some fundamental organic loss of ability—to learn new ways, to accept new attitudes, and especially to take on new responsibilities. In all professional persons, there is a general trend for productiveness to fall off past the age of fifty; this trend provides a seemingly physiological basis for the common practice of compulsory retirement at some arbitrarily set age.

15   Because of practical administrative necessities, it is probably reasonable and perhaps indispensable to make retirement compulsory at a fixed chronological age, but the choice of this age is influenced more by social considerations than by biological imperatives. There is, first, the well-recognized fact that

chronological age does not rigidly determine physiological age and therefore does not constitute a good criterion of ability to function—physically or mentally, individually or socially. Of even greater importance is the fact that the operation of mental faculties is largely independent of ordinary biological vigor. As long as the vascular bed and physiological functions remain capable of supplying the brain with all the oxygen and the sugar it needs, the clarity of mental processes is preserved, and the person can continue a fairly normal range of personal and social activities.

History is indeed replete with examples of persons who remained productive and effective until a late chronological age, even after their physical health had begun to deteriorate. Cervantes completed the second part of *Don Quixote* when he was sixty-eight. Goethe's second *Faust* was written in his eighties. Henry James wrote the famous novels of his "major phase" between the ages of sixty and seventy-three. Contrary to what is generally stated, many scientists also have made fundamental contributions in their later years. William Harvey published *De Generationes* at age seventy-three, and I could produce a long list of contemporary biologists who discovered important scientific facts and laws in their sixties, seventies, and even eighties. Suffice it to mention here the case of Oswald T. Avery, under whom I worked at the Rockefeller Institute. He established the role of DNA in the transmission of hereditary characteristics after his official retirement age, at a time when he appeared so frail that many of his colleagues believed, and said, that he had shot his bolt. Naturally, much of the work that led to Avery's monumental scientific achievement of his later years was carried out by some of his younger colleagues who were more familiar than he was with modern theories and techniques. Yet it was he who elected to focus the efforts of his laboratory on the transmission of hereditary characteristics and who contributed the experience and the continuity essential to the solution of the problem.

The names of Georges Clemenceau for the First World War and of Winston Churchill for the Second World War are sufficient to illustrate that nations have often depended on chronologically old men for the arduous tasks of political leadership during critical periods in their history. In fact, the same remark applies to more technical aspects of leadership. During the Second World War, many of the most important commanding officers of the American army and navy were in their sixties; Henry L. Stimson was seventy-seven when he became secretary of war.

18   The case of the Supreme Court justices is of special interest, not only because it provides many examples of old men who remained professionally active late in life, but also because it demonstrates that the desire for continued professional activity can be independent of financial rewards. Justices are permitted to retire from the bench at seventy, after ten years of service, and receive their full salary until the end of their lives. Very few of them, however, have taken advantage of this clause in their contracts. In fact, most of them have elected to stay on the bench way past seventy—indeed, into their eighties and nineties and often until death.

19   It is probable that, like the Supreme Court justices, many retired people in all walks of life would prefer to continue as long as possible some form of socially useful activity. A recent survey of "senior citizens" in Sweden gave results that could probably be duplicated in the United States and in other prosperous countries of Western civilization. In Sweden, persons over sixty-seven years of age now account for almost 20 percent of the total population and most of them are retired. When these retired people were interviewed, the prime wish they expressed was for conditions that would enable them to remain as active as possible in body and in mind; opportunities for travel and for engaging in handicrafts rated high among their requests. In fact, the local administrations of many Swedish communities provide senior citizens with elaborate programs of entertainment, such as travel to other cities, visits to museums, theaters, and movies, education in languages, dances, and various kinds of hobby work. Granted the usefulness of such programs, they have not yet been proven to be an adequate substitute for activities that allow a person to contribute to the life and welfare of the community.

20   In a profound way, there is some analogy between the biological and psychological needs of people at both ends of life. In the case of old people as well as of young people, the social

significance of the occupation is probably more important than simply being occupied.

The development of biological and mental faculties is conditioned by their use during the early stages of life; similarly the maintenance of these faculties depends upon their continued use during the later stages of life. The validity of the ancient dictum "Use it or lose it" has been recently confirmed by a biomedical investigation. Dr. Alexander Leaf, professor of medicine at Harvard University, studied people of three agrarian societies characterized by unusual longevity, great vigor even in old age, and remarkable freedom from chronic diseases. 21

These three societies have very different ways of life because they belong to entirely different ethnic and cultural groups. One is located in Hunza, on the borders of China and Afghanistan; one in the Soviet Republic of Georgia; and one in Vilcabamba, Ecuador. Despite ethnic and cultural differences, however, these three agrarian societies have a few characteristics in common. In all three, people have an extremely frugal diet, they engage regularly in vigorous physical work, and they are expected to play an active role in the affairs of their communities from early in life almost to its end. This latter role changes, of course, with age, but instead of degenerating into retirement spiced with entertainment, people remain socially productive and useful. 22

Frugality, continued physical activity, and the practice of engaging in socially useful tasks throughout life certainly contribute to the longevity of these people, as well as to their vigor and freedom from disease. Modern societies, in contrast, are moving further and further away from these characteristics, creating a situation in which the young and the old alike are more and more deprived of important social roles. In many cases, I realize, progressively removing them from the productive stream of social life is the consequence of generous intentions—such as restricting the labor market to adults who are in the heaviest period of familial responsibilities; giving young people a chance for a more extensive, or at least more prolonged, education; and allowing older people more time to enjoy leisure at the end of a laborious life. But I believe 23 that these motives, though good in theory, commonly misfire in practice. They cause a wasting of life at both ends and generate dangerous situations for the future.

24   I am aware of the economic and administrative difficulties involved in reintegrating young and retired people into a more socially useful life. I know too that our society cannot return to the agrarian ways of life studied by Dr. Alexander Leaf. The problem demands the formulation of new priorities based on the view that economic criteria should be subservient to the expression of human potentialities, instead of the other way around. We need social innovations to deal with the fact that there is more to human life than health, education, entertainment, and leisure. Whether rich or poor, young or old, weak or strong, all people desire to be needed, recognized, and valued.

Points for Discussion

1. Where does Dubos explicitly state his thesis? What is the function of the first two paragraphs of the essay?

2. A writer of persuasive pieces often "establishes credentials" by giving information to convince you that he speaks from knowledge. How does Dubos meet that requirement?

3. Where and how does Dubos set limits around his subject, showing readers that he (and they) should not be sidetracked by related but tangential concerns?

4. Effective persuasion often depends on skillful refutation. Where does Dubos deal with possible counterarguments?

5. Find paragraphs in the essay that are arranged *deductively*—generalization plus proof; find others that are arranged *inductively*—examples lead to a conclusion about them.

6. After reading the entire essay, go back and reread the two opening paragraphs. Then construct a diagram to show the movement from the specific situation at Harvard to the problem with

worldwide implications. Comment on the effectiveness of the narrative opener.

7. Compare the final sentence of paragraph 3 and the final sentence in the essay. What challenge do both give to society as represented by the reader?

Suggestions for Writing

1. Create several syllogisms showing the logic that underlies Dubos' reasoning. Here is one for a start:

> Society needs the creative work of experienced people.
> People over sixty have creativity and experience.
> Therefore, society should utilize the work of people over sixty.

2. Set up a paper in which you state a thesis and show the logic in the form of a syllogism or an enthymeme such as this:

> Because society needs experienced workers, it should utilize the experience of people over sixty.

Then develop the paper as a strong argument for your position. Consider your credentials as "expert," the context and limits of the situation, tone to convince an identified audience, supporting specifics from which you argue, refutation of possible objections, and the logical structure of the whole. You might use a topic related to the work force. For instance, should government or society furnish on-the-job training for young people rather than holding them in school longer? What kind of training should that be? What is the effect of the minimum wage laws on youth employment? Where might senior citizens serve without displacing workers in the mid-years when financial responsibilities are greatest (a point in Dubos' essay)? What do social security benefits contribute to incentives to retire in spite of a worker's physical, psychological, and intellectual abilities to serve? All these are questions you might pursue and rephrase to show a thesis.

7

PAPERS THAT REVIEW AND ANALYZE READING

Sometimes a social scientist writes about the writing of others—a summary, an evaluation, or a survey of the works by several authors.

When you are asked to perform this kind of task in a college course, you are usually expected to demonstrate your ability to identify the main points (the essence) of your reading and to convey that substance in highly condensed prose. On the other hand, scholars use the same form for still other purposes: to keep a summary of their reading or to share in capsule form important information that other scholars may not have found or read. These analyses may take various forms, depending upon their purpose.

1. *The Abstract.* An abstract summarizes an article or longer piece of writing, pointing out the major ideas and conclusions and sometimes showing how these ideas are organized.

2. *The Book Review.* A book review goes beyond mere reporting of content to examine critically the value of the book within its field. A writer of a review must always consider audi-

ence. As you will discover, the selection offered here from *Reviews in American History* is written for a specialized audience, while the article about *infiltration* is written for the more general audience of the *Saturday Review*.

3. *The Annotated Bibliography.* As the label implies, the annotated bibliography is more than a list of authors and titles, although it is arranged as a formal bibliography appended to a research paper might be. Actually this bibliography is a list of publications with informative notes under each entry. In making such a list, you show that you have read thoroughly and can describe the content briefly, thus capturing the gist of the material for yourself and for others. Occasionally, you may add a sentence or two estimating the value of a selection.

4. *The Literature Review (A Form of the Bibliographic Essay).* As a student you may begin a paper by making a survey of the literature on your subject, including in that survey a brief discussion of the articles and books you find on the topic you are investigating. The "literature review" resembles the bibliographic essays that appear in some professional journals. There the writer not only collects and explains the materials, but evaluates them in order to help readers understand more about the area. In a narrower way, you do the same thing by bringing together the materials that provide a context for your project or paper. Such surveys or essays may be organized in different ways—chronologically, building to importance, comparing useful and less useful—as the material itself dictates.

The Abstract

From *Abstracts in Anthropology*

1153. Benn, David W. THE WOODLAND CERAMIC SEQUENCE IN THE CULTURE HISTORY OF NORTH-

EASTERN IOWA. Mid-Continental Journal of Archaeology. 1978, 3(2):215–283.

The FTD site is multicomponent Woodland village on the Iowa bank of the Mississippi River at Effigy Mounds National Monument. A large surface collection of ceramics and test excavations at the site are described. This material, plus data from four other Iowa sites, provides the data for an analysis of northeastern Iowa Woodland ceramic types. This paper pursues four objectives: (1) major pottery types are defined, (2) ceramic types and wares are sequentially related, (3) types are placed in their cultural context, and (4) regional development of Woodland culture is discussed.

1155. Carmichael, David L. PRELIMINARY ARCHAEOLOGICAL SURVEY OF ILLINOIS UPLANDS AND SOME BEHAVIORAL IMPLICATIONS. Mid-Continental Journal of Archaeology. 1977, 2(2):219–251.

Preliminary archaeological survey is discussed for two areas of glaciated uplands in central Illinois. Kettle depressions and related glacial features are seen as the loci for prehistoric occupations. Survey yielded seventy-nine upland sites, mostly representing short-term Archaic foraging camps. While some show evidence of hunting behavior, it is hypothesized that most of the sites were located for the exploitation of plant and small game resources available during the summer season. The model is evaluated in terms of its relation to modern ethnographic accounts of hunter-gatherer behavior.

From *America, History and Life*

17A:4441. Stein, Harry H. AMERICAN MUCKRAKERS AND MUCKRAKING: THE 50-YEAR SCHOLARSHIP. *Journalism Q. 1979 56(1): 9–17.* Surveys scholarly commentary on the investigative, muckraking literature that has appeared in magazines, newspapers, and novels in the United States since the late 19th century. The study of muckraking has dwelt on the content, rather than the influence, of muck-rakers' writings, and it has been motivated primarily by scholars' own concerns over social progress. Furthermore, this scholarship, plagued by conceptual weakness, has generated few debates over the findings or approaches to the study. 23 notes.

R. P. Sindermann, Jr.

17A:4444. Stewart, James B. and Hyclak, Thomas. ETHNIC-ITY AND ECONOMIC OPPORTUNITY. *Am. J. of Econ. and Sociol. 1979 38(3): 319–335.* In this analysis, data from the 1970 Census of Population are used to determine whether ethnic discrimination has been an important factor contributing to differential economic performance among immigrant groups. The measures of economic performance employed in this investigation are mean family income and the extent of poverty among cohorts of immigrants. Stepwise multiple regression analysis is used to select among possible influences on these measures of economic performance. Dummy variables are defined in a manner that allows the impact of discrimination on economic performance to be measured directly. The results of this analysis support the hypothesis that discrimination against particular groups has been a major contributing factor to differential economic performance among groups. As a consequence, we are led to reject the competing explanation of differential economic performance advanced by some analysts that differentials in economic performance merely reflect skill differentials among groups.

J

17A:4453. Vidyasova, L. IMPRESSIONS OF AMERICA. *Int. Affairs [USSR] 1978 (10): 101–110.* Decides that the United States is beset by racism (although there have been some improvements in the last two decades), resurgent "cold-warism" (excepting a few largely unheeded voices), unemployment, inflation, increasing taxation, crime, drugs, pornography, militarism, misinformation, foreign relations failures, loss of confidence in the Carter administration, etc.

THE ABSTRACT

. . . is an economical piece of writing—no wasted words
. . . includes two kinds of information:
1. a complete citation
2. summary of the work

Suggestions for Writing

1. Choose an article you have recently read about a subject in the social sciences and write an abstract of it; remember to be economical yet informative.

2. As a group project when your class is reading articles about one topic—such as Indians of the Midwest or American History since W.W. II, topics about which abstracts are included here—compile a booklet resembling *Abstracts in Anthropology* or a similar publication. Assign some of the articles to several students so that you can compare summaries and edit the abstracts to come up with the one which best captures the essence of the article. The finished product should be a valuable reference tool for students in your class and for other classes as well.

The Book Review

The two book reviews that follow are directed to quite different audiences. Telford Taylor writes for a general publication, the *Saturday Review,* but because of the nature of the nonfiction book that he discusses, his audience is likely to be the reader who is interested in political history. David Brody, a professor of history, writes for a professional journal. Both writers, however, provide examples of the clear analysis and evaluation that are part of good reviewing.

■ TELFORD TAYLOR

If It Weren't for Himmler . . .

A Review of *Infiltration,* by Albert Speer, translated by Joachim Neugrosschel, Macmillan, 368 pp., $15

No student of the Third Reich or World War II should fail to read this third and latest book by Albert Speer (Hitler's personal architect and, after 1942, his Minister for Armament and Munitions), for it offers a wealth of detail and insights that augment understanding of decision-making in the Third Reich. But the general reader will find it hard going. In large part this is Herr Speer's fault, but neither the translation nor the editing has made the author's work any easier to digest.

1

As published in Germany, the book is entitled *Der Sklaven Staat* ("The Slave State") and subtitled "My Conflicts With the SS." According to the publisher, Speer himself suggested the title *Infiltration* for the American edition. "It was well known that one or more of Himmler's confidential agents occupied important posts in every ministry." Speer tells us, and much of the book concerns the activities of these "agents" in keeping Himmler informed and in promoting Himmler's aims within the government branches to which they were ostensibly responsible. In a foreword, Speer explains that:

2

> My original plan was to write a book about German armaments in the Second World War. I thought it best to begin with the most difficult chapter, that of the role of the SS in the armaments industry and in the war economy. While preparing this chapter, I stumbled upon the writings of the SS Reichsführer [Himmler] in the Federal Archives at Koblenz. . . . The material was so rich that it soon exceeded the scope of a chapter: hence I resolved to devote my book to the failure of SS industrial efforts.

And that is what he did, dividing his book in four parts. The first deals with the conflict between Himmler's ambition to create an SS industrial empire with a significant share in war production, and Speer's decision, as Minister for Armament and Munitions, to rely primarily on private management—the

3

policy of "industrial self-responsibility." The second and third parts recount Himmler's machinations, deceits, threats, and other nefarious tactics in furtherance of his ambitions, together with his fantasies and failures. These included support of preposterous projects such as using fir tree roots for oil and dandelion roots for rubber, and his mishandling of the long-range rocket program.

4   The fourth, and much the most interesting part, concerns the conflict between those who, like Speer, wished to use the Jews as a source of skilled labor, and the hard-line exterminators, among whom Speer numbers Hitler himself but, surprisingly, not Himmler:

> The dichotomy in this man, who was in charge of total mass murder and yet who constantly went against extermination policies, leads me to suspect that he was not the driving force in the murder of the Jews. I would point instead to Hitler, Joseph Goebbels, and that hate-filled mover [*Motor,* in the German] Martin Bormann.

5   The translator's use of the bland unidiomatic "mover," rather than "engine" or (figuratively) "dynamo," is an example of one of his failings. His English is dull and often confusing. Thus an SS officer is described as "disillusioning" instead of "disillusioned"; a chapter is opaquely entitled "The Disorderly Concern," although the German *Konzern* denotes what we would call a corporate combine or conglomerate, an explanatory footnote tells the reader that "The Armaments Inspection, under General Waeger, summed up and evaluated the work of the Armaments Inspections," whereas an accurate translation is: "In the Armaments Department, under General Waeger, the work of the Armaments Inspectorates was surveyed and evaluated."

6   The translator is also hopelessly inconsistent and inaccurate in his rendering of German ranks and titles. Army and SS ranks are sometimes given in German, e.g., *Obergruppenführer,* and sometimes in English, usually inaccurately. Thus "Squad Commander" is the rendering of *Gruppenführer,* although a "squad" is a small unit usually commanded by a noncommissioned officer, while a *Gruppenführer* was the SS equivalent of a major general.

7   As for the substance of the book, it seems to me unfortu-

nate that the author did not carry out his original intention to deal with the German war economy and armament generally. Relying on private business management as he did, Speer must have observed much of the behavior and attitudes of German civilian leaders confronted with the opportunities, responsibilities, hazards, and tensions of those times. But except for an occasional reference—such as to the efforts of Hermann Bücher of the General Electric Company to protect his Jewish employees—there is nothing. The detail of Speer's many difficulties with Himmler and his minions, now nearly 40 years in the past, is oppressive, and at times gives the impression that Speer, like some German generals, is telling us that, but for the interference of Hitler, Himmler, and their ilk, Germany could have won the war.

Probably this was not intended, for there is no lack of *mea culpa* in these pages. "Even now at seventy-five, decades after the events, I am still haunted by the thought that I could have made decisions in a minute that would have improved the situation of the unfortunate inmates" [of labor camps]. Speer discusses perceptively the atrophy of moral sensitivity among the Nazi administrators, and their use of wartime necessities as a device to block awareness of the meaning of their acts and decisions: 8

> Until the fall of 1944 I was one of those who put all qualms aside when the needs of war demanded it. Also, I was so deeply in Hitler's thrall that I would have suppressed any comments merely because of a look of disapproval on his face. Yet how often Hitler had threatened the Jews with annihilation. For me, the tens of thousands who disappeared into the ghettos were lost to the labor process. . . . Today, forty years later, it is incomprehensible to me that I thought the number of tanks produced more important than the vanished victims of racism.

Not quite all of the intended victims vanished. As Germany's military situation deteriorated, the demands for workers grew ever louder, and there was open resistance in the army supply agencies to the deportation to extermination camps of Jews whose industrial skills were contributing substantially to the output of munitions and other war material. General von Gienanth, the Military Commander in occupied Poland, was too outspoken and lost his job. By 1944 some Jews were being 9 brought back from Auschwitz to factories where the labor needs were especially urgent.

10   Furthermore, administration of the "final solution," like that of other SS programs, was far from uniformly efficient. For example, in the portions of Poland annexed to the Reich (the Warthegau and Upper Silesia), Jews continued to be employed until the approach of the Soviet armies in the fall of 1944. Aware of current "literature" denouncing the Holocaust as a hoax, Speer warns that these departures from the extermination policy lend no support to the arguments of "right-wing extremists," and endorses Raoul Hilberg's conclusion that three million Polish Jews were murdered.

11   *Infiltration* is indeed a mine of information and insight. Unfortunately, it reads like a spontaneous monologue spoken to a former colleague. Names of persons well known to top officials of the Third Reich, but meaningful today only to students of those times, are used throughout with little by way of identification or reminder. If ever a book cried out for glossaries of names, ranks, and offices it is this one, but the editors have given no help.

12   The book rambles on in a manner wholly uncongenial to the nature of the subject. Once again blaming Himmler, Speer explains:

> The disorderliness of Himmler's empire and the unsystematic nature of the material reflect the character of the events and not an inability on my part to put things in order. In short, the seeming disarray of the material in this book arises from the disorder inherent in that empire.

Like shortcomings of this review may similarly be attributed to the "disarray" *(Unordnung)* of Herr Speer's book.

■ DAVID BRODY

Taking on the Left

Aileen S. Kraditor. *The Radical Persuasion, 1890–1917: Aspects of the Intellectual History and the Historiography of Three American Radical Organizations.* Baton Rouge: Louisiana State University Press, 1981. ix + 381 pp. Notes and index. $37.50 (cloth), $12.95 (paper).

"Why Is There No Socialism in the United States?", Werner   1
Sombart entitled his famous article of 1905. His own answer stressed high living standards and the equalitarian social order. Others have added to the list, until in 1971 one scholar was able to enumerate twenty-eight distinct "obstacles" to the triumph of socialism in America. Stuff and nonsense, says Aileen S. Kraditor in this pugnacious book. Before talking about barriers, one ought logically to ascertain whether the American worker—John Q. Worker to Kraditor—was susceptible to radical appeals. The answer she gives back is a resounding "No." And from that conclusion she launches her reassessment of American radicalism between 1890 and 1917 and a ringing attack on American radical historiography.

This book is a notable example of how scholarly currents   2
circulate within the historical profession. Kraditor is, of course, an intellectual historian, known for her studies of the ideas of the woman suffrage and abolitionist movements. This book was projected as the third in her series on dissenting causes, focusing on the Socialist Labor party, the Socialist party, and the IWW. By now, however, she had fallen under the influence of the new social history. The world she finds in this scholarship scarcely corresponds to the abstractions of class struggle and a unified capitalist order—a "System"—that she sees in the rhetoric of the radical movements. Her social history reading yields for her two ruling concepts about American working class life. First, workers had autonomous and satisfying "belief-systems" that were rooted in ethnicity, community, family, and so on. Second, the larger society, exploitative

as it might have been, gave them the "social space" to live in accordance with those belief-systems.

3   Kraditor conjures up the image of "the millions of anonymous John Q. Workers who went to work every day and went home to their families every night and could never see the radicals' ideology as a better explanation for their lives than the ones that they subscribed to and that made their experiences meaningful to them" (p. 53). No proselytizers, radical or otherwise, were likely to make many converts, she argues, "simply because, unless a person's belief system has disintegrated in the face of experiences that it cannot accommodate, his most deeply held beliefs are not open to challenge from any quarter" (p. 16). Kraditor's book is not about working class culture. (What she has to say in substance on that score, drawn from extensive reading in the social-history literature, is properly relegated to an epilogue.) Rather, it serves as a base-line for reconsidering the history of American radicalism.

4   What strikes her, above all, is that the radicals "perceived [John Q. Worker] falsely." This was because their theories "had been formulated aprioristically. . . . It was the gap between the abstraction they called the Worker and the real John Q. Worker that, in the final analysis, defeated them" (p. 33). These conclusions are derived from, or at least are much buttressed by, extensive reading in the contemporary records of the SLP, the SP, and the IWW. All three conceived of themselves as a vanguard, privy to the scientific laws of social development, prophetic of the future, and locked in mortal combat with an omnipotent capitalist adversary. The prize over which the two sides contended was the working class, sometimes seen in radical rhetoric as heroic, more often as asleep, an inert mass, but about to awaken and to follow the radicals on to the barricades. The implications of radical "system-building" are spelled out most fully in Kraditor's treatment of racial and women's issues. These could not be accommodated within radical theory and were routinely dismissed with the assurance that racial and sexual injustice would disappear with capitalism. They were, in effect, left to individual judgment or idiosyncracy, reflective of the "private sphere" rather than "public sphere" in which radicals located their struggle. This inability to come to grips with racial and sexual exploitation, to treat

them as central concerns, Kraditor takes as powerful evidence
of the intellectual blinders on the radical mind.

Kraditor reserves her sharpest words for the historians of   5
American radicalism. They have, in her view, suffered from
the same intellectual afflictions as the movements they studied.
Kraditor devotes an entire chapter to specifying the fallacies
of radical historiography—that it has been counteractual and
tautological, antihistorical, teleological, and reductionist. All
of this follows the Sombartian mode, which can only ascribe
to "obstacles" the fact that the course of American working
class history did not obey the laws of Marxian theory. Old Left
historians have shown little interest in the real world of the
worker. The New Left, while not guilty of this omission, has
proceeded from the assumption that working class self-activity
was by definition radical. "Neither treats John Q. Worker's
life and belief system as having had meaning other than in relation to capitalist oppression and the historically assigned mission to destroy it" (p. 2). The alternative Kraditor proposes
is, of course, the empirical approach of the social historians,
"who do not begin with the 'system' paradigm . . . , who do
not search the data primarily for seeds of revolt or of the ideological hegemony of the ruling class," but who are prepared
to see and weigh working class life in all its dimensions, including those that fall outside the structures of economic and political power (p. 3).

This is strong medicine and, in certain ways, health-giving.   6
It can only be beneficial to have Kraditor's rigorous critique
of shoddy radical scholarship. Many a historian will read her
strictures with the uneasy thought, "Who, me?" There is
much to be said, too, for her efforts to reorient radical historiography so that, instead of being the lenses through which the
past is seen, radical movements become the object of study.
Her book makes an important contribution on that score. The
chapters devoted to "Perceptions" by the radicals of John Q.
Worker, of nonwhites and women, and of their own role as
radicals are richly detailed, laced with quotations, interspersed
by "Documentary Excursuses" on particular issues, and
backed up by a more massive collection of evidence deposited
at the Boston University Library. So far, so good. The reader
may want to make allowances for her hyperbole, but the basic

case she makes is strongly argued and solidly grounded. Unfortunately, Kraditor does not confine herself to the realm of ideas. She goes on to a full-scale reinterpretation of American radicalism in the Progressive era and, in so doing, overreaches herself.

7   The years 1890–1917, she argues, were a "shake-up period" in American history, a time of transition into advanced industrialism. This turbulent age produced two needs that the radical organizations were able to meet. The first was for "surrogate communities" for "mavericks from their own communities," "people whose inherited belief-systems had lost meaning for them as individuals" (p. 22). As in her explanation for the resistance of the working class majority, so here Kraditor injects a strong dose of psychology in accounting for the successes of radicalism. Its constituency was confined primarily to people with "the need to systematize inner and outer reality" (p. 277), seekers for an overarching theory that "gave the answers and obviated the need for empirical study" (p. 275). Insofar as there is an explanation for the intellectual stance of American radicalism, it comes down to the uses that outlook had for meeting the psychological needs of the nation's true believers. The second function of the Left, likewise evoked by the shake-up period, was to help the nation through its moral crisis. The radicals, Kraditor suggests, tested the boundaries of the country's norms and values, and in so doing expanded the options "from which a society hungry for adaptive changes could choose" (p. 88).

8   This interpretation, insofar as it is empirically grounded, derives from a close reading and logical exegesis of the rhetoric of American radicalism. The methodological problem comes down to this: can such an exercise form the basis for understanding a social movement? Consider, for example, the dilemma Kraditor finds in the IWW: "it could be a revolutionary organization or a union, but not both" (p. 26). As a theoretical construct, perhaps so, but as a functioning movement, why not? The syndicalist rhetoric had, in fact, powerful uses: it invested the IWW with the dynamic it needed to reach and mobilize the exploited Western workers. Not an intractable ideological dilemma, but state repression killed the IWW. And what of the role that Socialists played in the trade-union

movement? Is it of no account, of no significance, in estimating
the SLP into the 1890s and the SP thereafter, that Socialists
led and had large followings in many AFL unions? How is the
Socialist presence in Milwaukee and other cities to be accommodated within Kraditor's framework? Or the part they
played in forming the Non-Partisan League and the Minnesota
Farmer-Labor Party? The acid test is her success at treating
the SLP, SP, and IWW as a single phenomenon. Kraditor discusses at length their differences, but underlying she perceives
a common intellectual outlook. On the touchstone issue of
race, however, she must confront the fact that the IWW was
staunchly equalitarian. Aside from the lame suggestion that
the IWW "consciously cultivated iconoclasm," Kraditor can
only explain this by abandoning the basic premise of her argument. It was a practical matter, she concedes, for a movement
trying to organize the unskilled to advocate racial equality,
and equally expedient for the SLP and the SP to accommodate
to the prejudices of their political constituencies. This conces-
sion does not, however, seem to have raised any doubts about
the centrality of her common intellectual pattern for understanding the SLP, SP, and IWW as functioning movements.

Then there is the meaning that Kraditor finds in her social-history reading. For purposes of analyzing rhetoric and
historiography, it would have been sufficient to establish the
gap between radical abstractions and the complex working
class world uncovered by recent research. But she goes on to
sweeping conclusions as to the conservative nature of that
world. Was it true that the "belief-systems" of ethnic communities were so uniformly and sturdily resistant to socialism?
Kraditor acknowledges the Jews and Finns as exceptions, but
in fact ethnic identity was commonly the basis for radical organization—hence the growing importance of the for-
eign-language federations within the Socialist party. The En-
glish-speaking sector of the working class gets short shrift in
Kraditor's accounting. It would have come as a surprise to Eugene Debs, who could never bear to move away from Terre
Haute, that he had become a Socialist out of his need for a
surrogate community. Debs's career suggests another troubling problem with the way Kraditor conceives of the larger
setting: she denies the possibility that radicalism might have

been a rational response to naked repression or exploitation. There is thus no room in her analysis for Melvyn Dubofsky's explanation of the turn to socialism by the Western Federation of Miners or for the following the SP had among the Oklahoma tenant farmers that James R. Green has studied in his recent *Grass-Roots Socialism* (1978).

10   Something of a paradox pervades this book. Kraditor puts forth social history as a model for how to study American radicalism, but she in no wise adopts the model for herself. Celebrating the cautious empirical approach of the new scholarship, she leaps to generalizations that will astonish its practitioners. She applauds their multi-leveled probing into working class life, then interprets the radical movements through the single dimension of their rhetoric. *The Radical Persuasion* will prove valuable as an historiographical critique and as a study of radical thought. While it calls for a reorientation of radical historiography, the book is unlikely to be the starting point for that future work. There is more to the history of American radical movements than as way stations for the nation's alienated or as purveyors of daring propositions for the consideration of the larger society.

THE BOOK REVIEW

. . . evaluates a book in light of its contribution to the field
. . . usually includes specialized information when written for professional social scientists, but tends to omit that information when the audience is more general
. . . uses details and language suitable to the audience for whom it is written

Points for Discussion

1. What reveals that both writers are authorities on the areas represented by the books they consider?

2. What is the effect of quoting from the books themselves? Comment on the ways the writers work quotations into their own writing.

3. Show that by reading these reviews you know the thesis of each book. How do the reviewers let you know something about tone and style in each book?

4. Where do these reviewers offer criticism or express reservations? What are their final evaluations and where do they reveal their opinions?

Suggestions for Writing

1. Consult the *Book Review Digest* and report to your class about the benefits you might gain from familiarity with that reference tool.

2. Read a current book on a topic in the social sciences—one of your choice or one that is assigned—and write two reviews: direct one to a specialized audience, perhaps your classmates and teacher who are reading the same material; direct the other to a general audience, perhaps the readers of your city's daily newspaper.

3. As a class project, have everyone in the group collect several (two or three) reviews of the same book, using either magazines for the general public or special journals in your field of study as sources. Determine from reading those reviews which books you think you want to read or which might be most useful to you. If the reviews are not helpful or if you consider them misleading, report that to the class.

The Annotated Bibliography

The annotations here are the first few in a much longer list from *Writing in Subject Matter Fields* by Eva M. Burkett. These entries offer a model for annotation and bibliography form, but you might well consult the entire book to find many useful and interesting suggestions related to your area of study.

■ EVA M. BURKETT

From "The Writing of History"

1. Adams, James Truslow. "My Methods as a Historian," in *Writing for Love or Money.* Edited by Norman Cousins. New York: Longmans, Green, and Company, 1949, pp. 176–185.

Adams says that history is not a science since history is personal and science is impersonal. He believes that the philosophy of history is a combination of the great man theory and the influence of social forces. He thinks that the qualities of mind required to write sound history are more akin to those of the artist than to those of the scientist, but this does not mean that history should be written as fiction. "The historian must stick to his facts as he finds them, but in finding them and in weaving them together he needs not only the scientist's love of truth but delicate intuition, experience of men and affairs, and other qualities a scientist does not need in his work."

2. Bean, Walton. "Is Clio a Muse?" *Sewanee Review,* XLV (1937), 419–426.

Bean welcomes the broadening of the scope of history to include the whole economic, social, and cultural part of man. He says that it is difficult to distinguish between academic social history and popular art—literature, the dance, painting, etc.—and since Clio is a Muse, there should not be quarreling between historians and artists.

3. Beard, Charles A. "Written History as an Act of Faith," *American Historical Review,* XXXIX (January, 1934), 219–229.

Beard attacks the theory of history as objective actuality. History, he says, is thought about past actuality for total actuality is chaos. The historian must make choices and the extent of his influence depends upon the correctness of his decisions. He does not exclude the scientific method but thinks that it has its limitations.

4. Becker, Carl L. "Detachment and the Writing of History" (1910), in *Ten Contemporary Thinkers.* Edited by Victor E. Amend and Leo T. Hendricks. New York: The Free Press of Glencoe, 1964, pp. 220–237. Originally appeared in the *Atlantic Monthly,* CVI (October, 1910).

Becker thinks that complete detachment in historical writing is not likely and would produce few or worthless histories since the "really detached mind is a dead mind." It is the business of the historian to arrive at concepts and to select the facts that are important for the concepts. "When old landmarks are being washed away, and old foundations are crumbling to dust, it is doubtless useful and necessary to conceive the historical reality as continuous, causally connected, and changing only in response to forces largely remote from purposive human will."

5. Becker, Carl L. "What Are Historical Facts?" in *Ideas of History.* Edited by Ronald H. Nash. New York: E. P. Dutton and Company, Inc., II (1969), 177–193.

Becker asks and answers three questions: What is the historical fact? Where is the historical fact? When is the historical fact? He defines the historical fact as the affirmation about an event, a symbol that enables us to recreate it imaginatively. "The historical fact is in someone's mind or it is nowhere." The actual occurrence has passed. If the historical fact is present, imaginatively, in someone's mind, then it is now, a part of the present.

6. Blake, Nelson Manfred. "How to Learn History from Sinclair Lewis and Other Unknown Sources," in *American Character and Culture. Some Twentieth Century Perspectives.* Edited by John A. Hague. De Land, Florida: Everett/Edwards Press, Inc., 1964, pp. 33–47.

Blake discusses the relation of literature and other arts—architecture, painting, music, dance—to history. He says that the student of history must apply the same standards of historical criticism to these arts that he would apply to other historical sources: learn about the author or artist and why he created the work, determine the reliability of the artist's sources, consider the probable truth or accuracy of particular statements. He says that every great work of literature and art has both a timely quality and a timeless quality. The historian is interested in the data that the work reveals about the age in which it was created. Blake applies the principles he sets up to a discussion of *Elmer Gantry* as a document of social history.

7. Burnette, O. Lawrence, Jr. "Newspapers as Historical Evidence," in *Beneath the Footnote. A Guide to the Use and Preservation of American Historical Sources.* Madison: The State Historical Society of Wisconsin, 1969, pp. 265–284.
Burnette says that the portions of newspapers most used by historians are editorials, illustrations, and advertisements. The historian must apply the same tests to information found in newspapers that he uses to evaluate other historical material.

8. Gay, Peter. "Style in History," *The American Scholar,* XLIII (Spring, 1974), 225–236.
This essay is an introduction to Gay's book, *Style in History,* 1974, which centers on the style of Gibbon, Ranke, Macaulay, and Burckhart. Since the historian is both a professional writer and a professional reader, Gay says that the historian is under pressure to become a stylist, for he must give pleasure as well as information. He discusses the historian's use of various literary styles: emotional style, professional style, and his style of thinking. Gay says that style must be learned since writers are not born stylists but must fashion their style through effort. "It [style] is only in part a gift or talent; beyond that it is an act of will and an exercise of intelligence. It is the tribute that expressiveness pays to discipline." Gay says that style gives access to a writer's private, psychological world, and that study of the style of historians provides insight into their craft or profession as well as to culture itself.

9. Green, Constance McLaughlin. "The Value of Local History," in *The Cultural Approach to History.* Edited by Caroline F. Ware. Port Washington, N.Y.: Kennikat Press, Inc. Copyright 1940 by Columbia University Press, pp. 275–286.
Green thinks that American life should be studied from

the bottom instead of from the top. Therefore the writing and study of American local history is of primary importance. She suggests several kinds of studies involving local materials that would make contributions to American cultural history. But she warns about some of the difficulties involved in obtaining authentic local material.

10. Highet, Gilbert. "The Historian's Job," in *People, Places and Books.* New York: Oxford University Press, 1953, pp. 176–184.

Highet says that the historian's job is to tell us about the past, but this is a difficult if not impossible task. He discusses three types of history: memories set down by an eyewitness; reconstruction, a recreation from scant records; imaginative descriptions, selection and compression of facts from a large amount of data.

11. Kennan, George F. "The Experience of Writing History," *The Virginia Quarterly Review,* XXXVI (1960), 205–214.

Kennan discusses the difficulties encountered in writing history: the struggle to be objective since the describing of historical events is partly "an act of the creative imagination of the writer"; the study and writing of history as a lonely occupation; and the uncertainty whether what one does is worth doing and whether it will ever be read if it is.

AN ANNOTATED BIBLIOGRAPHY

. . . cites item in bibliographic form:
alphabetical arrangement by author's last name
book or article title
source or publisher
date
pages, where appropriate
. . . follows (somewhat more briefly) pattern of abstract
. . . occasionally includes brief evaluation or comment on usefulness of the item, usually by comparing it to others in the list

Suggestions for Writing

Compile an annotated bibliography related to a topic you are studying. Although the bibliography itself may be an assignment for which you receive class credit, there are several other purposes it may serve:

- a summary of your reading
- an opportunity to begin exploring a topic for further reading and writing
- background for a panel discussion or debate
- preparation for an oral history project (see pages 115–120)

The Literature Review

The following excerpts from two papers, one by a teacher writing for a professional publication, and the other by a student writing a class assignment, illustrate the review of literature offered to provide context or background.

■ NAN BAUER MAGLIN

From "The Demoralization Paper"

... As a base for this discussion, I will quickly synthesize two important articles: "Expansion and Exclusion: A History of Women in Higher Education," by Patricia Albjerg Graham, recently appointed dean of the Graduate School of Education at Harvard, and "Inside the Clockwork of Male Careers" by Arlie Russell Hochschild.[1]

Graham explains that the years between 1875 and 1925 were a good time for women in higher education, for it was during that period that "a strikingly heterogeneous array of acceptable and praiseworthy [educational] institutions existed in America" (p. 761), allowing women to enter and participate in a variety of ways. By World War II, however, a new monolith, the research university, emerged triumphant, and the "heterogeneous array" vanished. Not only were women not concentrated in the new institutions or allowed much access to them, but the teaching skills that were associated with women and "that characterized the revered professors of past generations" were no longer respected (p. 769). With this change came a new way of judging careers, which valued not only what you did but when you did it. And for a career in the university, like one in athletics, achievement is expected in the early thirties. As Hochschild outlines it:

> The academic career is founded on some peculiar assumptions about the relation between doing work and competing with others, competing with others and getting credit for work, getting credit and building a reputation, building a reputation and doing it while you're young, doing it while you're young and hoarding scarce time and minimizing family life, minimizing family life and leaving it to your wife. (p. 49)

> The career-self experiences time as linear and the career itself as a measured line, other parts of the self following along. Time

is objectified in the academic vita, which grows longer with each
article and book, and not with each vegetable garden, camping
trip, political meeting, or child. . . . What is won for the garden
is lost to the vita. (p. 62)

3   Who then would want Mira of *The Women's Room,* who
returns late in life to the university? But how even can I, for
example, at forty, with a four-year-old, keep up my career and
my child? As Hochschild keeps emphasizing, this should not
be perceived as simply a "role problem" or a "woman's problem," that is, one in which each woman must decide whether
to have children or not or how to be a wife, a mother, and
have a traditional career. Instead it should be understood as
a systemic problem in which the university is structurally in
opposition to the values and lifestyle that women in this society most often embody.[2] When Hochschild compared academic talk to women's talk, I was most struck by what this
means. "Women's talk is discriminated against for it is uncom-
petitive, undressed, non-product, supportive talk" (p. 66). I
began to understand the silence of women students, of myself
at English department meetings and at MLA conventions.

4   The hostility and discrimination against women is intensified when women do women's studies in the university, that
is, when in their lives and work they are feminists (and it is
further complicated when they are, for example, black feminists or lesbian feminists). These women are told that their
work is not good enough, is not "seminal," is not "hard" research, is too interdisciplinary, too political, too descriptive.
But women's studies at its best has been interdisciplinary,
based on a collective effort designed to contribute to the
group, to a sense of community. It has of necessity been descriptive, working out the taxonomy of centuries of ignored
phenomena. It has found politics a necessity in order to win
allowances to do its proper work.[3]

5   Hochschild writes that "academic life reflects a market-
place. Ideas become products that are 'owned' or 'borrowed'
or 'stolen' from their owners, products that through talk and
in print rise and fall in market value, and products that have
become alienated from their producers" (p. 66). While
women's studies unfortunately now often reflects this same hi-

erarchical, individualistic, competitive system, this is not the value system through which women's studies grew. . . .

Notes

1. Hochschild's essay is cited in footnote 5 [not included in this excerpt]; Graham's is published in *Signs*. 3 (1978), 759–73.

2. Hochschild says that "nearly half the women who remain in academic life solve the problem by not marrying or not rearing children at all" (p. 69).

3. See Linda Gordon, "A Socialist View of Women's Studies: A Reply to the Editorial, Volume 1, Number 1," *Signs,* 1 (1975), 559–66.

■ ADA SKYLES

From "Problem-Solving Interventions in Treating Negative Effects of Stepmothers"

1   Historically, the stepfamily was the result of the death of one
parent (Cherlin, 1978). The new spouse was expected to assume parental responsibilities out of love for the partner. Most
of the time the stepfather was ignored and his role in the family was minimal (McCormick, 1974; Rallings, 1976). The
stepfather, whose parental role was undefined, enjoyed positive regard for assuming economic responsibility for a family
that was not his. The stepmother, on the other hand, had to
contend with the explicit expectations of motherhood (Mad-
dox, 1975) and with negative stereotypes (Pfleger, 1947).

2   The current situation of stepmothers has not improved.
Our society expects the stepmother to have instant love for
the stepchildren (Schulman, 1972), an immediate knowledge
of parenting skills (Capaldi, 1979), and the ability to be both
wife and mother (Bernard, 1956). She is to occupy a central
position in the family although she lacks the power base for
achieving this goal (Capaldi, 1979). Whether the natural
mother is alive or not, the stepmother usually begins as an out-
sider entering an on-going group (Bernard, 1956). As a consequence, she has to be prepared for rejection, hostility, jeal-
ousy and criticism from others. She is often surrounded by a
judgmental atmosphere in which people are prone to exaggerate any mistake she makes. Thus, behavior which is acceptable
in natural mothers is often criticized in stepmothers; they must
be better than natural mothers to be successful in their role
(Bernard, 1956).

3   Most research studies, concerned with the welfare of the
child in the stepfamily, have compared stepfathers with step-

mothers. Jessie Bernard (1956) found that stepmothers were less likely than stepfathers to have an affectionate relationship with their stepchildren. She attributed this finding to the fact that stepmothers usually have more time with the children and therefore encounter more opportunities for disharmony. Bowerman and Irish (1962) studied 2145 stepchildren. Their conclusions were that the homes with step-relationships were more likely to have stress, ambivalence and low cohesiveness than were homes of nuclear families. The stepmother role, they found, was more difficult because society gives assistance to the male stepparent and males are therefore more likely to find social acceptance in the step role. The stepchildren believed that the stepparents were less fair to them (stepmothers discriminated more than stepfathers) and that stepmothers approximated real mothers less than stepfathers resembled real fathers.

Fast and Cain (1966) who studied the families of 50 step-   4
children, also felt that the stepfamily was particularly vulnerable to stress and breakdown, and, most importantly, that the stepparent could never totally succeed as a parent. However strong the stepparent's determination to be a parent and however skillful the efforts, social norms, they concluded, made it inappropriate for the stepparent to completely assume the parent role. They cautioned that the stepparent must be prepared to share the role with the natural parent. The stepparent was described as having contradictory functions as a parent, stepparent and non-parent simultaneously.

Later studies confirmed some of the earlier findings. Lu-   5
cille Duberman (1975) studied 88 families. She also found that the stepfather, rather than the stepmother, was more likely to create and maintain good relationships with the stepchild. Duberman (1973) noted that the stepmother has the more difficult role because of proximity to the child and the nature of her role. Messinger (1976), basing her conclusions on 70 interviews with stepfamily couples, described the couples' underestimation of the emotional upheaval involved in becoming a stepfamily and the role ambiguity and role overload they experienced. They found relationships with the ex-spouse a major difficulty and a cause of marital stresses. Margaret Draughon (1975) suggested three role identifications

from which the stepmother might choose: "primary" mother, the "other" mother and the "friend." She commented that one of the most difficult aspects of being a stepmother was that no social guidelines exist for the relationship between the step-mother and stepchild.

6   Two studies have focused exclusively on stepmothers. Janice Nadler (1976) investigated the psychological stress of stepmothers by comparing part-time, full-time and natural mothers. She concluded that part-time and full-time stepmothers experienced more feelings of anxiety, depression, and anger than natural mothers did, and she hypothesized that this psychological stress emanated from the stepmother's lack of support within the family and society. Irene Sardanis-Zimmerman (1977) compared 35 stepmothers and 35 natural mothers. She found that while stepmothers tended to be slightly more self-confident than natural mothers, they were also more ambivalent towards their stepchildren and felt more jealous of them.

7   The literature is specific about how the stepmother is at risk for emotional disturbance and distress. Unfortunately, the literature is not specific about the means by which the step-mother is to be helped. In particular, it suggests no treatment interventions to assist the stepmother who is experiencing low self esteem, negative self-statements, and depression as a reaction to her family situation.

THE LITERATURE REVIEW

. . . incorporates in the text of a paper a review of related articles and books

. . . provides accurate citation and all necessary documentation using bibliography or footnotes as stipulated by course work or publication

. . . evaluates literature reviewed to show relevance to general topic

. . . gives necessary authority (background) of writers cited (information about research, methods, and so on)

. . . exhibits variety of style, clarity, and brevity

Points for Discussion

1. Explain how Maglin and Skyles each relates the articles or books she reviews to the subject of her article or paper. What can you as reader tell about the importance of the materials cited?

2. What is the effect of quoting directly as Maglin does? Show two ways in which she incorporates the quotations into her own writing.

3. How does Maglin make use of *summary?* Using one paragraph from the selection here, mark off sentences that summarize and other sentences that are Maglin's comments to develop her topic.

4. What reveals that Skyles is *selecting* rather than summarizing material from her sources? What is the purpose of such focused reading and analysis here?

5. Find methods by which both writers avoid repetition of words such as "The author says," a phrase commonly used in writing about literature. What evidence can you find of the authority or credentials of the writers reviewed?

6. How do the methods of citation in these reviews differ? What is the importance of dates in Skyles' paper?

Suggestions for Writing

1. As you prepare for writing a paper, read two or three works (books, sections of books, articles) on your topic. Keep notes and bibliographical information; incorporate comments about these works and their relationship to your topic in your paper. You may or may not place your review in the introductory section of your paper.

2. From reading articles assigned as part of your work in any course, discover the use writers make of related literature. In a paragraph or two of analysis show how and why such references strengthen scholarly work; or present your conclusions in a discussion with others in your class.

Part Three

| LONGER
| PROJECTS

8

DIFFERENT VIEWS OF THE SAME SUBJECT

A writer is always asking questions: *Why* am I writing this particular piece? *What* am I writing about? *What* is my attitude toward this subject? *How* do I sound on paper? *To whom* am I writing? Different answers to each question result in various kinds of writing. If, for example, you intend to persuade a general audience of your view on a subject, your paper will be different from what it would be if you decide to explore a topic for a specialized audience. Or if you decide to use a formal tone for a term paper, you will avoid language which might be appropriate for a letter to a friend but not necessarily for a paper in a sociology course.

The following selections represent different writing about the same subject. All the articles deal with poverty, but they differ considerably in purpose, tone, audience, and writers' attitudes. Examine each piece carefully, watching the ways in which the authors choose language, marshal evidence, and write to their particular, identifiable audiences. As you read, ask yourself the *why, what, how,* and *to whom* questions that the writers probably faced as they composed. And as you write, you should ask similar questions about your papers.

OSCAR LEWIS

Anthropologist Oscar Lewis, who died in 1970, wrote this
essay for *Scientific American* in 1966.

The Culture of Poverty

Poverty and the so-called war against it provide a principal
theme for the domestic program of the present Administration. In the midst of a population that enjoys unexampled material well-being—with the average annual family income ex-
ceeding $7,000—it is officially acknowledged that some 18
million families, numbering more than 50 million individuals,
live below the $3,000 "poverty line." Toward the improve-
ment of the lot of these people some $1,600 million of Federal
funds are directly allocated through the Office of Economic
Opportunity, and many hundreds of millions of additional dollars flow indirectly through expanded Federal expenditures in
the fields of health, education, welfare and urban affairs.

Along with the increase in activity on behalf of the poor
indicated by these figures there has come a parallel expansion
of publication in the social sciences on the subject of poverty.
The new writings advance the same two opposed evaluations
of the poor that are to be found in literature, in proverbs and
in popular sayings throughout recorded history. Just as the
poor have been pronounced blessed, virtuous, upright, serene, independent, honest, kind and happy, so contemporary
students stress their great and neglected capacity for self-help,
leadership and community organization. Conversely, as the
poor have been characterized as shiftless, mean, sordid, violent, evil and criminal, so other students point to the irrevers-
ibly destructive effects of poverty on individual character and
emphasize the corresponding need to keep guidance and control of poverty projects in the hands of duly constituted authorities. This clash of viewpoints reflects in part the infighting
for political control of the program between Federal and local
officials. The confusion results also from the tendency to focus
study and attention on the personality of the individual victim

1

2

of poverty rather than on the slum community and family and from the consequent failure to distinguish between poverty and what I have called the culture of poverty.

3   The phrase is a catchy one and is used and misused with some frequency in the current literature. In my writings it is the label for a specific conceptual model that describes in positive terms a subculture of Western society with its own structure and rationale, a way of life handed on from generation to generation along family lines. The culture of poverty is not just a matter of deprivation or disorganization, a term signifying the absence of something. It is a culture in the traditional anthropological sense in that it provides human beings with a design for living, with a ready-made set of solutions for human problems, and so serves a significant adaptive function. This style of life transcends national boundaries and regional and rural-urban differences within nations. Wherever it occurs, its practitioners exhibit remarkable similarity in the structure of their families, in interpersonal relations, in spending habits, in their value systems and in their orientation in time.

4   Not nearly enough is known about this important complex of human behavior. My own concept of it has evolved as my work has progressed and remains subject to amendment by my own further work and that of others. The scarcity of literature on the culture of poverty is a measure of the gap in communication that exists between the very poor and the middle-class personnel—social scientists, social workers, teachers, physicians, priests and others—who bear the major responsibility for carrying out the antipoverty programs. Much of the behavior accepted in the culture of poverty goes counter to cherished ideals of the larger society. In writing about "multiproblem" families social scientists thus often stress their instability, their lack of order, direction and organization. Yet, as I have observed them, their behavior seems clearly patterned and reasonably predictable. I am more often struck by the inexorable repetitiousness and the iron entrenchment of their lifeways.

5   The concept of the culture of poverty may help to correct misapprehensions that have ascribed some behavior patterns of ethnic, national or regional groups as distinctive characteristics. For example, a high incidence of common-law marriage

and of households headed by women has been thought to be distinctive of Negro family life in this country and has been attributed to the Negro's historical experience of slavery. In actuality it turns out that such households express essential traits of the culture of poverty and are found among diverse peoples in many parts of the world and among peoples that have had no history of slavery. Although it is now possible to assert such generalizations, there is still much to be learned about this difficult and affecting subject. The absence of intensive anthropological studies of poor families in a wide variety of national contexts—particularly the lack of such studies in socialist countries—remains a serious handicap to the formulation of dependable cross-cultural constants of the culture of poverty.

My studies of poverty and family life have centered largely in Mexico. On occasion some of my Mexican friends have suggested delicately that I turn to a study of poverty in my own country. As a first step in this direction I am currently engaged in a study of Puerto Rican families. Over the past three years my staff and I have been assembling data on 100 representative families in four slums of Greater San Juan and some 50 families of their relatives in New York City.

Our methods combine the traditional techniques of sociology, anthropology and psychology. This includes a battery of 19 questionnaires, the administration of which requires 12 hours per informant. They cover the residence and employment history of each adult; family relations; income and expenditure; complete inventory of household and personal possessions; friendship patterns, particularly the *compadrazgo,* or godparent, relationship that serves as a kind of informal social security for the children of these families and establishes special obligations among the adults; recreational patterns; health and medical history; politics; religion; world view and "cosmopolitanism." Open-end interviews and psychological tests (such as the thematic apperception test, the Rorschach test and the sentence-completion test) are administered to a sampling of this population.

All this work serves to establish the context for close-range study of a selected few families. Because the family is a small social system, it lends itself to the holistic approach of anthropology. Whole-family studies bridge the gap between the conceptual extremes of the culture at one pole and of the individual at the other, making possible observation of both culture and personality as they are interrelated in real life. In a large metropolis such as San Juan or New York the family is the natural unit of study.

9   Ideally our objective is the naturalistic observation of the life of "our" families, with a minimum of intervention. Such intensive study, however, necessarily involves the establishment of deep personal ties. My assistants include two Mexicans whose families I had studied; their "Mexican's-eye view" of the Puerto Rican slum has helped to point up the similarities and differences between the Mexican and Puerto Rican subcultures. We have spent many hours attending family parties, wakes and baptisms, responding to emergency calls, taking people to the hospital, getting them out of jail, filling out applications for them, hunting apartments with them, helping them to get jobs or to get on relief. With each member of these families we conduct tape-recorded interviews, taking down their life stories and their answers to questions on a wide variety of topics. For the ordering of our material we undertake to reconstruct, by close interrogation, the history of a week or more of consecutive days in the lives of each family, and we observe and record complete days as they unfold. The first volume to issue from this study is to be published next month under the title of *La Vida, a Puerto Rican Family in the Culture of Poverty—San Juan and New York* (Random House).

10   There are many poor people in the world. Indeed, the poverty of the two-thirds of the world's population who live in the underdeveloped countries has been rightly called "the problem of problems." But not all of them by any means live in the culture of poverty. For this way of life to come into being and flourish it seems clear that certain preconditions must be met.

11   The setting is a cash economy, with wage labor and production for profit and with a persistently high rate of unemployment and underemployment, at low wages, for unskilled labor. The society fails to provide social, political and economic organization, on either a voluntary basis or by government imposition, for the low-income population. There is a

bilateral kinship system centered on the nuclear progenitive family, as distinguished from the unilateral extended kinship system of lineage and clan. The dominant class asserts a set of values that prizes thrift and the accumulation of wealth and property, stresses the possibility of upward mobility and explains low economic status as the result of individual personal inadequacy and inferiority.

Where these conditions prevail the way of life that develops among some of the poor is the culture of poverty. That is why I have described it as a subculture of the Western social order. It is both an adaptation and a reaction of the poor to their marginal position in a class-stratified, highly individuated, capitalistic society. It represents an effort to cope with feelings of hopelessness and despair that arise from the realization by the members of the marginal communities in these societies of the improbability of their achieving success in terms of the prevailing values and goals. Many of the traits of the culture of poverty can be viewed as local, spontaneous attempts to meet needs not served in the case of the poor by the institutions and agencies of the larger society because the poor are not eligible for such service, cannot afford it or are ignorant and suspicious.

Once the culture of poverty has come into existence it tends to perpetuate itself. By the time slum children are six or seven they have usually absorbed the basic attitudes and values of their subculture. Thereafter they are psychologically unready to take full advantage of changing conditions or improving opportunities that may develop in their lifetime.

My studies have identified some 70 traits that characterize the culture of poverty. The principal ones may be described in four dimensions of the system: the relationship between the subculture and the larger society; the nature of the slum community; the nature of the family, and the attitudes, values and character structure of the individual.

The disengagement, the nonintegration, of the poor with respect to the major institutions of society is a crucial element in the culture of poverty. It reflects the combined effect of a variety of factors including poverty, to begin with, but also segregation and discrimination, fear, suspicion and apathy and the development of alternative institutions and procedures in the slum community. The people do not belong to labor unions or political parties and make little use of banks, hospitals, department stores or museums. Such involvement as there is in the institutions of the larger society—in the jails, the army and the public welfare system—does little to suppress the traits of the culture of poverty. A relief system that barely keeps people alive perpetuates rather than eliminates poverty and the pervading sense of hopelessness.

16   People in a culture of poverty produce little wealth and receive little in return. Chronic unemployment and underemployment, low wages, lack of property, lack of savings, absence of food reserves in the home and chronic shortage of cash imprison the family and the individual in a vicious circle. Thus for lack of cash the slum householder makes frequent purchases of small quantities of food at higher prices. The slum economy turns inward; it shows a high incidence of pawning of personal goods, borrowing at usurious rates of interest, informal credit arrangements among neighbors, use of secondhand clothing and furniture.

17   There is awareness of middle-class values. People talk about them and even claim some of them as their own. On the whole, however, they do not live by them. They will declare that marriage by law, by the church or by both is the ideal form of marriage, but few will marry. For men who have no steady jobs, no property and no prospect of wealth to pass on to their children, who live in the present without expectations of the future, who want to avoid the expense and legal difficulties involved in marriage and divorce, a free union or consensual marriage makes good sense. The women, for their part, will turn down offers of marriage from men who are likely to be immature, punishing and generally unreliable. They feel that a consensual union gives them some of the freedom and flexibility men have. By not giving the fathers of their children legal status as husbands, the women have a stronger claim on the children. They also maintain exclusive rights to their own property.

18   Along with disengagement from the larger society, there is a hostility to the basic institutions of what are regarded as the dominant classes. There is hatred of the police, mistrust of government and of those in high positions and a cynicism

that extends to the church. The culture of poverty thus holds a certain potential for protest and for entrainment in political movements aimed against the existing order.

With its poor housing and overcrowding, the community 19 of the culture of poverty is high in gregariousness, but it has a minimum of organization beyond the nuclear and extended family. Occasionally slum dwellers come together in temporary informal groupings; neighborhood gangs that cut across slum settlements represent a considerable advance beyond the zero point of the continuum I have in mind. It is the low level of organization that gives the culture of poverty its marginal and anomalous quality in our highly organized society. Most primitive peoples have achieved a higher degree of sociocultural organization than contemporary urban slum dwellers. This is not to say that there may not be a sense of community and *esprit de corps* in a slum neighborhood. In fact, where slums are isolated from their surroundings by enclosing walls or other physical barriers, where rents are low and residence is stable and where the population constitutes a distinct ethnic, racial or language group, the sense of community may approach that of a village. In Mexico City and San Juan such territoriality is engendered by the scarcity of low-cost housing outside of established slum areas. In South Africa it is actively enforced by the *apartheid* that confines rural migrants to prescribed locations.

The family in the culture of poverty does not cherish childhood as a specially prolonged and protected stage in the life cycle. Initiation into sex comes early. With the instability of consensual marriage the family tends to be mother-centered and tied more closely to the mother's extended family. The female head of the house is given to authoritarian rule. In spite of much verbal emphasis on family solidarity, sibling rivalry for the limited supply of goods and maternal affection is intense. There is little privacy.

The individual who grows up in this culture has a strong 21 feeling of fatalism, helplessness, dependence and inferiority. These traits, so often remarked in the current literature as characteristic of the American Negro, I found equally strong in slum dwellers of Mexico City and San Juan, who are not segregated or discriminated against as a distinct ethnic or racial group. Other traits include a high incidence of weak ego structure, orality and confusion of sexual identification, all reflecting maternal deprivation; a strong present-time orientation with relatively little disposition to defer gratification and plan for the future, and a high tolerance for psychological pathology of all kinds. There is widespread belief in male superiority and among the men a strong preoccupation with *machismo*, their masculinity.

22   Provincial and local in outlook, with little sense of history, these people know only their own neighborhood and their own way of life. Usually they do not have the knowledge, the vision or the ideology to see the similarities between their troubles and those of their counterparts elsewhere in the world. They are not class-conscious, although they are sensitive indeed to symbols of status.

23   The distinction between poverty and the culture of poverty is basic to the model described here. There are numerous examples of poor people whose way of life I would not characterize as belonging to this subculture. Many primitive and preliterate peoples that have been studied by anthropologists suffer dire poverty attributable to low technology or thin resources or both. Yet even the simplest of these peoples have a high degree of social organization and a relatively integrated, satisfying and self-sufficient culture.

24   In India the destitute lower-caste peoples—such as the Chamars, the leatherworkers, and the Bhangis, the sweepers—remain integrated in the larger society and have their own panchayat institutions of self-government. Their panchayats and their extended unilateral kinship systems, or clans, cut across village lines, giving them a strong sense of identity and continuity. In my studies of these peoples I found no culture of poverty to go with their poverty.

25   The Jews of eastern Europe were a poor urban people, often confined to ghettos. Yet they did not have many traits of the culture of poverty. They had a tradition of literacy that placed great value on learning; they formed many voluntary associations and adhered with devotion to the central community organization around the rabbi, and they had a religion that taught them they were the chosen people.

26   I would cite also a fourth, somewhat speculative example

of poverty dissociated from the culture of poverty. On the basis of limited direct observation in one country—Cuba—and from indirect evidence, I am inclined to believe the culture of poverty does not exist in socialist countries. In 1947 I undertook a study of a slum in Havana. Recently I had an opportunity to revisit the same slum and some of the same families. The physical aspect of the place had changed little, except for a beautiful new nursery school. The people were as poor as before, but I was impressed to find much less of the feelings of despair and apathy, so symptomatic of the culture of poverty in the urban slums of the U.S. The slum was now highly organized, with block committees, educational committees, party committees. The people had found a new sense of power and importance in a doctrine that glorified the lower class as the hope of humanity, and they were armed. I was told by one Cuban official that the Castro government had practically eliminated delinquency by giving arms to the delinquents!

Evidently the Castro regime—revising Marx and Engels—did not write off the so-called *lumpenproletariat* as an inherently reactionary and antirevolutionary force but rather found in them a revolutionary potential and utilized it. Frantz Fanon, in his book *The Wretched of the Earth,* makes a similar evaluation of their role in the Algerian revolution: "It is within this mass of humanity, this people of the shantytowns, at the core of the *lumpenproletariat,* that the rebellion will find its urban spearhead. For the *lumpenproletariat,* that horde of starving men, uprooted from their tribe and from their clan, constitutes one of the most spontaneous and most radically revolutionary forces of a colonized people." 27

It is true that I have found little revolutionary spirit or radical ideology among low-income Puerto Ricans. Most of the families I studied were politically conservative, about half of them favoring the Statehood Republican Party, which provides opposition on the right to the Popular Democratic Party that dominates the politics of the commonwealth. It seems to me, therefore, that disposition for protest among people living in the culture of poverty will vary considerably according to the national context and historical circumstances. In contrast to Algeria, the independence movement in Puerto Rico has 28 found little popular support. In Mexico, where the cause of independence carried long ago, there is no longer any such movement to stir the dwellers in the new and old slums of the capital city.

29   Yet it would seem that any movement—be it religious, pacifist or revolutionary—that organizes and gives hope to the poor and effectively promotes a sense of solidarity with larger groups must effectively destroy the psychological and social core of the culture of poverty. In this connection, I suspect that the civil rights movement among American Negroes has of itself done more to improve their self-image and self-respect than such economic gains as it has won although, without doubt, the two kinds of progress are mutually reinforcing. In the culture of poverty of the American Negro the additional disadvantage of racial discrimination has generated a potential for revolutionary protest and organization that is absent in the slums of San Juan and Mexico City and, for that matter, among the poor whites in the South.

30   If it is true, as I suspect, that the culture of poverty flourishes and is endemic to the free-enterprise, pre-welfare-state stage of capitalism, then it is also endemic in colonial societies. The most likely candidates for the culture of poverty would be the people who come from the lower strata of a rapidly changing society and who are already partially alienated from it. Accordingly the subculture is likely to be found where imperial conquest has smashed the native social and economic structure and held the natives, perhaps for generations, in servile status, or where feudalism is yielding to capitalism in the later evolution of a colonial economy. Landless rural workers who migrate to the cities, as in Latin America, can be expected to fall into this way of life more readily than migrants from stable peasant villages with a well-organized traditional culture, as in India. It remains to be seen, however, whether the culture of poverty has not already begun to develop in the slums of Bombay and Calcutta. Compared with Latin America also, the strong corporate nature of many African tribal societies may tend to inhibit or delay the formation of a full-blown culture of poverty in the new towns and cities of that continent. In South Africa the institutionalization of repression and discrimination under *apartheid* may also have begun to pro-

mote an immunizing sense of identity and group consciousness among the African Negroes.

One must therefore keep the dynamic aspects of human   31
institutions forward in observing and assessing the evidence
for the presence, the waxing or the waning of this subculture.
Measured on the dimension of relationship to the larger society, some slum dwellers may have a warmer identification with
their national tradition even though they suffer deeper poverty than members of a similar community in another country.
In Mexico City a high percentage of our respondents, including those with little or no formal schooling, knew of Cuauhté-
moc, Hidalgo, Father Morelos, Juárez, Díaz, Zapata, Carranza
and Cárdenas. In San Juan the names of Rámon Power, José
de Diego, Baldorioty de Castro, Rámon Betances, Nemesio
Canales, Lloréns Torres rang no bell; a few could tell about
the late Albizu Campos. For the lower-income Puerto Rican,
however, history begins with Muñoz Rivera and ends with his
son Muñoz Marín.

The national context can make a big difference in the play   32
of the crucial traits of fatalism and hopelessness. Given the advanced technology, the high level of literacy, the all-pervasive
reach of the media of mass communications and the relatively
high aspirations of all sectors of the population, even the poorest and most marginal communities of the U.S. must aspire
to a larger future than the slum dwellers of Ecuador and Peru,
where the actual possibilities are more limited and where an
authoritarian social order persists in city and country. Among
the 50 million U.S. citizens now more or less officially certified
as poor, I would guess that about 20 percent live in a culture
of poverty. The largest numbers in this group are made up
of Negroes, Puerto Ricans, Mexicans, American Indians and
Southern poor whites. In these figures there is some reassurance for those concerned, because it is much more difficult to
undo the culture of poverty than to cure poverty itself.

Middle-class people—this would certainly include most   33
social scientists—tend to concentrate on the negative aspects
of the culture of poverty. They attach a minus sign to such
traits as present-time orientation and readiness to indulge im-
pulses. I do not intend to idealize or romanticize the culture
of poverty—"it is easier to praise poverty than to live in it."

Yet the positive aspects of these traits must not be overlooked. Living in the present may develop a capacity for spontaneity, for the enjoyment of the sensual, which is often blunted in the middle-class, future-oriented man. Indeed, I am often struck by the analogies that can be drawn between the mores of the very rich—of the "jet set" and "café society"—and the culture of the very poor. Yet it is, on the whole, a comparatively superficial culture. There is in it much pathos, suffering and emptiness. It does not provide much support or satisfaction; its pervading mistrust magnifies individual helplessness and isolation. Indeed, poverty of culture is one of the crucial traits of the culture of poverty.

34   The concept of the culture of poverty provides a generalization that may help to unify and explain a number of phenomena hitherto viewed as peculiar to certain racial, national or regional groups. Problems we think of as being distinctively our own or distinctively Negro (or as typifying any other ethnic group) prove to be endemic in countries where there are no segregated ethnic minority groups. If it follows that the elimination of physical poverty may not by itself eliminate the culture of poverty, then an understanding of the subculture may contribute to the design of measures specific to that purpose.

35   What is the future of the culture of poverty? In considering this question one must distinguish between those countries in which it represents a relatively small segment of the population and those in which it constitutes a large one. In the U.S. the major solution proposed by social workers dealing with the "hard core" poor has been slowly to raise their level of living and incorporate them in the middle class. Wherever possible psychiatric treatment is prescribed.

36   In underdeveloped countries where great masses of people live in the culture of poverty, such a social-work solution does not seem feasible. The local psychiatrists have all they can do to care for their own growing middle class. In those countries the people with a culture of poverty may seek a more revolutionary solution. By creating basic structural changes in society, by redistributing wealth, by organizing the poor and giving them a sense of belonging, of power and of leadership, revolutions frequently succeed in abolishing some of the basic

characteristics of the culture of poverty even when they do not succeed in curing poverty itself.

Points for Discussion

1. How does Lewis define the term "the culture of poverty"? Why doesn't he simply use the word "poverty"?

2. What is Lewis's attitude toward social scientists? Where does he reveal this view?

3. In describing his studies of poverty and family life, Lewis explains both how he conducts the study (his methods) and why he proceeds in the way he does (his objective). Summarize the methods and explain how they are especially appropriate to the objective.

4. What, in Lewis's view, are the preconditions for the culture of poverty to flourish? How can this culture be both "adaptation" and "reaction"?

5. Summarize the four categories Lewis uses to analyze the traits that characterize the culture of poverty. What is Lewis's tone in this categorizing?

6. At the conclusion of his article, Lewis cites four examples of poor people who do not belong to the culture of poverty. What are these examples? Why does Lewis mention them? Why do you think he brings these examples up at the end of his analysis rather than at the beginning?

7. Examine Lewis's consideration of the ways in which the culture of poverty is affected by national context and historical circumstances (pars. 26–30). How would you describe his tone in the last sentence of this section: "In these figures . . . itself"? Pay special attention to such words as "some reassurance."

8. Examine Lewis's conclusion, a contrast between the future of the culture of poverty in countries like the United States and its

future in underdeveloped countries. How does tone in the final section reflect attitudes throughout the article?

Suggestions for Writing

1. Oscar Lewis's article is an analytical piece about the culture of poverty, a subject he obviously believes is misapprehended, written for an educated audience interested in science and social science. His tone is therefore suitable for handling this subject for a particular audience. To change an aspect of this relationship (for instance, to write for an audience other than readers of *Scientific American*) would require revision.

Assume that you have been asked to rewrite "The Culture of Poverty" for one of these audiences:

- social workers in your geographic area—city, county, state
- the welfare department of your state
- teachers in the high school from which you graduated
- a minority coalition (you can decide on its components)
- undergraduate sociology majors at your college or university

First analyze the audience you choose, determining interest in and attitude toward the culture of poverty. Using Lewis's article as a base, make changes (additions, deletions, alterations in tone) as you write for the readers you want to reach.

2. Write a proposal for remedying one of the conditions that result from "the culture of poverty." Or write proposing a method for alleviating one of the causes contributing to poverty in society today.

WILLIAM RYAN

William Ryan's *Blaming the Victim,* the source of this selection, bears a date ten years later than Lewis's essay on poverty. Ryan's book is often required or supplementary reading in sociology classes.

Learning to Be Poor

I

"Do you want your prize to be one Hershey bar today or two Hershey bars next Wednesday?"

A social scientist asks the question solemnly. He is conducting an experiment in an elementary classroom, and his subjects and listeners are the school children who have just been playing the simple game he has presented to them—perhaps a silly, or even boring game, but a considerable relief from the task of memorizing the capitals and principal products of Ecuador and Peru. The experimenter is no more interested in the game than the children are; he is eager to hear what the prize-winner will choose: one if he takes it now, two if he can contain himself and wait until next week.

"If you unexpectedly got a windfall of two thousand dollars, what would you do with it?"

The young lady asking the question holds her clipboard in standard fashion, casually, planted in the crook of her left arm. She is a pretty cog in the public opinion industry doing her part in the intricate business of conducting an attitude poll. After she conscientiously writes down the response, it will be coded, and processed, and fed into a computer, and the information will be transformed into one of two simple answers to a question that intrigues her employers—that two grand that just fell into your lap, will you save it or will you spend it?

These are two examples of the ways that behavioral scientists try to find out how much ability different persons have to *wait* to have their needs gratified. Like most human charac-

1

2

3

4

5

teristics, this trait is presumed to be variably distributed throughout the population: some people can wait, others must have their reward immediately.

6   Academic and political experts on poverty and the poor have given wide currency to the proposition that this distribution is highly related to social class position. The pattern of behavior characterized by ability to delay need-gratification—what has been called the Deferred Gratification Pattern (D.G.P.)—is supposedly characteristic of the middle classes. Members of the lower classes, in contrast, are usually rumored to display the Non-deferred Gratification Pattern (N.G.P.). The formula has all the force and simplicity of a classical cigarette advertising commercial: M.C./D.G.P.; L.C./N.G.P. All it lacks is a catchy tune.

7   The consumer of tobacco is deliberately assaulted with such a message to create in his mind a preference for one brand of cigarettes. Now, no one accuses the academic and political intellectuals who transmit the slogans about deferred need-gratification of having such a deliberate intent. They would be outraged—and properly so—at such an accusation. The fact is, however, that the effect is really very similar. The consumer of popularized social science is no more immune to brainwashing than is the consumer of tobacco; he can hardly resist developing a preference for the behavior patterns attributed to the middle class person, who is pictured as a mature man of prudence and foresight, able to plan ahead and reap the long-term rewards of virtue. He looks particularly good in contrast to the portrait of the lower classes—feckless folk indeed, thoughtless and impulsive, with a childish, if not immoral insistence on gratification now.

8   There is vast sociological literature detailing the supposed differences between the poor and the middle class on such variables—including values, child-rearing practices, level of aspiration, sexual behavior, and so forth. As in the case of ability to deter gratification, it is found that the middle class come out on top every time—they are said to have greater commitment to education, achievement, orderly family lives, sexual regularity, and to rear their children in such a way as to impel them to do likewise.[1] More recently, these ideas have been pulled together into such packages as the "culture of pover-

ty"[2] and the "lower class culture."[3] And here is where we start to run into ideological trouble. Viewed simply as descriptions, all these different portraits of poor people might simply be dismissed as stereotypes or exaggerations. They might be left to the ministrations of a Poor People's Anti-Defamation League, if there were one. But aficionados of the culture of poverty go several steps further into very dangerous territory. They identify the culture of poverty and lower class culture and the presumed life styles of the poor as themselves *causes* of continued poverty. This theme in the writing of Oscar Lewis—otherwise exciting and insightful when viewed as highly sensitive descriptions of some families living in poverty—is, to me, very disturbing. He makes such statements as:

> Once the culture of poverty has come into existence it tends to perpetuate itself. By the time slum children are six or seven they have usually absorbed the basic attitudes and values of their subculture. Thereafter they are psychologically unready to take full advantage of changing conditions or improving opportunities that may develop in their lifetime.[4]

In fairness, it should be stressed that Lewis' thinking along these lines is quite cautious. He states that by no means all of the world's poor live in the culture of poverty (and is inclined to think it may be essentially absent in some of the socialist countries), and that, in the United States, only a small minority of the poor—no more than one in five—can be placed within it. Those who quote Lewis so freely and simplify his ideas so readily are much less cautious. In my judgment, this is because they share neither his genuine empathy for the poor nor his conviction that social changes of a structural nature are necessary to deal with the problem of poverty.

The extent to which these ideas have penetrated the thinking of the social welfare establishment and that of its pet academics can be grasped rather well by reading a revolting government publication, a little pamphlet called *Growing Up Poor*[5] (which might well have been subtitled *Dick and Jane Go Slumming*). In its 108 pages, Catherine Chilman has managed to pack every nefarious idea about the poor that has ever been dreamed up in the past thirty years, up to and including, incredible as it may seem, the question of the poor's "social acceptability." It is a downright emetic book, yet every person concerned about these questions should read it in order to understand what social workers and social scientists are whispering to each other behind their cupped hands.

11   Let me provide a preview with a few choice quotations:

> With all its faults, the middle class way, compared to that more typical of the very poor, seems to be more in harmony with present-day economic realities. The middle class approach has played importantly into the building of this system and has been built by it.[6]

> Thus, both for the benefit of a number of the poor themselves and for the rest of society, it would appear that, among other things, methods should be found within the democratic framework to help many lower-lower class parents raise their children in a way that, in the light of available evidence, would seem to be predictive of a greater likelihood of success and fulfillment in today's society.[7]

> The subcultural adaptation to poverty would seem to interact with the poverty situation to perpetuate lower-lower class status. For the welfare of many of the very poor, as well as for the welfare of the rest of society, it seems to be necessary to help a large group re-adapt its life styles to more effective patterns.[8]

> However, the school is also an important part of the child's social world and the low-income child in the mainly middle class school room is generally observed to be a social outcast.[9]

> As in the case of the generally accepted criteria for "good adjustment" or positive mental health, so the characteristics of the socially acceptable child are solidly middle class.[10]

> As in the case of other substantive areas discussed in this paper, the child-rearing patterns more characteristic of the very poor seem poorly calculated to develop "good moral character" in many of their children.[11]

> "No cheating in school" is often used as a criterion of honesty by researchers. With the educational cards generally stacked against the very poor child, his failure record might well be worse than it usually is, if he consistently abstained from cheating.[12]

In addition, Dr. Chilman goes on to list no fewer than   12
fifty-one characteristics of the way of life of the lower-lower
class that are specifically handicapping to any one of them who
might want to achieve such middle class characteristics as
being well-adjusted, well-educated, socially acceptable, of
good moral character, and involved in sound family life.
Among them are (I swear!):

> Fatalistic, apathetic attitudes
> Magical, rigid thinking
> Pragmatic, concrete values
> Poor impulse control
> Ambivalent attitudes toward property rights
> Little value placed on neatness and cleanliness
> Little verbal communication and discussion
> High divorce and separation rates
> Income less than $3,000 a year

Growing Up Poor can be thought of as a somewhat adulter-   13
ated, but reasonably accurate distillate of the culture of poverty ideology—a popularization of this new version of the idea
that poverty is a resultant of the characteristics of the poor
themselves. This can be contrasted with the idea that poverty
is most simply and clearly understood as a lack of money. One
might formulate this idea in a more elegant way—"poverty
is an economic status etiologically related to absence of both
monetary input and access to income-generating resources"—but the message is the same. Being poor is having
no cash in hand and damned little on the way. Put in these
terms, poverty in the United States is almost a picayune problem. A redistribution of about fifteen billion dollars a year
(less than two per cent of our Gross National Product that is
now pushing toward one trillion dollars annually) would bring
every poor person above the present poverty line. This is less
than half our annual expenditure on the Viet Nam War.

But if poverty is to be understood more clearly in terms   14
of the "way of life" of the poor, in terms of a "lower class
culture," as a product of a deviant value system, then money
is clearly not the answer. We can stop right now worrying
about ways of redistributing our resources more equitably,
and begin focusing our concern where it belongs—on the
poor themselves. We can start trying to figure out how to

change that troublesome culture of theirs, how to apply some tautening astringent to their flabby consciences, how to deal with their poor manners and make them more socially acceptable. By this hard and wearying method of liquidating lower class culture, we can liquidate the lower class, and, thereby, bring an end to poverty.

15   It all comes perilously close to putting into reality the satire of a comic greeting card that was published when President Johnson first decided to go into the poverty business. The front cover of the card showed a bedraggled old lady, with a raggedy skirt and a shawl over her head, saying, "I hear there's going to be a War on Poverty." The inside of the card shows her, arms spread wide in great concern, continuing, "Does that mean they're going to shoot me?"

Notes

1. For a detailed bibliography of this literature see the footnote references in Catherine Chilman's *Growing up Poor* (Washington, D.C.: Welfare Administration Publication No. 13, U.S. Department of Health, Education, and Welfare, U.S. Government Printing Office, 1966).

2. Oscar Lewis, "The Culture of Poverty," *Scientific American,* CCXV, No. 16 (October, 1966), pp. 19–25.

3. Walter Miller, "Lower Class Culture as a Generating Milieu of Gang Delinquency," *Journal of Social Issues,* XIV, No. 4 (1958), pp. 5–19.

4. Oscar Lewis, *op. cit.,* p. 7.

5. Chilman, *Growing Up Poor.*

6. *Ibid.*

7. *Ibid.*

8. *Ibid.*

9. *Ibid.*

10. *Ibid.*

11. *Ibid.*

12. *Ibid.*

Points for Discussion

1. What is the effect of opening with the two examples of the social scientist and the pollster?

2. Many words and phrases suggest Ryan's tone—for example, "feckless folk indeed" (par. 7) and "The formula has all the force

and simplicity of a classical cigarette advertising commercial . . . All it lacks is a catchy tune" (par. 6). Find and discuss other examples that reveal Ryan's attitude.

3. How does Ryan use secondary materials—especially those of Lewis and Chilman—to indicate his own attitude?

4. What is the effect of the following two parenthetical expressions: "a little pamphlet called *Growing Up Poor* (which might well have been subtitled *Dick and Jane Go Slumming*)" (par. 10) and "Among them are (I swear!)" (par. 12)? Find similar expressions that are appropriate in this selection but might not be in more formal writing.

5. Examine Ryan's comment on the way language is used to be elegant ("poverty is an economic status etiologically related to absence of both monetary input and access to income-generating resources") or to be direct ("Being poor is having no cash in hand and damned little on the way") (par. 13). Although he does not state it explicitly, what do you think is Ryan's view of social science jargon? How does jargon relate to tone?

6. What clues tell the reader that Ryan's last two paragraphs are satirical?

Suggestions for Writing

1. William Ryan begins and ends this essay with examples that reveal contemporary attitudes toward poverty. He could have analyzed these examples in detail, pointing out what he considers fallacies; instead he chooses to be ironical, thus attempting to persuade readers to see the humor and limitations of a point of view.

Try your hand at this technique by choosing a subject of current general interest that you feel strongly about—for example, a politician, censorship, inflation, the Equal Rights Amendment, costs of medical care. Assume that you have been asked to write a report for a group that disagrees with your position. For instance, if you are in favor of some form of censorship, report to the American Civil Liberties Union; if you are opposed to the ERA, report to the National Organization for Women. Not wanting to alienate your audience, you will need to pay special attention to tone, perhaps using some of the techniques Ryan uses.

2. Read "A Modest Proposal" by Jonathan Swift, a wide-ly-known satire on conditions of poverty in eighteenth-century Ireland. Write a short paper comparing the content and techniques in Swift's essay and those in Ryan's "Learning to Be Poor."

The persuasive tone of this recent "comment"—an editorial from *The Progressive*—is interestingly juxtaposed with the articles and research of Lewis and Ryan.

" 'Welfare Reform' Forever" from *Comment—The Progressive* (September, 1981)

All but lost in the uproar over the Reagan Administration's budget and tax-cut proposals have been the President's notions of "welfare reform." Congress will be asked to require all "able-bodied" welfare recipients who have no children under the age of six to work for their benefits. The change is intended to reduce welfare costs and to give welfare recipients the kind of "training and self-esteem" that will integrate them into the regular work force.

Jimmy Carter, and Richard Nixon before him, had similar notions of welfare reform. Like Ronald Reagan's, they were announced with much fanfare, then faded. The problem is that such proposals are based on false assumptions about who is on welfare and why. Recent studies have reaffirmed that most welfare recipients are not members of a permanent class of idle misfits and cheats; they are adults who must depend on welfare to supplement seasonal low-wage jobs. In any five-year period, about one-fifth of all American families will be on welfare at some point, though the average welfare family receives benefits totaling less than $1,000 a year.

Perhaps the greatest fallacy surrounding welfare reform schemes is that they can serve to funnel recipients into the regular labor market. People are on welfare not because they are deficient, but because our economy increasingly fails to provide an adequate number of jobs that pay a living wage. The

Reagan Administration is surely deluded if it believes forcing recipients to work at low wages as cafeteria help, school crossing guards, and park attendants will provide the training needed to launch individuals on more profitable careers in the private sector.

4   But despite their lack of contact with reality, "welfare reform" proposals come up again and again. Service industries, fast food chains, many retail outlets, and giant agribusiness concerns all have an interest in preserving a pool of poor workers who have no choice but to work for extremely low wages. If welfare is kept as tight, demeaning, and tough as possible, such enterprises can keep their wage bills low and their profits high.

5   Still, welfare reform is clearly a popular cause among many unionized industrial workers who have concluded from their own frustrating experience with unfulfilling jobs that work is a form of punishment that all citizens must be willing to bear. Many unionized workers have been induced to see cuts in welfare spending as about the only way they can cut their own tax bills.

6   For the Left, welfare poses an acute dilemma: Surely the cruel cuts inflicted on the poorest must be resisted, but welfare and social service activists must also broaden their focus to encompass Reagan cuts in such programs as Trade Relocation Assistance and unemployment compensation. These cuts are designed to enlarge the ranks of poor industrial workers and thus undercut the wages and bargaining power of unionized workers. Similarly, unions must address the ways in which a pool of poor seasonal workers helps create conditions that depress wages and power on the shop floor throughout the U.S. economy. Only a full-employment economy can give labor the power to negotiate adequate pay and a human work environment.

7   Only when workers have fashioned an economy in which a sufficient number of remunerative and fulfilling jobs is always available can the mean politics of "welfare reform" be ended once and for all. Until we manage to build effective coalitions around such broad concerns, "welfare reform," however ineffective, will, like the poor, always be with us.

Points for Discussion

1. What in this selection indicates that it is an article voicing an editorial opinion? What elements "date" it as current and recent? What in the content places the situation in a wider context, one of many times?

2. How much evidence does the writer give to support the ideas and suggestions offered? What is the relationship (structurally as well as in content) between paragraphs 3 and 7?

3. Compare this editorial-article to the selections by Lewis and Ryan. How would you characterize the tone in this final selection on poverty? To what extent do you find the editorial persuasive, and why?

Suggestions for Writing

1. Write an editorial or comment of your own on some recent development proposed by state or national government in efforts to deal with poverty, unemployment, or a closely related problem.

2. Write a report on an economic aspect of unemployment or poverty. An example might be found in paragraph 4 of "'Welfare Reform' Forever," the statements about the relationship between service industries, employment policies, and welfare reform. Or you might check statistics on numbers of local persons on welfare and compare those figures to national records. Be sure to use well-founded evidence in statistics, perhaps presenting your findings in the form of tables, charts, or graphs.

9

| PAPERS OF EXTENDED RESEARCH

When you are asked to compose longer papers of extended research, you will use most of the same skills and ask virtually all the same questions that apply to other forms of writing. You are still concerned with defining an area of investigation, discovering a problem to solve, developing and proving a hypothesis. And in writing the paper you also give attention to audience, voice, and style. In fact, the only difference between this kind of paper and most others is technical: here you will show and document your research findings more completely. For this reason, all writers of extended research rely upon manuals that remind them of techniques for gathering data, keeping track of sources, footnoting information, and compiling bibliographies.

After gathering your data—through interviews, observation, reading—you begin to shape the paper, asking questions like the following about using and interpreting your sources.

USING SOURCES:

1. How do I select materials that are both representative and pertinent? (This of course means being honest and not ignoring anything that might disprove the thesis.)

2. How can I incorporate the research to show how I arrived at my conclusions?

3. How should I arrange the materials so that the reader can follow my train of thought?

4. In what ways should I present the specifics of my research (evidence, data, other authorities):

- in discursive prose
- in graphs, lists, charts, diagrams
- through direct quotations
- through paraphrases or short summaries that distinguish between the source and my interpretation?

INTERPRETING SOURCES:

1. Am I giving enough information from the sources, but not overdoing it?

2. Am I being honest, avoiding distortion?

3. Am I demonstrating the significance of the evidence and conclusions?

Some points, addressed in all writing, that you should consider when writing your paper are

- viewpoint—Since this is not a personal paper, the focus should be upon the subject matter, but it is not uncommon to use first person, as the writer of the following anthropology paper did.
- clarity—You must choose your language carefully so the reader can understand just how you are integrating your ideas with those of your sources.
- editing—In addition to the typical editing tasks, you should doublecheck the ways in which you have used and footnoted your sources. Inaccurate citations will threaten your credibility as a writer.

The following papers, written by undergraduate students in psychology and anthropology classes, should give you some ideas for gathering data and communicating it in written form. While the writers differ in some of their techniques—for example, footnote and bibliography forms and viewpoint from which the material is presented—they both prove their theses about Gestalt psychology and animism through careful use and interpretation of sources.

■ MARIE J. BEYER

Gestalt Psychology: Its Principles and Historical Antecedents

1   The Gestalt Psychology of Max Wertheimer, Wolfgang Köhler, and Kurt Koffka[1] maintains that perception, memory and recall, learning, motivation and emotion, and motor activity, as psychological facts, cannot be understood without reference to the total field in which the individual operates. This means that factors in the environment and within the person interact in a dynamic, organizing interplay of external and internal events which result in mental life that is somehow more than would be expected if its parts were simply summed up as separate, isolated facts. Underlying Gestalt theory are several assumptions and principles which will be presented, followed by a discussion of the historical antecedents of the theory. In many respects the organization of a presentation along these lines is difficult because the principles of Gestalt, as discussed by Köhler,[2] its most important spokesman, are at times direct results of reactions against certain trends which were active at the time the Gestalt theory was formulated. Thus, the introductory outline of Gestalt theory in this presentation may seem somewhat sketchy; however, it is hoped that the subsequent discussion of Gestalt Psychology's antecedents will more clearly define the theory itself.

2   *Principles of Gestalt Psychology.*   The first assumption of Gestalt theory as set forth by Köhler is that the world can be and is directly experienced (Köhler, 1947; Madden and Boring, 1965). This is not to say that the physical objects that exist "out there" are experienced per se, because certain physical processes mediate in the experiencing of external events and things. However, and this is a second important assumption of Gestalt theory, because the objective experience of the

world is directly given and to some extent is a reliable impression of the physical world, psychology can learn from data gathered by direct experience through introspection. This particular form of introspection will be discussed more fully in the historical portion of this paper, so for now it is only briefly outlined. Gestalt introspection is a phenomenological method; it leads to descriptions of experience as given, without abstraction. Köhler felt that introspection was a viable way in which to discover the important factors and their relationships which result in the complex mental and behavioral phenomena of psychological events. Introspection would thus allow the formulation of testable hypotheses which could then be experimentally verified. Thus, psychology must rest on a basis of both careful introspection and experimentation.

According to Köhler, objective experience is the result of "physical events which stimulate sense organs" and "physiological events." Gestalt is primarily interested in the physiological events, and since objective experience depends on these physiological events, the experience itself must contain information regarding the nature of the underlying physiological processes (Köhler, 1947). This is the Gestaltists' principle of psycho-physical isomorphism. This principle holds that objective experience is directly related to underlying physiological processes in the nervous system which correspond to the experience. These physiological processes mirror the physical world to some extent, but not in all cases, as evidenced by perceptual illusions. Experiences themselves are ordered, and this order is also experienced and corresponds to an ordering of the physiological processes underlying experience. Thus isomorphism rests on other principles. These, as stated by Köhler, include a principle of spatial order: "Experienced order in space is always structurally identical with a functional order in the distribution of underlying brain processes" (Köhler, 1947, p. 39). A similar principle may be applied to the experience of temporal order: "[E]xperienced order in time is always structurally identical with a functional order in the sequence of correlated brain processes." Further, the fact that some units of experience are felt to go together rests on an isomorphic principle: "[U]nits in experience go with functional units in the underlying physiological processes" (Madden and Boring, 1965, pp. 259–261). Experienced order is, then, "a true representation of a corresponding order in the processes upon which experience depends" (Madden and Boring, 1965, pp. 189–193).

4   Gestalt theory also assumes that experience results from dynamic processes. Thus objective experience is more than can be explained in terms of local stimuli alone. An indication of this can be seen in the results of Wertheimer's phi-phenomenon experiments. In these experiments, the stimuli were two separate, distinct lighted bars. However, when the bars were lit alternately at certain speeds, subjects reported experiencing perceived motion where no movement actually existed. It is the dynamic processes in the nervous system that result in this perception of movement and not any characteristic of the stimuli themselves. In explaining the phi-phenomenon, Wertheimer referred to physiological "cross functions," a sort of short circuit which allows a transfer of stimulation between areas in the nervous system and sense organs (Madden and Boring, 1965).

5   The dynamics of the nervous system have an organizing effect on experience. The nervous system favors regular wholes and closed areas, and exhibits preference for certain types of organization. Isomorphic physiological processes correspond to spatial and temporal order for visual, audio and tactile sensory experience, and depend on such factors as proximity, intensity and quality. This organization is not entirely determined by stimuli or their arrangement in the perceptual field. It can be qualitatively altered by such things as attitudes which result in "a real transformation of sensory facts" (Köhler, 1947, pp. 82–100). Such processes underlie not only sensory experience, but also learning, recall, motivation, emotion, intellectual activity, and behavior. The actual mechanisms behind these mental and behavioral explanations are beyond the scope of this paper, but are discussed fully by Köhler.

6   *The Antecedents of Gestalt.*   Gestalt theory is both an extension and elaboration of some earlier concepts and a reaction against others. Thus an historical discussion of Gestalt could be organized around various positive and negative influences.

However, because the historical facts are so closely related to an understanding of the theory, the antecedents of Gestalt theory will be discussed here in terms of their relation to the assumptions and principles of the theory. Also, with few exceptions, the Gestalt theorists never mention specific earlier theorists as having influenced them. Therefore, the antecedents below are based on writings of historians of psychology rather than the words of the Gestaltists themselves. In some cases, in fact, theorists named as predecessors of Gestalt theory are given rather harsh treatment by Köhler.[3]

Direct Experience, Phenomenology and Introspection. The assumption that experience is immediately given is, according to some authors, a case of German nativism (Madden and Boring, 1965), although Köhler denies that nativistic principles need be cited (Köhler, 1947). The insistence of the Gestalt theorists that processes in the nervous system favor certain forms of organization does, however, appear to be a nativistic idea. We are born with nervous systems that operate in a particular way. In any case, this assumption is clearly a reaction against British empiricism and associationistic theories which stated that sensory elements are all that are experienced and that through association they are combined into more complex phenomena (Madden and Boring, 1965).

The related idea of phenomenology can be traced in Germany back to Goethe, the poet and philosopher. It is a methodological tool which relies on a free, unbiased, immediate description of experience as it happens, without analyzing or abstracting (Schultz, 1975). In this regard, Ewald Hering preceded Gestalt. He believed that description and observation would lead to insight into events and that spatial relations, for example, are given innately with sensations. Stumpf, a student of Hering, was a phenomenologist and taught Koffka and Köhler. Another predecessor was Husserl, a student of Brentano and Stumpf, who believed experience should not be analyzed into elements but taken for what it appears to be. David Katz, a student of G. E. Müller, conducted a phenomenological study of color perception and arrived at the conclusion that color perception could not be reduced to sensations and attributes. Külpe, a student of Wundt who rejected Wundtian analyzation of experience into elements, believed that an "impalpable awareness" existed in mental life that could be studied phenomenologically (Madden and Boring, 1965; Watson, 1979; Schultz, 1975).

9   Gestalt introspection, being phenomenological, is different from and is a reaction against the elementist form of introspection of Wundt, Titchner and others (Madden and Boring, 1965). Traditional Wundtian introspection was analytic and sought to resolve all experience into sensations or other elements (Boring, 1929). In this area, Brentano preceded the Gestalt psychologists. Brentano held that Wundtian introspection was artificial in its abstraction of elements; he favored a less rigid and more direct observation of experience as it occurs (Madden and Boring, 1965; Schultz, 1975). It must be noted that the Gestaltists did not deny that experience *could* be analyzed into elements; they simply felt that such abstraction could not tell the whole story or explain certain phenomena, such as illusions. Indeed, as mentioned above, Köhler admitted that the observer's attitude could actually change perception. One could introspect and discover elements, but this is only due to one's conscious attempt (in other words, one's attitude) to discover such elements.

10   Finally, an implication of Gestalt reliance on direct experience and phenomenological introspection is its implicit assumption that the consciousness can and should be studied. The processes underlying consciousness could explain behavior. This is in direct opposition to the Behaviorists' view which developed at the same time as Gestalt. The Behaviorists not only did not rely on consciousness to study behavior, they completely ignored it. Only behavior was observable, they said, and therefore it was the only valid object of scientific study for psychology (Schultz, 1975; Köhler, 1947).

11   *Emphasis on Organization and Wholes.* The idea of unity in psychology can be traced back to the philosophy of Aristotle, who maintained, in opposition to Plato's plurality of souls, that the soul, while having several faculties, is unitary and indivisible into parts. Descartes also posited a unitary sort of mind in his mind-body interactionism (Boring, 1929). Kant also argued that sensory elements are organized into a perceptual

unity through active organization by the mind rather than through mechanical processes such as association (Schultz, 1975).

The 1890 publication of William James' *Principles of Psychology* predated Gestalt by stating that elements or simple sensations do not exist in experience, but he did not offer a valid alternative (Lowry, 1971). Like James, the Gestalt emphasis on organization was a reaction against the elementarism of Hume and Helmholtz and against what the Gestalt theorists called Wundtian "brick and mortar" psychology or the "bundle hypothesis." The elementarists held that elements are the basis of sensory experience and that these elements are collected or combined through association, that separate stimuli give rise to separate sensations which are integrated on the basis of past experience. In contrast, Gestalt held that objects, not elements, are experienced. Resulting perceptions are something new and not contained in the sum of the elements. Further, the entire field is experienced rather than isolated stimuli (Schultz, 1975; Madden and Boring, 1965; Peters, 1965). Previously, Holt had argued against the "bead theory" that "causally connected events, strung out along a line," can adequately describe behavior. Dewey's argument against using the reflex-arc as a basis for behavior because behavior is continuous with sensory and motor factors blending into one another is another antecedent in this respect, as is Kant's argument for a "sensory manifold" as opposed to Humean elementism. Ward's "presensational continuum" also predates the Gestalt movement, and Stout posited that "spatio-temporal forms and other types of unity" are as much real ingredients of the total field as are separate sensations (Madden and Boring, 1965; Peters, 1965).

In this respect, perhaps the most important predecessors of Gestalt are Ernst Mach and Christian von Ehrenfels. As early as 1885, Mach considered spatial patterns and temporal patterns as having sensations, independent of their elements, which corresponded to their form, and which he called space-form and time-form. Other qualities of stimuli, such as color or size, could be altered without changing the nature of the form quality. Even if the observer's orientation to an object changed, the form would not change in perception.

12

13

Ehrenfels and the Austrian school followed in the same vein. Ehrenfels suggested a Gestalt or form quality inherent in the specific arrangement of stimuli. He illustrated this idea by the fact that a melody played in two different keys is still recognized as the same melody, but that a rearrangement of the notes of a melody, even if played in the same key, results in a totally new melody. The discrete stimuli (notes) cannot fully explain the resulting perception, for the arrangement in which the stimuli are presented is also important. Gestalt qualities were believed to be constructed out of sensory data by the individual, but Ehrenfels was unable to prove that form qualities could not be a result of association. Thus, form quality, as defined by Mach and Ehrenfels, was little more than a new element (Schultz, 1975; Peters, 1965).

14   Finally, a discovery from outside the science of psychology influenced the Gestalt movement. This was the trend in physics at the end of the nineteenth century toward a concern with newly discovered fields of force, such as magnetism, which were not readily suited to Galilean-Newtonian explanations. Such forces could operate over distances and had spatial extension and configuration or patterns. They were considered "structural entities" rather than collections of elements; physics was therefore dealing with organic wholes. In fact, Köhler, in his discussion of Gestalt Psychology, uses many analogies and illustrations from field physics, especially in relation to vectors and the processes of the nervous system (Schultz, 1975, p. 264; Köhler, 1947).

15   *Isomorphism.*   The principle of psychophysical isomorphism was first outlined by Wertheimer in a 1912 paper that initiated Gestalt theory. This view was preceded by R. H. Lotze in 1852 in his discussion of "qualitative relations," by H. Grassman's 1853 discussion of series of colors, and by Fechner in 1860 and Mach in 1865 in a more general way. Hering, in 1878, in a discussion of color theory, suggested that light entering the sense organs causes chemical changes in the sensory nerves and in the brain which allow the perception of color. Mach, in his psycho-physical axioms stated that, "Every state of consciousness is based upon a material event, a so-called psychophysical process . . ." Equivalence, similarity, differ-

ences, and changes in sensation correspond to equivalence, similarity, differences and changes in the physiological processes. Müller hypothesized that chemical reactions in retinal processes underlie the perception of color, and the structure of the system restricts the number of factors which must be considered in the construction of hypotheses (Madden and Boring, 1965; Watson, 1979).

The Dynamic Nature of Mental Processes.   Like Gestalt introspection and emphasis on organization, the view that the processes in the nervous system are dynamic is a reaction against the static Wundtian elementism, the "psychology of content." At the end of the nineteenth century, this view had already been challenged by the Act Psychology of Brentano and the Austrian School. Brentano's Act Psychology emphasized the process of experiencing rather than the content of experience or elements. However, in one regard, Wundtian psychology recognized process. In his principle of creative synthesis, Wundt admitted that new qualities could appear when elements are combined into wholes (Schultz, 1975; Peters, 1965).

    Field physics also influenced this view as did discoveries in the field of chemistry. Köhler makes many references to these sciences. He points out that in physics and in chemistry, reactions of elements depend on the particular characteristics of the elements and on their relationships to one another. This, he says, is analogous to the relationships in experience, where the stimuli in the environment, their particular arrangement in relation to one another, and processes and factors in the individual must all be considered in order to understand resulting mental and behavioral phenomena (Köhler, 1947).

Conclusion.   As can be seen, Gestalt Psychology was a more or less natural outcome of various theories and studies of the time. It was able to explain phenomena which could not be understood in empiricistic, associationist, or elementarist terms, and it drew on sources both within and outside of psychology. While some psychologists derided the Gestalt reliance on introspection, they could hardly deny the evidence Gestaltists presented from experimentation. Gestalt's wide range of application, its ability to explain unexplained phenomena, its supporting experimentation, and its basis in facts both inside and outside psychology added to the impetus which made it a major movement of its time.

Reference Notes

1. The field theory of Lewin is also often included as a form of Gestalt Psychology. Due to space limitations, Lewin is not discussed here. The reader is referred to Peters, R. S., ed., *Brett's History of Psychology,* (Cambridge: The M.I.T. Press, 1965), pp. 724–715. Also see Heidbreder, E., "Lewin's Principles of Topological Psychology," in Henle, M., Jaynes, J., and Sullivan, J. J., eds., *Historical Conceptions of Psychology* (New York: Springer Publishing Co., Inc., 1973), pp. 257–266.

2. Except where otherwise specified, the principles and assumptions of Gestalt theory have been taken from Köhler, W., *Gestalt Psychology: An Introduction to New Concepts in Modern Psychology* (New York: The New American Library, 1947).

3. See, for example, references to William James, in Köhler, pp. 80, 198–199.

References

Boring, E. G. *A History of Experimental Psychology.* New York: The Century Co., 1929.

Henle, M., Jaynes, J., and Sullivan, J. J. (Eds.) *Historical Conceptions of Psychology.* New York: Springer Publishing Co., Inc., 1973.

Köhler, W. *Gestalt Psychology: An Introduction to New Concepts in Modern Psychology.* New York: The New American Library, 1947.

Lowry, R. *The Evolution of Psychological Theory: 1650 to the Present.* New York: Aldine Publishing Co., 1971.

Madden, E. H., and Boring, E. G. (Eds.) *A Source Book in the History of Psychology.* Cambridge: Harvard University Press, 1965.

Peters, R. S. (Ed.) *Brett's History of Psychology.* Cambridge: The M.I.T. Press, 1965.

Schultz, D. *A History of Modern Psychology,* 2nd ed. New York: Academic Press, 1975.

Watson, R. I. *Basic Writings in the History of Psychology.* New York: Oxford University Press, 1979.

■ PAT HONSBERGER

Notes on Animism in Native North American Cultures

The native cultures of North America were an integral part   1
of nature's system. As such, they were intimately affected by
the vagrancies of nature—the abundance or shortage of game
animals and the mildness or severity of weather conditions—in ways that we, with our high level of technology and
control over the extremes of the elements, cannot appreciate.
It is no surprise, then, that these people's lifestyles were
shaped so drastically by their animistic beliefs.

Animism may be defined as "the doctrine that the phe-   2
nomena of animal life are produced by a soul or spiritual force
distinct from matter" or "the doctrine that inanimate objects
and natural phenomena possess a personal life or soul." In the
following paragraphs I will relate some examples of how animism affected the cultures of our native North American peoples—from the Eskimo in the far North to the Maya in Me-
soamerica.

These people's day-to-day existence was permeated with   3
invisible powers and supernatural forces which they perceived
and felt at all times in nature—the success or failure of an enterprise, the well-being or misfortune of a community, the life
and death of its members—all these depended upon powers,
"spirits," and influences which constituted the real masters of
their destinies.

Animism consists of two dogmas: first, concerning souls   4
of individual creatures, capable of continued existence after
death or destruction of the body; second, concerning other
spirits upward to the rank of powerful deities (Tylor 1877:
426). Since the incidences of animistic beliefs, both animate
and inanimate, are so numerous, I shall stress primarily the
animate phase of this subject.

In the early North American hunting and gathering cul-   5
tures, the ideas of a divine "master of animals" and a "protec-

tor of game" stand out clearly. The game protector concept is illustrated by the following Labrador Eskimo tale:

> There was once a great shaman who wanted to find out the place where the caribou went when they moved in great herds to the interior. His guardian spirit led him there in a journey which took two months. After sunset the shaman saw a big house built of sod and stones. In the door stood a big caribou. He was the king of the caribou. He stood so tall that the other caribou could walk underneath him without touching. The caribou came in great herds to pass underneath him into the house. When the last caribou had gone in, the big caribou lay down before the door and guarded the others (Jensen 1963: 137).

6   The "master of animals" is perceived in various forms in native Indian cultures: it may be a particularly large animal of a species important as game or an anthropomorphic being of striking appearance, often tall or dwarfishly small. Since he is the protector of all game, however, he generally determines the relationship between hunter and prey, for without his approval and assistance the food quest would be unsuccessful. It is not surprising, then, that a prime concern of these people is the dispositions of the "master of animals" or the animal spirits themselves, for the game quest is the essential form of human sustenance in the upper latitudes of North America.

7   The Sedna tale of the Eskimo is a good example of the "master of animals" concept. Sedna, the goddess of the sea, has the power to withhold sea animals as a result of offense both to the animals themselves and to Sedna. When a seal or whale is killed, its soul remains with the body for three days before returning to Sedna's underworld abode, to be sent forth again by her.

8   Various tribes have many propitiatory rites or practices destined to maintain their animal spirits or the "master of animals" in favorable moods. This, of course, resulted in the establishment of certain practices and taboos regulating the capture of game animals. One example of this concern for animals' dispositions deals with the Eskimo's treatment of seals and whales. Since they live in salt water, they are continually thirsty. They have no means of getting fresh water, so a seal will allow himself to be killed by a hunter who will give him

a drink of water in return. Thus a dipperful of water is always poured into the seal's mouth when it is brought ashore. If the hunter neglects to do this, all the other seals know about it and no other seal will allow himself to be killed by that hunter. This example illustrates the importance of treating game animals with "respect," for an animal accorded proper treatment upon capture would apprise the other world of animals (in which dwelt the souls of animals not yet liberated to earthly existence) of the good conduct of men on earth, thereby granting hunters plentiful game in the future (Weyer 1969: 334, 339).

A dominant theme in the Eskimo system of taboos related   9
to the separation of land and sea animal products. Caribou and seal were not to be eaten on the same day; caribou and fresh-water fish should not be cooked over driftwood (which comes from the sea); and the sewing of caribou skins was prohibited (except for necessary mending) while the Eskimo was living on the ice or hunting walrus. All pertain to the fundamental principle: the differentiation of the marine realm from the terrestrial.

Many of the Sub-Arctic tribes prohibited the feeding of   10
the meat of trapped animals to their dogs, while certain taboos were imposed with respect to human consumption of parts of various animals. A common practice involved throwing salmon and beaver bones back into the water so that they might return to the village as a food source once more. Some Indian tribes of the Southeast carefully preserved the bones of the animals they ate and burned them, and the bones of animals caught in a snare or trap were not thrown away but hung up or placed on the roof of the house; such practices were thought to conciliate the appropriate spirits.

In contrast to the animals which allowed themselves to be   11
killed if man accorded them the proper "respect," there were also animals generally regarded as hostile to man. Some of the Sub-Arctic tribes avoided the frog, mink, otter, wolf, and wolverine (they possessed malevolent spiritual powers and were almost never killed or eaten), while the Creeks would not willingly kill a wolf or a rattlesnake. The Delaware Indians considered the giant bear and the great horned serpent evil, although several tales referred to the bear and otter as having

strong spiritual powers, capable of curing illness. The Maya considered poisonous snakes the devil himself and also feared a mythical group of beasts that fed on human flesh. The killing of these "evil" animals promised illness or misfortune to the person responsible.

12   Because animals possessed supernatural powers, there were common beliefs in their abilities to aid or hinder man in various activities. Animal "guardian spirits" were common in the Sub-Arctic, the eastern plains and the southeastern United States. Boys were encouraged, at an early age, to solicit the "protection" of an animal. This was accomplished by a period of isolation and deprivation in the bush or through a vision or dream wherein an animal, manifesting human attributes, spoke to the boy. A successful solicitation of animal power brought a person assistance in hunting and/or the ability of shamanistic curing. Once the person obtained this power, certain eating taboos were imposed with respect to parts of the animal from which the power was obtained.

13   The horned snake was a favorite "assistant" in hunting or war for the Creek Indians. Water snakes were able to bring on or withhold rain; and red-headed woodpeckers and hoot owls were able to foresee events and indicate them by their cries or mere presence. A Delaware Indian often wore a charm around his neck which represented his guardian animal (i.e., a bear or eagle claw, a bird bill or animal tooth), and no one else could touch it. Thus the guardian animal was considered "sacred" by the protected person but, to others, it was the same as any other animal.

14   Since these native peoples believed that animals possessed souls, there were occasions when the animal assumed what might be called a "helper spirit" role. These are instances when an animal was slain, upon his master's death, in order to do service to his master in the other world. The Plains Indian's horse was slain and buried with him so that he would be ready to ride again in the happy hunting grounds. The Canadian Indian's dog was slain and buried also so that he would be able to serve his master in the other world. Some Eskimos buried a dog's head with a small child, so that the soul of the dog (which always finds its way home) could guide the helpless infant to the land of souls.

Since the belief was widespread that animals possessed   15
souls, the idea of man's soul transmigrating into an animal's
body was common. It was believed that men had previously
existed in the forms of birds, animals and fishes, or that these
had the spirits of men in their bodies and, after death, they
would pass again into the bodies of the animals they occupied
in this former state. It followed, then, that since man could
be reincarnated in animal form, animals could understand
human speech, and one was therefore careful about what was
said in the presence of an animal. Among the Iroquois it was
a common belief that witches could change their form into that
of an animal, bird or reptile (the most frequently reported
forms being owls, ravens, and cats). The Creeks felt that, if
an animal were properly killed, death was only a temporary
thing; the animal would be reincarnated in identical form. The
Delawares, believing in the immortality of the soul, likened
themselves to corn; when thrown out and buried in the soil,
it comes up and grows.

An interesting aspect of this universal respect for animals   16
is the instances of totemism that are found among these native
peoples. Totemism implies a great respect for the animal for
which a clan is named. The Indians might consider the animal
their ancestor, or believe that their anthropomorphic ancestor
changed himself into the animal, or he may have had a specific
encounter with the particular animal. Creek clans were named
for animals or natural forces (Wind, Bear, Panther, Raccoon,
Alligator, Deer) with each member of the clan having descended from a female ancestor called Bear-woman, Pan-
ther-woman, etc. The Delaware believed that, at one time, the
world was entirely flooded and all men perished. The turtle,
however, able to live on land and in water, survived and again
peopled the world. Hence, the Turtle Tribe was the most important.

Respect for animal superiority is also evidenced by the fol-   17
lowing tale which ascribes animal qualities to men—the tale
of The Universal Mother:

> . . . the Universal Mother again descended to earth. She selected
> for her husband . . . a very subtle owl, who was the half-brother
> of a bear and a wolf, the cousin of a dog and a deer, and distantly

related to the panther, the fox, the eagle, and the adder. Men take their qualities from the beasts, to whom they are related, and most from those of whose blood they have in their veins. If they have most of their great father's, the owl, they are wise; if the wolf predominates they are bloody-minded; if the bear, they are dirty and sluggish, great eaters and love to lick their fingers; if the deer, they are exceedingly timorous and feeble; if the fox, cruel and sly; the eagle, bold, daring and courageous; and the adder, treacherous (Jones 1970: 98, Vol. 2).

18   Animals are of maximum importance where climates are cold or dry and thus unfavorable for vegetable growth. These conditions applied to the Eskimo and the Sub-Arctic tribes, but the tribes in the eastern plains/woodland areas and in the southeastern United States relied on an agriculture-based subsistence pattern where game animals were supplementary to their primary crops of beans, corn and squash. The Mayans practiced extensive agriculture, and game animals were relatively unimportant in their economy.

19   As the subsistence patterns changed as a function of the environment, so did the social organization of the groups. These changes correlated to the groups' perceptions of the types of spirits important to their daily activities. The number of spirits relating to natural phenomena (such as the wind, rain, fire, sun and moon) assumed greater importance as the dependence upon agriculture increased. This degree of horticulture/agriculture among North American Indian societies can be measured by the number and complexity of ceremonies associated with crops and the attendant natural phenomena. The Iroquois Confederation tribes, the tribes in the Southeast, and the Mayans reflected this idea.

20   It was a widespread belief that "man must not exploit the children of Mother Earth unduly. He must take no more than he needed from animal or plant and give back thanks and respect" (Underhill 1965: 49). Thus, rituals and ceremonies became important in Indians' lives as a means of returning thanks to the beings of their world, both natural and supernatural. Numerous annual ceremonies pertaining to crops (Corn, Green Corn, Maple, Strawberry) were held by the Iroquois in order to thank the spirits for this food. The Southeastern tribes also held ceremonies in which crops played dominant

roles. The Mayan culture was replete with ceremonies. They believed that everything in nature belonged to the gods, that man used the products of nature only if he had divine permission and help, and that the gods must be recompensed for such privileges. (Their most important god was the maize god, god of all vegetation, and it was also necessary to be on good terms with the "winds" or malign spirits.) Out of these beliefs grew the practices of agricultural, animal and human sacrifices.

While the hunters and gatherers killed animals as a means   21
of self-preservation, a major part of the hunter's ceremonial is oriented, not toward glorifying the act of killing, but to nullifying and negating the unavoidable deed. They did not view killing as a desirable act but one forced on them by their environment as a means of sustenance. However, ceremonial killing of animals was practiced in some of the agricultural tribes. An important ritual during the Iroquois Midwinter Rites was the White Dog Sacrifice. A white dog was strangled, its body spotted with red paint and adorned with feathers and wampum, then suspended on a pole for five days, after which it was burned. This ritual signified the transfer of the community's sins, or purging of evil therein, to the sacrificed animal.

Through my readings in preparation for this paper, I ran   22
across the idea of animatism, which is the belief in a supernatural force which can bestow prowess or holiness on animate and inanimate objects alike. This force might be illustrated by the force of *mana,* an invisible force, perhaps like magnetism or electricity, which may bring good luck or misfortune. This, then, is considered a less sophisticated religious belief than that of animism. Edward Tylor, in his book *Primitive Culture,* classified animism as "the groundwork of the philosophy of religion." Might not, then, we look at the subject of religious beliefs as a series of progressions from animatism, to animism, to polytheism, then on to the advanced cultures' beliefs in monotheism, as we have applied the criteria of adaptation to the biological and social aspects of mankind? Would it be improper to compare this progression of religious beliefs to that of the social order (i.e., the band, the tribe, the chiefdom, then the state)?

It appears that many of the beliefs of the "primitive" or   23
less complex societies have analogous relationships to those

of our "advanced" societies. Certainly these ideas and practices have been modified and refined to a certain degree, but might they not have had their roots in the old beliefs of animatism or animism? I feel these ideas and practices can be pictured as having grown up within their local groups, in turn using tradition and some borrowed elements, and then adapting, through the generations, to local needs and knowledge.

24   Might not we still see traces of the "primitive" man/animal relationship or totemistic concept in our culture when we speak of the "heart of a lion," the "eye of an eagle," or "wise as an owl"? Or perhaps some of our religious practices are rooted in the "primitive" religions; might the "patron saint" or "guardian angel" found in Catholicism be an out-growth of the animal guardian belief? Of course, there are still cultures in the world where belief in guardian spirits can be found. The Lahu of Northern Thailand erect an altar to their House Spirit which protects the household members and all their property from misfortune (Walker 1976). Might the "lamb of God" found in Catholicism be a refinement of the sacrificial animal of the "primitive" ceremonies? Indeed, might not many of today's religious practices be analogous to those of the "primitive" religious beliefs, our modern practices having been refined and "evolved" from these older forms?

25   This leads me to believe, then, that, as a society's social organization is largely affected by its environmental constraints, so then may our system of religious beliefs be structured in relation to its social order—from the individualistic man/spirit relationships of the northern climes to the group ceremonial activities of the sedentary agricultural societies.

26   To the American Indian, nature was good and man was a part of nature. The entire universe—men, animals and spirits—was unified in one cosmic interdependency. His religious beliefs, then, focused primarily on this relationship with nature instead of toward his fellow humans. However, as man learned to control more and more the vagrancies of nature and as his social structure grew more complex, religious methodology also "adapted."

27   Thus, man is a part of both nature and culture, and his concept of nature, and also his exploitation of it, is stamped by

the culture of his community. So, then, are man's religious beliefs a function of this attempt to deal with both his environmental and social constraints in a meaningful, symbolic manner? ". . . [W]hat instinct does for animals, religion does for man, by aiding his intelligence in opposing to it in critical situations intellectual representations. Ultimately it is a product of an instinctual urge, a vital impulse which, combined with intelligence, ensures man's survival and his evolutionary climb to ever greater heights" (Evans-Pritchard 1965: 116).

References

Jensen, Adolf E.
1963
Myth and Cult Among Primitive Peoples. The University of Chicago Press, Chicago.

Jones, James A.
1970
Traditions of the North American Indians. Literature House, New York.

Spencer, Robert F. and Jesse D. Jennings, et al.
1977
The Native Americans, 2nd ed. Harper and Row, New York.

Student papers
1976
Davis, J. "Religion in the Americas"
Moron, R. "Religion and Ceremonial Life of the North American and Southern Mexico Indians"

Tooker, Elisabeth.
1970
The Iroquois Ceremonial of Midwinter. Syracuse University Press, Syracuse.

Tylor, Edward B.
1977
Primitive Culture. Henry Holt and Company, New York.

Van Stone, James W.
1974
Athapaskan Adaptations: Hunters and Fishermen of the Sub-Arctic Forests. Aldine Publishing Company, New York.

Walker, Anthony R.
1976
"Red Lahu Rites of Spirit Exorcism in North Thailand." *Anthropos,* 71: 3–4.

Part Four

TOOLS FOR THE SOCIAL SCIENCE WRITER

TOOLS FOR THE SOCIAL SCIENCE WRITER

A Guide to Reference Materials in the Social Sciences

Using reference materials is a little like being Sherlock Holmes: you search for clues, you uncover the hidden, you put pieces together until, finally, you can propose a solution to the mystery. This section is a guide to help you search and discover. Neither inclusive nor specialized, this guide does not mention every possible reference tool and does not provide detailed information about reference materials in each discipline considered a social science, though the final category does list some specific guides to the seven areas emphasized in this book. Instead, it is a general list of reference materials—from books to computerized systems—that can help you before you write, as you compose, and when you revise your work.

Guides. These sources examine all forms of information pertinent to a discipline. In effect, this entire part of the book is a brief guide to the social sciences. In this specific section of the guide, we list five items which cover the entire field of the social sciences, though not every item includes all the disciplines we consider social sciences—for example, history is not included in each guide. Because they present in an organized way all forms of reference tools that students and scholars may need to examine in the course of their research, guides are extremely valuable materials. In addition, they frequently make evaluative statements regarding the relative merits and strengths of specific tools. Finally, in some cases they explain the unique way in which social scientists use materials. To find out if a guide is useful for your particular needs, read its introduction.

Friedes, Thelma. *Literature and Bibliography of the Social Sciences.* Los Angeles: Melville Publishing Co., 1973. 254 p.

Hoselitz, Bert F., ed. *A Reader's Guide to the Social Sciences.* Rev. ed. New York: Free Press, 1970. 425 p.

Lewis, Peter R. *The Literature of the Social Sciences; An Introductory Survey and Guide.* London: The Library Association, 1960. 222 p.

Stevens, Rolland E. and Davis, Donald G. Jr. *Reference Books in the Social Sciences and Humanities.* Champaign, Ill.: Stipes Publishing Co., 1977. 189 p.

White, Carl M. and Associates. *Sources of Information in the Social Sciences; A Guide to the Literature.* 2d ed. Chicago: American Library Association, 1973.

Bibliographies. The bibliographies included in this section contain lists of books in the social sciences and also references to lists of books in specific disciplines within the social sciences. Different from guides, bibliographies usually contain lists, lack evaluative comments, and frequently have lengthier lists than guides. They are usually organized in topical or chronological ways so that it is necessary for you to examine only the sections of the bibliographies pertinent to the area of research you're involved in. One value of bibliographies is their currency since they are frequently updated with supplements; therefore, if you're looking for sources on a contemporary issue, you probably should check the supplement. Another value is the method of citation used for the title: normally, bibliographies contain the most authoritative title. If you have a general idea of the title of a work but do not have its exact citation, you should consult a bibliography. Always good sources for building a list of references to consult in your research, bibliographies are sometimes annotated.

Bibliographies of Bibliographies
Gray, Richard A. and Villow, Dorothy. *Serial Bibliographies in the Humanities and Social Sciences.* Ann Arbor, Mich.: Pierian Press, 1969. 345 p.

Index Bibliographicus. Vol 2. Social Sciences. 4th ed. The Hague: FID, 1964. 34 p.

Bibliographies
American Behavioral Scientist. *The ABS Guide to Recent Publications in the Social and Behavioral Sciences.* New York, 1965. 781 p.

Recent Publications in the Social and Behavioral Sciences: The ABS Guide Supplement, 1966–75. Beverly Hills, California: Sage, 1966–75.

International Bibliography of the Social Sciences. (Bibliographie internationale de Sociologie.) 1951– . London: Tavistock; Chicago: Aldine, 1952– . Annual.

London Bibliography of the Social Sciences. (. . . comp. under the direction of B. M. Headicar and C. Fuller, with an introd. by Sidney Webb (Lord Passfield). London: London School of Economics, 1931–32. 4 vols., and suppl. (v.5–31), 1934–75. (London School of Economics. Studies in economics and political science: Bibliographies, no. 8)

_____. Supplement, First 1929/31– . London: British Library of Political and Economic Science, 1934–68: Mansell, 1970– .

Indexes and Abstracts.   While most written materials contain indexes and some may also have abstracts, the titles in this section direct you to indexes of periodical or serial publications. In other words, these are indexes to magazines and scholarly journals. All the items in this list are organized by subject and some by author or title. In addition, the frequency of publication of each item is noted. A few words about each subdivision:

1. *Indexes.* Like the familiar *Readers' Guide to Periodical Literature,* the three indexes in this list are organized mainly by subject or topic—for example, Vietnam War or banking and finance. They are normally subdivided by chronological period or subdivisions of the topic. You will often find proper names used as a topic—for example, Ronald Reagan. Each citation contains the journal in which the article is found, and the volume and page numbers.

2. *Contents Reproductions.* As the term suggests, this reference tool contains a list of the title page or contents page of a given journal. If, for example, you're looking for articles in the *Journal of Economic History,* you'll find the title page with a list of every article and author. *Current Contents* is particularly valuable for very current material because it is assembled before the subject indexes are ready; it is less useful for anything in print over a year—normally you should use indexes or citation indexes for less current topics because they have been more carefully analyzed. *Current Contents* is also valuable if you are trying to follow the work of a specific author or policy of a given journal.

3. *Citation Index.* A recent form of periodical indexing, the *Social Sciences Citation Index* is more detailed and complete than previous tools of this nature. It analyzes the contents of a journal and the bibliographies attached to each article published in that journal, as well as linking for you the sources of the articles used by the author of the single journal article you're using. This format provides an immediate bibliography on a topic, allowing you to identify authors who write frequently on the same topic and guiding you without further searching to additional citations on the topic. The *Social Sciences Citation Index* also includes the names and addresses of authors of articles, as well as information about professional organizations and institutes.

4. *Abstracts.* Though it is not a new concept, abstracting has been more widely used in the last twenty years than ever before; in fact, many articles in scholarly journals are now prefaced by abstracts. Abstracts are normally brief, usually no more than one hundred to two hundred words, and if well done provide the thesis, argument, and conclusions of an article. Of obvious value to students and scholars, abstracts allow you to determine whether the full article is sufficiently useful to pursue.

5. *Indexes and Abstracts for Microform Collections.* Because the volume of printed literature has increased enormously in the past thirty years, commercial organizations have begun producing printed materials in microform fashion. In organizing these materials for easy access, the organizations have prepared index volumes and abstract volumes. Normally the student or scholar begins by using the index, moves to the abstract volume, and finally selects the microform needed. The indexes are arranged topically, sometimes numerically (House Bills 1, 2, 3, 4, 5) or by agency or institution. *The American Statistics Index* (ASI), the *Congressional Information Service* (CIS), and the *Statistical Reference Index* (SRI) contain a wide range of information, particularly in the areas of government documents and statistical sources, which are otherwise difficult to find.

Indexes
Humanities Index. New York: Wilson, 1974– . Quarterly with annual cumulations.

Public Affairs Information Service Bulletin. New York: PAIS, 1915– . Semi-monthly with quarterly and annual cumulations.

Social Sciences Index. New York: Wilson, 1974– . Quarterly with annual cumulations. Formerly *International Index of Periodicals.* 1907–1965. Later, *Social Sciences & Humanities Index,* 1966–1974.

Contents Reproductions
Current Contents: Social and Behavioral Sciences. Philadelphia: Institute for Scientific Information, 1969– . Weekly.

Citation Index
Social Sciences Citation Index, 1972– . Philadelphia: Institute
for Scientific Information, 1973– . 3 per year with annual cumulations.

Abstracts
*Social Science Abstracts: A Comprehensive Abstracting and Indexing
Journal of the World's Periodical Literature in the Social Sciences.* New York: Social Science Abstracts, Columbia University, 1929–1933. 5 vols.

Indexes and Abstracts for Microform Collections
American Statistics Index. Washington: Congressional Information Service, 1973– . Monthly, annual cumulation.

Congressional Information Service. Washington: Congressional
Information Service, 1969– . Monthly, annual cumulation.

Statistical Reference Index. Washington: Congressional Information Service, 1980– . Monthly, annual cumulation.

Periodicals. Journals, magazines, annual reviews, and the
like—these are periodicals. Because they are continuously
published, they are different from books or monographs. This
section lists three kinds of tools to help you use periodicals:

1. *Periodical Guides.* These contain alphabetical listings, in
proper citation form, of journals held in libraries and other
research institutions of the northern hemisphere. The *Union
List of Serials* and the *New Serial Titles* are especially useful in
finding a journal's proper title, any changes in the title, and
the libraries in which the journals are held.

2. *Periodical Indexes.* The usefulness and organization of
indexes is described in the previous section.

3. *Periodicals in the General Area of the Social Sciences.* The
three titles listed here are standard and well-known journals
in the general area of the social sciences. For more complete
and detailed lists of journals in the specific disciplines, refer to the *Social Sciences Citation Index and the Social Sciences
Index.*

Periodical Guides
New Serial Titles, A Union List of Serials Commencing Publication After Dec. 31, 1949. Washington, D.C.: Library of Congress, 1953–   . Monthly with annual cumulations.

Union List of Serials in Libraries of the United States and Canada. 3d ed. Edited by Edna Brown Titus. New York: Wilson, 1965. 5v. 4649 p.

Periodical Indexes
Nineteenth Century Readers' Guide of Periodical Literature, 1890–1899, with supplementary indexing, 1900–1922, ed. by Helen Grant Cushing and Adah V. Morris. New York: H. W. Wilson, 1944, 2v.

Poole's Index to Periodical Literature, 1802–1881. Rev. ed. Boston: Houghton Mifflin, 1891. pref. 1891, c. 1882. 2v. (Repr, N.Y.: P. Smith, 1935; Gloucester, Mass.: P. Smith, 1963).

Readers' Guide to Periodical Literature. New York: H. W. Wilson, 1905–   . Cumulated.

Periodicals in the General Area of the Social Sciences
American Academy of Political and Social Science Annuals, Philadelphia: The Academy, 1890–   . Bimonthly.

American Behavioral Scientist. Beverly Hills, Cal.: Sage Publications, 1957–   . Bimonthly.

International Social Science Journal. Paris: UNESCO, 1949–   . Quarterly.

Newspapers. Newspapers, which are actually periodicals, are very important for social scientists because of their frequency, currency, easy access, and combined objective and subjective presentations. They are indexed in basically the same way as periodicals. While the following list includes indexes for five major newspapers, the necessity for indexing papers is widely recognized, and most papers have indexes for at least some of the years of their publication. Additionally, the *New York Times* not only has a standard index of its contents, but also specific indexes—for example, obituaries, theater reviews, book reviews, and the like. A particularly useful tool, *NewsBank* gathers articles pertaining to thirteen major subject categories from newspapers throughout the country. The categories are Business and Economic Development, Consumer Affairs, Education, Environment, Government, Structure, Health, Housing and Urban Renewal, Law and Order, Political Development, Social Relations, Transportation, and Welfare and Poverty.

Directories
American Newspapers, 1821–1936; A Union List of Files Available in the United States and Canada, ed. by Winifred Gregory under the auspices of the Bibliographical Society of America. New York: H. W. Wilson, 1937. 791 p. (Repr, N.Y.: Kraus, 1967).

Newspapers on Microfilm: A Union Check List. Washington, D.C.: Library of Congress, 1963. George Schwegman, Jr., ed.

Indexes
Christian Science Monitor Index. Subject index of the *Christian Science Monitor.* Boston: 1960– . Monthly, with semiannual and annual cumulations.

NewsBank. Stamford, Conn.: NewsBank, Inc., 1974– . Monthly, quarterly cumulations.

New York Daily Tribune Index. New York: Tribune Association, 1876–1907. 31v.

New York Times Index. New York Times, 1913–Present. Semimonthly, with annual cumulation.

Official Index to The Times [of London]. London: 1907–Present.

Palmer's Index to The Times [of London] *Newspaper, 1790–1943.* London: 1868–1943.

Wall St. Journal. Index. 1958– . N.Y.: Dow Jones, 1959– . Monthly with annual cumulations.

Data Base Bibliographic Services. The most recent access tool for students and scholars is on-line data base searching. Many of the printed sources already described have been read into the memories of computers and are now accessible through computer terminals. The information is exactly the same and the results are frequently identical to those obtained in manual searches; however, this is a much quicker method, though the usual service charge for using computers prompts the social scientist to balance time against cost. No list of data base bibliographic services can be complete since the range of indexes and journals that can be searched increases each day. Predictably, in the future most research will be done in this, the most efficient method. The output can be a simple citation (similar to that in the *Social Science Index*), abstracts, or, in some cases, full texts of articles.

Economics	ABT/IMFORM
	ACCOUNTANT'S INDEX
	ASI
	FOREIGN STATISTICAL AB-STRACTS
	INTERNATIONAL ANNUAL TIME SERIES
	INTERNATIONAL ECONOMIC ABSTRACTS
	PREDICASTS, INC.
	SCANP and SCIMP
	U.S. ANNUAL TIME SERIES
	U.S. REGIONAL TIME SERIES
	U.S. STATISTICAL ABSTRACTS
Government, Political Science, Public Affairs, Law	CIS
	CRECORD
	FEDERAL INDEX
	FEDERAL INDEX WEEKLY
	FEDREG
	FOUNDATION DIRECTORY
	FOUNDATION GRANTS INDEX
	GRANTS
	MONTHLY CATALOG OF U.S.

	GOVERNMENT PUBLICA-TIONS
	NATIONAL FOUNDATIONS
	PAIS INTERNATIONAL
	USPSD
	WORLD AFFAIRS REPORT
History	AMERICA: HISTORY AND LIFE
	HISTORICAL ABSTRACTS
News, Current Affairs	BELL & HOWELL NEWSPAPER INDEX
	DOW JONES NEWS/RETRIEVAL
	ENVIROLINE
	MAGAZINE INDEX
	NEW YORK TIMES
	NEWS SEARCH
	QUEBEC-ACTUALITE
Social Sciences,	CHILD ABUSE AND NEGLECT
Behavioral Sciences,	POPINFORM
Population, Psychology	PSYCHOLOGICAL ABSTRACTS
	SOCIAL SCISEARCH
	SOCIOLOGICAL ABSTRACTS

Encyclopedias. Encyclopedias in the social sciences serve the same purposes as general encyclopedias: they contain articles of varying lengths which provide an overview of the topic. The two titles listed here—considered the best standard encyclopedias in the field—contain long, carefully researched, signed articles which are frequently accompanied by bibliographies.

Encyclopaedia of the Social Sciences. Ed. in Chief, E. R. A. Seligman; assoc. ed., Alvin Johnson. New York: Macmillan, 1930–35. 15v.

International Encyclopedia of the Social Sciences. David L. Sills, ed. New York: Macmillan and the Free Press, 1968. 17v.

Dictionaries. Within the social sciences, specialized dictionaries serve the same purpose as *Webster's International* or other reputable dictionaries: they offer brief, sometimes technical definitions of the vocabulary of the field. One particular advantage of these two dictionaries is that they describe highly connotative words in the way frequently used by social scientists.

Gould, Julius and Kulb, William L., eds. *A Dictionary of the Social Sciences.* New York: Free Press, 1964. 761 p.

Zadrozny, John Thomas. *Dictionary of Social Science.* Washington, D.C.: Public Affairs Press, 1959. 367 p.

Biographies.   Biographies usually come in two forms:
   1. Reasonably long, evaluative articles about notable people in the field which sometimes contain bibliographies citing works of or about these people. The *Dictionary of National Biography* and the *Dictionary of American Biography* are examples of this type of biography.
   2. Brief articles, containing the name, address, and family history of the person. Most of the titles in this section, with the exception of the DNB and DAB, are in this format.
   If a biography you consult does not contain sufficient information, check the *Biography Index* to find the source of other biographical articles—for example, the *New York Times* may have printed a biographical article, or a magazine may have done a memorial edition about the person you are researching.

Bibliographies of Biographies
Biography Index; A Cumulative Index to Biographical Material in Books and Magazines. New York: Wilson, 1947–   . Quarterly with annual and 3-year cumulations.

Biographical Dictionaries: Master Index. Detroit: Gale Research, 1975.

Biographies (British)
Dictionary of National Biography. Leslie Stephen and Sidney Lee, eds. Oxford: Oxford University Press, 1908–   . Supplement, Boston: G. K. Hall, 1966.

Who's Who. London: Black; N.Y.: St. Martin's, 1849–   . Annual.

Who Was Who, 1897–1970. London: Black, 1929–72. 6v.

Biographies (American)
American Men and Women of Science. 14th ed. New York: Jacques Cattell Pr./Bowker, 1979. 1st–11th eds., 1906–68.

Dictionary of American Biography. New York: Scribner; London: Milford, 1928–37. 20v. and Index. 1928–58, (Repr, N.Y.: Scribner, 1943. 21v.; 1946, 11v. on thin paper).

Directory of American Scholars. 7th ed. New York: Bowker, 1978. Previous editions published with the cooperation of the American Council of Learned Societies.

National Cyclopaedia of American Biography. Ann Arbor, Mich.: University Microfilms, 1967. (N.Y.: White, 1892–1971. v.1–53. il. [In progress] Some volumes issued in rev. ed.)

Who's Who in America. Chicago: Marquis, 1899–   . Biennial.

Who Was Who in America, 1897–1981. Chicago: Marquis, 1942–1981. 8v.

Who Was Who in America: Historical Volume, 1607–1896. Chicago: Marquis, 1963. 670 p.

Who's Who of American Women. Ed. 1–   . Chicago: Marquis, 1958–   . Biennial.

Biographies (International)
Chamber's Biographical Dictionary. J. O. Thorne, ed. Rev. ed. New York: St. Martin's Press, 1969.

Current Biography. New York: H. W. Wilson, 1940–   . Monthly (except Aug.).

International Who's Who. London: Europa, Publs. and Allen & Unwin, 1935–   . Annual (slightly irregular).

New York Times Obituaries Index, 1858–1968. David I. Eggen-
berger, ed. New York: Times, 1970. 1136 p.

Yearbooks. The yearbooks listed here are directories of detailed information about nations and international organizations, containing comprehensive materials about people, finances, publications, and international activities. For instance,
if you need to know the GNP of a country, how much wheat
it exports, the names of ambassadors or consuls, or the address
of a leading newspaper, one of these three yearbooks should
help you find this information. The articles in these books are
rather long, and while the information is objective, these are
not merely sources for facts; narrative presentations frequently
supply valuable information.

Europa Year Book. London: Europa Publishing, 1959– . Annual.

*Statesman's Year-Book; Statistical and Historical Annual of the
States of the World, 1864–* . London, New York: Macmillan, 1864– . Annual.

Worldmark Encyclopedia of the Nations. 5th ed. New York: Worldmark Press, 1976. 5v.

Statistical Sources. Social scientists rely heavily on statistical
information in analyzing topics, and the titles listed
here—including the official governmental and international
organizations' publications—are especially useful. Until you
are familiar with the works, you should rely on the index or
contents pages to find the section you need since the data may
be scattered throughout the book—for example, birth rates
may be contained in different form in different categories. The
information in these sources is not limited to the year the book
is issued; the crime rate for the year of the book's publication,
for instance, is often compared with earlier statistics.

Demographic Yearbook; Annuaire démographique, 1948– . New
York: 1949–Present. Annual.

Gallup Poll. Wilmington, Delaware: Scholarly Resources Inc.,
1935– .

Statistical Abstract of Latin America. Los Angeles: UCLA Latin American Center Publications, 1955– . Annual.

U.S. Bureau of the Census. *Statistical Abstract of the United States, 1878–* . Washington, D.C.: GPO, 1879– . Annual.

United Nations. Statistical Office. *Statistical Yearbook; Annuaire statistique, 1948–* . New York, 1949– . Annual.

Wasserman, Paul, and others. *Statistical Sources: A Subject Guide to Data on Industrial, Business, Social, Educational, Financing and Other Topics for the United States and Selected Foreign Countries.* Rev. 7th ed. Detroit: Gale Research, 1982.

Government Publications.   The United States government is the single largest publisher in the United States, and since many of its publications deal with the common weal, social scientists will find a wealth of information and documentation in its publications. Much the same can be said of international agencies, particularly the United Nations. Many sources mentioned earlier are government documents—for example, CIS or *Statistical Abstracts* published by the U.S. Bureau of the Census. Listed here are indexes or guides to the literature, not the publications *per se,* and they are organized by agency and in some cases by subject. The *Monthly Catalog of United States Government Publications* is to government documents what the card catalog is to books in the library. It is organized by subject, author, and title, with the author frequently a government agency.

International Agencies
Guide to League of Nations Publications; A Bibliographical Survey of the Work of the League, 1920–1947. Hans Aufrecht, comp. New York: Columbia University Press, 1951. 682 p.

United Nations Documents Index. v. 1–24, Jan. 1950–Dec. 1973. [New York] 1950-B. Monthly.

U.S. Government Publications

U.S. Superintendent of Documents. *Monthly Catalog of United States Government Publications.* Washington, D.C.: Government Printing Office, 1895–Present. Monthly.

U.S. Superintendent of Documents. *Catalog of the Public Documents of Congress and of Other Departments of the Government of the United States for the Period March 4, 1893–Dec. 31, 1940.* Washington, D.C.: Government Printing Office, 1896–1945. v. 1–25.

United States Government Publications Relating to the Social Sciences: A Selected, Annotated Guide. Joseph K. Lu, ed. Beverly Hills, Ca.: Sage Publications, 1975.

Unpublished Materials. Many valuable materials in the social sciences are available only in the original form—handwritten documents, typed materials, sketches and the like which have never been organized and published by government, scholarly, or commercial sources. These materials contain a wealth of information and originality since frequently they are unedited and uncorrected expressions of the drafters. Collections of unpublished materials are often found in university libraries and in the National Library (the Library of Congress or the National Archives). Most nations, international organizations, major companies, universities, and scholarly organizations maintain archives. In this list, the first three items are guides to the places where archival collections can be found. Organized by subject, these guides will list the address of the archive and give some idea of the size and extent of its holdings. The last two items in this list are indexes, organized by subject and author, of university dissertations, which differ from archival materials because they are refined expressions of their authors' ideas.

Archives

Library of Congress. *The National Union Catalog of Manuscript Collections, 1959/61.* Ann Arbor, Mich.: Edwards, 1962– . (Publishers vary.)

U.S. General Services Administration. National Archives and Records Service. *Guide to the National Archives of the United States.* Washington, D.C.: GPO, 1974.

U.S. National Historical Publications and Records Commission. *Directory of Archives and Manuscript Repositories in the United States.* Washington, D.C.: National Archives and Records Service, 1978.

Current Research
American Doctoral Dissertations, 1955/56– . Completed for the Association of Research Libraries. Ann Arbor, Mich.: University Microfilms, 1957– . Annual.

Dissertation Abstracts International. Ann Arbor, Mich.: University Microfilms, 1938– . Monthly.

Photocopied and Nonprinted Sources. Just as data base bibliographic services are certainly to become increasingly important research tools, particularly in the social sciences, so photocopied and nonprinted sources will continue to grow in importance. The following items are just a few of these valuable resources.

American Historical Association. *Guide to Photocopied Historical Materials in the United States and Canada.* Richard W. Hale, ed. Ithaca, N.Y.: Cornell University Press, 1961.

Library of Congress Catalogue: Motion Pictures and Filmstrips. Washington, D.C.: Library of Congress, 1953–Present. Annual.

List of National Archives Microfilm Publications. Washington, D.C.: National Archives and Records Service, 1961.

The Oral History Collection of Columbia University. New York: Columbia University Oral History Research Office, 1964.

Oral History in the United States, A Directory. Gary L. Shumway, comp. New York: Oral History Association, 1971.

Picture Sources: An Introductory List. Helen Faye, ed. New York: Special Libraries Association, 1959.

Reference Department. *Guide to the Special Collections of Prints and Photographs in the Library of Congress.* Paul Vanderbilt, ed. Washington, D.C.: Government Printing Office, 1955.

Union Library Catalogue of the Philadelphia Metropolitan Area Committee on Microphotography. *Union List of Microfilms.* Ann Arbor, Mich.: J. W. Edwards, 1951.

Guides in Specific Disciplines. Guides exist for most of the specific disciplines commonly considered the social sciences. What follows are some representative works.

Anthropology	Frantz, Charles. *The Student Anthropologist's Handbook: A Guide to Research, Training and Career.* Cambridge, Mass.: Schenkman, 1972.
Economics	Daniells, Lorna M. *Business Information Sources.* Berkeley: University of California Press, 1976.
Geography	Brewer, J. Gordon. *The Literature of Geography: A Guide to Its Organisation and Use.* Rev. ed., London: Clive Bingley LTD, 1978.
History	Paulton, Helen J. *The Historian's Handbook: A Descriptive Guide to Reference Works.* Norman: University of Oklahoma Press, 1972.
Political Science	Brock, Clifton. *The Literature of Political Science: A Guide for Students, Librarians, and Teachers.* New York, London: R. R. Bowker Col, 1969.
Sociology	Bart, Pauline and Linda Frankel. *The Student Sociologist's Handbook.* 2d ed. Morristown, N.J.: General Learning Press, 1976.

Graphics and Visual Techniques

Social scientists frequently write about ideas and quantitative information that must be communicated in a special way, usually through some kind of visual technique or graphic. A picture is not always worth a thousand words, but a well-chosen graphic carefully incorporated into a writer's prose can often communicate what words alone cannot. Consider demographic studies, for instance. Writers who use graphs and tables to accompany their words about population trends will probably convey their information more clearly and quickly than they might in straight prose.

Graphics rarely substitute for words; they should, instead, enhance or illustrate what your prose communicates. When you include visuals in your writing,

1. present them as essential parts of your message, not as mere appendages or ornaments;
2. use them sparingly, for too many graphics can detract from your prose;
3. choose them carefully, with your purpose and audience in mind;
4. select them appropriately, based on the kind of material you are presenting—the most common visuals used by social scientists are *maps, photographs, tables, graphs,* and *charts.*

Maps.   Social scientists usually use maps to present information about geography—climatic data, for instance.

Photographs.   At times a photo enhances prose about objects, persons, or places. An article about Indian artifacts, for example, might be enlivened by a picture of the archaeological find.

Tables.   A table is an example of the "small is beautiful" concept since it uses a brief space to show large amounts of data. Examine the article by William Graybeal (pp. 99–112). Compiling the statistical information in tables and graphs, the author shows in a few pages what would take many more paragraphs of prose to present.

Graphs. A way of showing comparisons among numerical data, graphs illustrate cycles, trends, and distributions. Because they are not as precise as tables, graphs are often used with tables which give specific numbers (see the way Graybeal uses both graphs and tables). The most common graphs are line graphs, bar graphs, pie graphs, and picture graphs.

Line graphs. By plotting points in relation to two axes, a writer can connect the points to show a relationship between two sets of numbers. The illustration on page 102 is an example of this kind of linear diagram, the most common form of graph.

Bar graphs. Bar graphs use horizontal or vertical bars to show some quantity.

Picture graphs. Picture graphs are like bar graphs, the difference being the way in which the item is represented. Picture graphs, as the name suggests, use symbols with numerical quantities—for example, symbols of people to show demographic trends or symbols of oil wells to represent the number of drillings in different countries or states.

Pie graphs. Sometimes called circle graphs, these illustrations present data in circular form, dividing the total quantity into wedge-shaped sections.

Charts. Organizational charts and flowcharts, probably the most common types of charts, show the relationship, not of numbers, but of persons, departments, units, and the like. Sociologists and anthropologists frequently use charts to diagram ideas about social, cultural, and institutional groups.

Some Writing Resources

Handbooks and Writing Guides

Barzun, Jacques and Henry F. Graff. *The Modern Researcher.* New York: Harcourt, Brace, and World, Inc., 1970.

Barzun, Jacques. *Simple and Direct: A Rhetoric for Writers.* New York: Harper and Row, 1976.

Brusaw, Charles, et al. *The Business Writer's Handbook,* 2d ed. New York: St. Martin's Press, 1982.

Corder, Jim W. *Handbook of Current English,* 6th ed. Glenview, Illinois: Scott, Foresman, 1981.

Crews, Frederick. *The Random House Handbook.* New York: Random House, 1980.

Fear, David E. *Technical Writing,* 2d ed. New York: Random House, 1978.

Ebbitt, Wilma R. and David R. Ebbitt. *Writer's Guide and Index to English,* 7th ed. Glenview, Illinois: Scott, Foresman, 1982.

Hodges, John C. and Mary E. Whitten. *Harbrace College Handbook.* New York: Harcourt Brace Jovanovich, 1977.

Glorfeld, Louis, et al. *A Concise Guide for Writers.* New York: Holt, Rinehart and Winston, 1980.

Harris, John S. and Reed H. Blake. *Technical Writing for Social Scientists.* Chicago: Nelson-Hall, 1976.

Strunk, William and E. B. White. *The Elements of Style.* New York: Macmillan, 1979.

Trimble, John. *Writing with Style: Conversations on the Art of Writing.* Englewood Cliffs, New Jersey: Prentice-Hall, 1975.

Williams, Joseph. *Style: Ten Lessons in Clarity and Grace.* Glenview, Illinois: Scott, Foresman, 1981.

Style Manuals

American Psychological Association Publication. *Manual of the American Psychological Association.* Washington, D.C.: American Psychological Association, 1974.

Gibaldi, Joseph and Achtert, Walter S. *MLA Handbook for Writers of Research Papers, Theses, and Dissertations.* New York: Modern Language Association, 1980.

Turabian, Kate L. *A Manual for Writers of Term Papers, Theses, and Dissertations.* Chicago: University of Chicago Press, 1973.

The University of Chicago Press. *A Manual of Style.* Chicago: University of Chicago Press, 1982.

Chapter 3

"Shakespeare in the Bush" by Laura Bohannan. Copyright © 1966 by Laura Bohannan. Reprinted by permission of the author.

"California's Children of Divorce." Adapted from *Surviving the Breakup* by Judith S. Wallerstein and Joan Berlin Kelly © 1980 by Judith S. Wallerstein and Joan Berlin Kelly. Published by Basic Books, Inc., New York. Reprinted by permission.

"Creative Contradictions" by Albert Rothenberg, *Psychology Today,* June 1979. Reprinted by permission of the author.

"How Changes in Enrollment Will Affect Higher Education" by William Graybeal, *Today's Education,* February-March 1981. Copyright © 1981 by Today's Education. Reprinted by permission.

"Eli Luster." From *First-Person America,* by Ann Banks. Copyright © 1980 by Ann Banks. Reprinted by permission of Alfred A. Knopf, Inc.

Chapter 4

"A Zero-Sum Game." From *The Zero-Sum Society: Distribution and the Possibilities for Economic Change* by Lester C. Thurow. Copyright © 1980 by Basic Books, Inc., New York. Reprinted by permission of the publisher.

"Freedom of Speech" from *Everyman His Own Historian* by Carl L. Becker. Copyright 1935 by F. S. Crofts & Co. Reprinted by permission of Frederick D. Becker.

"Stereotypes-Their Use and Misuse" by Philip H. Rhinelander. Reprinted from *The Key Reporter,* Volume XLIII, Number Two, Winter 1977-1978. Copyright © 1977 by The United Chapters of Phi Beta Kappa. By permission of the publishers.

From *Eichmann in Jerusalem* by Hannah Arendt. Copyright © 1963, 1964 by Hannah Arendt. Reprinted by permission of Viking Penguin, Inc. Pp. 135-138, excerpts pp. 277-279.

"The Hedgehog and The Fox" from *The Hedgehog and the Fox* by Isaiah Berlin. Copyright © 1953 by Isaiah Berlin. Reprinted by permission of Simon & Schuster, a Division of Gulf & Western Corporation.

Chapter 5

From "Political Technology: The Constitution" in *The Republic of Technology* by Daniel J. Boorstin. Copyright © 1978 by Daniel J. Boorstin. By permission of Harper & Row, Publishers, Inc.

Reprinted from *The Work Ethic in Industrial America 1850–1920* by Daniel T. Rodgers by permission of The University of Chicago Press. © 1974, 1978 by The University of Chicago. Excerpts pp. 155-160.

"Presidents then and now" by Henry Steele Commager. Reprinted with permission from *Modern Maturity.* Copyright © 1980 by the American Association of Retired Persons.

Chapter 6

"Social Science vs. Government: Standoff at Policy Gap" by Amitai Etzioni, *Psychology Today,* November 1978. Reprinted by permission of the author.

"The Liberal Arts Religion" from *The Case Against College* by Caroline Bird. Copyright © 1975 by Caroline Bird. Reprinted by permission of the author.

INDEX TO MAJOR WRITING TECHNIQUES

S indicates Suggestions for Writing.